T0156438

KIPLING'S CANADIAN

Colonel Fraser Hunter, MPP, Maverick Soldier–Surveyor in "the Great Game"

by David Newton.

Order this book online at www.trafford.com
or email orders@trafford.com

Most Trafford titles are also available at major online book retailers.

© Copyright 2009 David Newton.
All rights reserved. No part of this publication may be reproduced, stored in a retrieval system, or
transmitted, in any form or by any means, electronic, mechanical, photocopying, recording, or
otherwise, without the written prior permission of the author.

Note for Librarians: A cataloguing record for this book is available from Library
and Archives Canada at www.collectionscanada.ca/amicus/index-e.html

Printed in Victoria, BC, Canada.

ISBN: 978-1-4251-9141-2 (sc)
ISBN: 978-1-4251-9143-6 (e-book)

*Our mission is to efficiently provide the world's finest, most comprehensive book publishing
service, enabling every author to experience success. To find out how to publish your book, your
way, and have it available worldwide, visit us online at www.trafford.com*

Trafford rev. 8/3/2009

 www.trafford.com

North America & international
toll-free: 1 888 232 4444 (USA & Canada)
phone: 250 383 6864 ♦ fax: 812 355 4082

Frederick Fraser Hunter, from Durham, Ontario, who played a key role in the final stages of "Great Game" and rose to be a major figure in India's secret service.

"If you can talk with crowds and keep your virtue
Or walk with Kings - nor lose the common touch,
If neither foes nor loving friends can hurt you,
If all men count on you, but none too much;
*   If you can fill the unforgiving minute*
With sixty seconds worth of distance run,
Yours is the earth and everything that's in it,
And - which is more - you'll be a Man, my son!"
Rudyard Kipling

FOR PAMELA.

ACKNOWLEDGEMENTS

So far as I am aware Hunter left behind no papers. Although he assiduously mapped Arabia, Persia and India his own life contains uncharted areas in which the guidance of others was invaluable. I must thank Victor Winstone, biographer of Gertrude Bell and Captain Shakespear and historian of British intelligence gathering in the Middle East, for his early encouragement and advice.

Others to whom I am particularly indebted include Mrs. Marlaine Elvidge of Durham, Ontario for the considerable information she provided on the town of Durham and the Hunter family. When I visited Durham, driven there by Peter Gamble, Mrs. Wilma Coutts, who had known Hunter well, shared her memories of him with me. She kindly gave me a photograph taken in Isfahan of Hunter as a young man with Persian officers. Charles Moffat, Elmer Clarke and Ina Milne were equally generous of their time and memories when I spent a pleasant few hours with them at the Durham Legion and Tom Firth took me to the cemetery where the Hunter family is buried.

I particularly appreciate the help of Dr. Floreeda Safiri of Oxford, England, who allowed me to borrow her papers on the South Persia Rifles; Lord Edmund Ironside of Bromwood Manor, England, who gleaned the unpublished pages of his father's diaries for mentions of Hunter; Captain MacKenzie of the Royal Military College of Canada in Kingston, Ontario for his constant willingness to bring to my attention items which might be relevant; Dr. Malcolm Yapp and Dr. Stephanie Cronin of the School of Oriental and African Studies at London University, Dr Desmond Morton of the University of Toronto, Mr. Harry Creagan of Kingston, Ontario for his information about early flying, Ursula Dufour for information on the Voluntary Aid Detachment and the Honourable Denny Burchill and Dr Jim O'Brien for their helpful suggestions. I also thank my daughter, Laura, for her suggestions and advice on how best to use the computer to access information, and Major and Mrs. Houlton-Hart for their unstinting generosity to me when I visited England to research this project.

I have made use of biographies of those involved recognizing, however, that autobiographies tend to be self-serving. General Sykes, for example, who wrote a two-volume history of Persia, covers his own campaign there in some detail in the second volume. Although he mentions a number of officers who were with him he largely ignores the role played by Fraser Hunter. This was certainly a consequence of their ultimately acrimonious relationship and is unfair to Hunter. I have attempted to redress the balance.

There are many others whose assistance has been considerable. I particularly mention staff of the Imperial War Museum and the National Army Museum in London; Miss Gillian Grant at the Middle Eastern Institute at St Anthony College in Oxford; the Yale University Library for access to the Wiseman Papers, Mrs. Christine Kelly, archivist at the Royal Geographical Society in London, the Toronto Globe and Mail, the Library and Records Department of the Foreign and Commonwealth Office in London, the Motor Museum at Beaulieu in England, the archivist of Upper Canada College and the United States Military History Institute at Carlisle, Pennsylvania. Most of all I thank my wife, Pamela, for her enduring patience with what became my obsession, her helpful suggestions and her meticulous editing of my copy.

Absolutely invaluable have been the archives of the India Office in London, England, particularly their Political and Secret files for the period covered, the British Library and the Public Records Office.

However, since this book is intended for the general reader rather than the academic researcher I have not included in the endnotes references to file series available at the Public Records Office. Most general readers find such information tiresome rather than illuminating. The great majority are in the Foreign Office series FO248, 371 and 395, the War Office series WO 106, and the Oriental and India Office Political and Secret files, particularly those in the L/P and S/10 series. Any researcher seeking more information should contact this author.

Photo Credits.

(Cover Photo) I am indebted to the Ontario Archives for their permission for me to use the photograph of Hunter taken when he was a Member of the Provincial Parliament representing Toronto, St Patrick riding.

Cadets at RMC, Kingston and of Hunter's graduation photograph are reproduced by kind permission of the archives and library of the Royal Military Academy, Kingston. The photograph of Hunter and other officers of the Duke of Connaught's Own Bombay Lancers is reproduced by courtesy of the Council of the National Army Museum, London and that of officers of the South Persia Rifles including Sir Percy Sykes and Lt Colonel Hunter is reproduced with permission of the Middle East Centre, St Anthony's College, Oxford, England.

Chronology

1876. Fraser Frederick Hunter born Durham, Ontario.

1898. Graduates from Royal Military College, Kingston.

1899. Joins Indian Army.

1900. To China and Boxer Rebellion.

1905. Joins Survey of India.

1906. Map of Arabia.

1914. "Great War" begins.

1916. South Persia Rifles

1917. Hunter to Russia.

1918. To New York and Western Front.

1920. With Persian Cossacks.

1920. Rejoins Survey of India.

1929. Retires.

1934. Elected Member of Ontario Provincial Parliament.

1943. Political career ends.

1959. Fraser Hunter dies and is buried in Durham, Ontario.

Contents

INTRODUCTION

Many years ago, during my "salad days", I was arrested by a unit of the Afghan Army and detained for a few days in Herat in the northwest of Afghanistan. They suspected that I was on a spying mission close to the Oxus River. They were wrong but the incident did churn up memories of schoolboy stories about the Great Game, that concern of so many in Victorian and Edwardian years.

The Great Game was the military and political preoccupation of Britain and Russia for most of the nineteenth century and some of the twentieth. While the armies of those countries never met in Central Asia, it was fear that Russia might try to annex Afghanistan or press through Persia to the Gulf, or that British and Indian troops might march on Khiva that kept the lamps burning in offices in Delhi, London and St Petersburg. It was our grandfathers' Cold War.

In the sporting metaphors of the nineteenth century, metaphors that cloaked the harsh realities, it was called "the Great Game". One of the players was Frederick Fraser Hunter of Durham, Ontario. Kipling would have loved to portray him. Hunter played hard in the Game, principally in Persia, throughout his professional career and before returning to Ontario and provincial politics. Though he antagonized some he grasped every opportunity to contribute to the defense of Britain and India.

There are a few similarities - albeit superficial - in Hunter's career and my own. Hunter graduated from the Royal Military College in

Kingston, Ontario, I from the Royal Military Academy at Sandhurst in England. As a young officer I, like Hunter, was elected a Fellow of the Royal Geographical Society and, like him, saw active service in the Far East. I also traveled a little in Persia and became, as was he, a devoted Canadian nationalist. But the similarities soon end. His career encompassed a level of individual drama scarcely possible in the latter half of the twentieth century.

Hunter was certainly close to many involved in secretive activities in Asia - but what was his precise role? Much of his career remains shrouded in mystery. What were his Secret Service connections? Was it confined to the gathering of topographical intelligence? Probably not, but he only once, to my knowledge, publicly admitted to being a member of India's Secret Service. Was he an "ear" in the East for Lord Curzon or for the Foreign Office at times when the government in India was at odds with the government in London? What is quite certain is that before returning to Canada Fraser Hunter had become head of India's equivalent of British MI.4 and was responsible for all topographical and related intelligence in countries adjacent to India through which an enemy might pass. Prior to that his career was full of drama.

This portrait does not intend to be a work of academic scholarship - although it does contain much original research. Rather it is for general reading and that which concerns the origins and progress of the Great Game would have been known to every schoolboy just a few decades ago - certainly to Fraser Hunter at Upper Canada College.

I call this story a portrait of Hunter rather than a biography because the passage of time and the shredding of sensitive government documents have left periods in his life that cannot be filled with certainty and must be speculative. Where that is necessary it has been done only after careful evaluation of those facts that are available. For example, a Toronto newspaper wrote in the nineteen thirties that Hunter was involved in an attempt to rescue the Czar from Ekaterinburg. Hunter was not in Russia when the Czar was imprisoned there. However, he was in Petrograd when the Czar and his family were confined just a few miles south but I have found no reports of any rescue attempts at this time.

It has often struck me as a shame that so many are unaware of the role played by Canadians in the epic events of recent times. There were many who in their own tenacious way have influenced the course of history.

The Royal Military College at Kingston has in the past one hundred years produced a large share of them.

This story confines itself to the career of Frederick Fraser Hunter of Durham, Ontario. Hunter immersed himself in the adventure of his age and was able to continue with his specialty through most of the Great War and beyond it.

Much of the story remains untold. It has been buried too deeply in the Political and Secret Files of the India Office. Anomalies remain. For example, Hunter was in Russia immediately prior to the October Revolution. But earlier, when he made contact with the Russian-led Persian Cossacks, he could already speak fluent Russian. Had he been there before? The records are mystifying not because of what they say but because of what they do not. What was the linkage between Hunter and David Hogarth, "eminence grise" of Middle Eastern espionage and sponsor of T.E. Lawrence? The files are silent.

His career was dominated by the politics of Central and Southern Asia. The year in which Hunter graduated from the Royal Military College at Kingston, Britain and Russia were near the brink of war over a loan to China and Kitchener was pressing southwards through the Sudan. These and earlier events would have made an indelible impression on a young Ontarian seeking the romance of adventure. He found it. He became a player in the final stages of the Great Game. His name would be known in hill stations in the Punjab and among the tribes of southern Persia. He organized and was part of the longest march across Persia since the days of Alexander the Great, he charged into battle alongside the Cossacks, and escaped Russia across the icy wastes of Siberia.

SPIRIT OF THE GAME

"As soon as histories are properly told
there is no more need of romances." -
Walt Whitman.

The "Great Game" was, for generations of young middle and upper class Victorians and Edwardians, an exhilarating, dangerous and purposeful adventure that attracted the brightest and best of an age. It cast British attitudes to enterprises such as espionage and guerrilla warfare in a mould, which may not yet have been broken.

This "Game" even influenced the arts - and certainly the evolution of the geographic and natural sciences. It helped colour British attitudes towards India for a hundred years.

In the span of Empires - Roman, Ottoman or British - not long has passed since the British left India. Yet today most people have forgotten, or never knew, of the immense influence of the Empire in general and India in particular on the thinking of the people of the nineteenth and the early twentieth century - and not just Englishmen but on all the British, as Canadians were then. This influence shows up in the writers of the period. From the schoolboy stories of G.A Henty and A.E.W. Mason to Conan Doyle, Rudyard Kipling and E.M. Forster, British thinking was bent towards imperial duty. It may have been the duty gently lampooned by Gilbert and Sullivan - Frederick, in the "Pirates of Penzance" was a "slave to duty" - but it profoundly influenced thousands, millions of British. This "duty" was to establish "order", for order is necessary to safety. The safety that was sought, then and now, was not only from internal enemies but also from external. And in India that meant safety from the so-called barbarians beyond the passes. These barbarians, the Russians north of the passes, had to be kept as far away as possible.

In fiction the game was played with élan. Kipling's Kimbal O'Hara managed to set askew the devious plans of the Czar's Intelligence Service. In reality as well, the attention of many a restless young man, Canadian as well as English, was focused beyond the passes, on that vast emptiness between the expanding British Empire in India and the expanding Russian Empire to the north. Many made reality of their dreams. Their names were not as well known as Kim's and some would die brutal deaths in the wilderness, supported only by the knowledge that their concept of duty had been done and that they had played a part in the great adventure of their times. Cold comfort perhaps, but from the disastrous First Afghan War through to Indian Army cavalry fighting on the edges of the Kara Kum in 1919, the Game was played, sometimes anonymously, but always with verve.

Eric Newby, in his book, <u>A Short Walk in the Hindu Kush,</u> describes how he found in the British Consulate in Meshed in 1956 an old map of Central Asia and marked, in the bleak desert well inside Russian territory, the inscription, "Captain X, July '84?". Although we may today read of the various Afghan wars and the tribal campaigns along India's Northwest Frontier, we may not know that there were also scores of anonymous players; a network of intelligence agents acting as surveyors, political officers, traders and archaeologists. They worked for the army, the navy, the Indian Civil Service's Foreign Department and Survey of India.

Their battlegrounds were varied; sometimes they ferreted their way through the bleak mountain passes of the Caucasus or through the Hindu Kush between the Pamirs and Baluchistan; sometimes they were drawn to the raw uplands of Afghanistan or the gritty deserts of Persia. The Game was played in the crowded bazaars or deserted alleys of medieval Central Asian khanates and along the caravan routes where once trod the men of Ghengis Khan and Tamerlane. The players almost literally put Central Asia on the map. The public became aware of places such as Tashkent and Merv - in one confrontation with the Russians a newspaper labeled the anxiety the crisis created as "mervousness". Earlier, romantic Victorian ladies had knitted woolens for Shamyl's Circassian highlanders fighting to keep the Czar's troops out of the Caucasus and thus bar the overland route to India. When James Elroy Flecker wrote,

"We travel not for trafficking alone,
By hotter winds our fiery hearts are fanned;
For lust of knowing what should not be known
We make the Golden Journey to Samarkand."

most people knew where Samarkand was.

The singers of the pub songs added a new word to the English language when the Russians sought an outlet to the warm waters of the Mediterranean by gaining Constantinople. The word was "jingoism" which is now defined by the dictionary as "favouring an aggressive foreign policy which might lead to war with other nations." The word was born of the song,

"We don't want to fight,
But, by jingo if we do,
We've got the ships,

We've got the men,
We've got the money too.
We've fought the Bear before
And while Britons shall be true
The Russians shall not have Constantinople."

The Great Game, with its secret agents and high adventure in lonely places, set two styles that linger still - at least in the public imagination. At the forefront, the players of the Great Game were the officers of the Indian Political Service and the Survey of India to whose ranks were attracted some of the very best, the most intelligent, shrewd and educated graduates of Oxford and Cambridge. Hence the Game tended to draw to its front those who were, at least in the nineteenth century, of the upper class and had private money. And when the British built their MI.4, MI.5 and Secret Intelligence Service, prominent in the ranks were those who were experienced at espionage - those who played in the Great Game.

Then there were the soldiers and sailors, men like Robert Baden-Powell, founder of the Boy Scout movement, who held the art of spying in highest regard and helped create the image of the upper class nit when he drew Turkish fortifications into the sketch of a butterfly which he had caught while stumbling around the Turkish coast in the guise of an ornithologist. Baden Powell later remarked that spying "would be an intensely interesting sport even if no great results were obtainable from it".

Well before he became, as Lord Tweedsmuir, Governor General of Canada, John Buchan had two fictional heroes based on real Great Game figures. Richard Hannay in "The Thirty-Nine Steps", "Greenmantle", and "Mr. Standfast" and Sandy Arbuthnot in "Greenmantle" were modelled on Edmund Ironside and Aubrey

Herbert. Edmund Ironside - later to become Field Marshal Lord Ironside - had met Buchan in South Africa. Ironside could speak fourteen languages, had fought in the Boer War and had been an intelligence agent in German South West Africa. He accompanied a German military expedition against an African tribe while disguised as a Boer transport driver and so well could he speak their language that even the other Boers did not suspect him. Before escaping to British South Africa he was awarded a German military medal. He spent the Great War on the Western Front, then commanded the Allied Expedition to Archangel. Later he commanded troops in North Persia and was in contact with Fraser Hunter, when he engineered the removal of the Persian Cossack commander - Colonel Staroselski. The Honourable Aubrey Herbert was an aristocratic wanderer who had drifted through some of the world's wilder places and would eventually become - with T.E. Lawrence - a key figure in the Arab Bureau.

The purpose of the Great Game was to block Russian expansion towards India. In the west that meant keeping the Ottomans - despicable though they were - in control of the Bosphorous. Further east it meant ensuring that - once the Russians had conquered the Caucasus, something they did quite early on - Persia remained neutral. Further east still it meant slowing the Russian advance through the independent Khanates and towards Afghanistan. Most easterly of all, in the high Himalayan passes and in the icy wilderness of Tibet and Chinese Turkestan, it meant playing a sinister, devious and intensely dangerous game of politics with tribal chieftains and mountain warlords.

The Game was not the exclusive preserve of Englishmen. Far from it. Native Indians played the major role. What few know, however, is that Canadians too were active in this early Cold War. Canadians had for some time been involved in many aspects of the imperial adventure. The most eminent, a railwayman and administrator in Africa, was certainly Montrealer, Sir Percy Girouard, Kitchener's "right hand man" in the campaign against the Mahdi's followers in the Sudan. But there were many others whose names are less easily found in the history books or the archives. General Heneker, who graduated from the Royal Military College at Kingston, commanded the army of southern India. One graduate of the College, Captain Stairs, was a member of Henry Morton Stanley's expedition to rescue Emin Pasha. He later annexed Katanga for the Belgians. A considerable number of Canadians - some forty of them - were with General Dunsterville's campaign in north Persia and south Russia. Some went with him to briefly hold Baku, others trained Assyrians to fight the Turks, one crossed the Caspian and for a short time commanded the British force holding Krasnavodsk against the Bolsheviks. Half a dozen Canadian pilots operated over the Caspian in 1919, while earlier three young pilots from Ontario campaigned against the tribesmen north of the Khyber Pass.[1]

The Royal Military Academy in Kingston, Ontario, has since its foundation produced many who have influenced the course of history. This is the story of one.

SOMEWHERE EAST OF SUEZ.

In mid-September, 1898, the ship that arrived in Bombay from England contained the usual contingent of India hands; civil servants, soldiers, employees of the mercantile houses. There were even a few young ladies of the so-called "fishing fleet" - women who, no longer in their early twenties, hoped to find in the bachelors of British India, marriage and possibly even romance.

Among them all, his heart bursting with romance, but the romance of adventure to come and of the east, was Second Lieutenant Frederick Fraser Hunter, serious, bony faced and sporting a military-required moustache which made him look younger rather than older as intended. Fraser Hunter, as he preferred to call himself, born and raised in Durham, Ontario, was temporarily posted to the Shropshire Light Infantry, then stationed in India, while waiting for a vacancy in the Bengal Presidency Army.

He was greeted by the pungent Indian smells of cardamom and pepper, cinnamon, cloves and garlic, fresh ginger, and other spices that wafted across the water and cancelled out the less pleasant odors. Hunter found the approach to berthing made more dramatic by the panorama, which with the Malabar Hills as a backdrop, is among the finest in the world. His excitement was intense.

After landing Hunter may have found the natural beauty diminished by the buildings along the waterfront and in the city. Some found the jumble quite hideous; Gothic competed with Doric,

Romanesque with Corinthian. And infused among it all, dignified or shambling, were the buildings of Asia, Hindu and Moslem.

Bombay, at the turn of the century the largest city in India, was where east and west met. But it was, without any doubt at all, an Indian city. From the bustle of small manpowered bumboats ferrying provisions or passengers between ship and shore, to the Towers of Silence where the Parsees exposed their dead until eaten by vultures, the city was Indian. Kipling had been born there on December 30th, 1865 and would return there briefly as a young man on his way to his first writing job in Lahore. But Bombay was different from the cities which one today associates with imperialism or Kipling. Bombay, like Calcutta, was not a city in which Anglo-Indian society was dominated by government officials; people like the Collectors, District Officers, Superintendents of Police, and Commissioners. Pre-eminent in Bombay were the business tycoons, often immensely rich. Their godowns, as the warehouses were called, were jammed with the bales of a cotton industry that had boomed thirty years earlier because of shortages in Europe caused by the American Civil War. These tycoons dominated not only the great business and trading houses of the city, but the social life as well.

The Bombay in which Hunter found himself throbbed with the vitality of the continent, despite the bubonic plague that had taken thousands of lives in the past few years and a famine that struck rural areas. In a sense Bombay matched his own excitement for the contrasts that enveloped his life in just the past few months could scarcely have been greater. Only a couple of months before he had made his farewells to his family and friends in Durham, Ontario and set out on his great adventure.

In Bombay Hunter was quickly swallowed up by the pressing crowds and their urgent business. In Durham he was known to almost everyone.

Hunter's family had been long established in Durham. Hunter's grandfather, Archibald, was forty years old when with wife, Elizabeth, their eighteen-year-old daughter Elizabeth, fifteen and twelve year old sons, William and Archibald and the newly born James, they left their village in Renfrewshire, Scotland and sailed for New York in 1840.

Almost immediately Archibald, leaving his family behind in New York, headed north to Ontario accompanied by his son William, a Mr. Jamieson and his son and a William Pullin. They had heard that there was free land available and their destination was an un-surveyed wilderness known as the Queen's Bush. There was little there but trees. The nearest settlement was the village of Fergus and the government had surveyed what was called the Garafaxa Road with free land grants on either side. Hunter and his party met one of the surveyors of this "road" when they passed through Oakville and he told them that the best potential farmland was beyond Fergus.

The party walked from Oakville to Guelph and then on to the Saugeen River that they managed to cross. Climbing a hill they found a deserted Indian wigwam. It was May 1842 and Archibald Hunter had come far enough. Land claims were made, trees cut and Hunter, father and son, built a log house on the Glenelg side of the Garafaxa Road. This was the first building in what would become the town of Durham.

After their first winter the two Hunters went back to New York, gathered up the rest of the family and returned to Ontario to begin the long labor of clearing land and creating a farm in the wilderness.

Ontario was opening up. More and more settlers were heading along the surveyed routes seeking land grants and many passed the Hunter property on their way to what is now Owen Sound - the village that, to the chagrin of Durham, became in 1850 the County Town.. The Hunters frequently let these travelers stay at their house, as there was no inn in the area. Soon they decided to build a hotel that could accommodate the growing number of travelers and in 1854 this, the British Hotel a substantial two and a half story building with a walk around second floor balcony, was opened. At the north end of the building was a store and both it and the hotel were soon a success, in large part due to the amiable nature of Mrs. Hunter. There were frequent social gatherings. There was fiddle playing and step dancing, quadrilles, waltzes, polkas and reels. As more young people saw in it a relief from the daily slog of land clearing, it became a social centre for the area.

The baby born in Scotland, James Hill Hunter, thrived in this vigorous environment and, when he was twenty-eight married the twenty-four year old Katherine MacDonald. James was successful, first in business then in politics and in 1875 was elected a Member of the Ontario Provincial Legislature. This new generation of Hunters had five children, the youngest, christened Frederick Fraser, was born on August 7th, 1876 - the same year in which the Royal Military College was established at Kingston.

When Frederick Fraser was about eight years old the Canadian government agreed to help Britain with its Nile Campaign. This expedition was led by General Lord Wolsely who, fourteen years earlier, had led a joint Anglo-Canadian military force against Louis Riel during the Red River Rebellion. Wolsely remembered the Canadian "voyageurs" and thought he could use men like these to advantage in his attempt to rescue General "Chinese" Gordon, besieged at Khartoum by the Mahdi and his dervishes. Enthusiasm ran high throughout Ontario and young Hunter would have been aware of it - 400 Canadians were recruited under the leadership of Lieutenant Colonel Frederick Denison, a Toronto alderman and a member of the Governor-General's Body Guard. Wolsely failed to rescue Gordon, arriving at Khartoum two days after the city had fallen and Gordon killed.

Less than a year later, however, came an event closer to home and one that most certainly influenced Hunter. In March of 1885 Louis Riel and his supporters clashed with a party of North West Mounted Police. Almost immediately a campaign was mounted. More than three thousand Canadians, principally militiamen, headed west to join militiamen from Manitoba and volunteers from the Northwest Territories. One would-be volunteer was particularly young. Nine-year-old Frederick Hunter ran away from home to the nearest militia unit in Owen Sound to offer his services. Though they declined his assistance in putting down the Riel Rebellion he was taken on as an honorary boy bugler in the 31st Grey Battalion and was surely soon dreaming of the untraveled road which lay before him. So began Hunter's military career and he remained an enthusiastic member of the militia until 1896 - during which short span he was promoted to second lieutenant at the age fifteen.

He would have been well aware of the writings of his age that focused on the energetic imperial expansion of the times. Much adventure was occurring in Africa led by people such as Henry Stanley. But the African theatre was a stage for freelances backed by commercial or religious concerns while east of Suez drew the soldiers and administrators.

While Hunter was a teenager Kipling's <u>Barrack Room Ballads</u> appeared. Campaigns on India's turbulent Northwest Frontier were a pattern of ambush and raid that continued unabated for decades. The British and Indian Army military expeditions, now using magazine loading Lee Metford rifles supplemented by Gatlings and Maxim guns, encouraged the Pathan[2] tribesmen to use stealth rather than the earlier favored mass charge. The army in India, in Hunter's teen years, actively campaigned against the Black Mountain tribes, up into the Zhob, and against the Hunza; they campaigned in the Chitral and Malakand and they fought Mohmands, Orakzais, Afridis, Mahsuds and Tochi Waziris - a rich recipe for a young Ontarian dreaming of a military career.

Hunter's parents had prospered in Durham and the education of their children was a matter of concern. There were excellent private schools in the vicinity of Toronto and Hunter's parents sent him, as they had his older brother, to the most celebrated - Upper Canada College – that was established nearly sixty years earlier. Again, Hunter's military interests predominated and he was soon put in command of the school's cadet corp, a branch of the militia called the Upper Canada College Rifles. It was no surprise to anyone, either at the school or his home, that on leaving UCC at the age of eighteen he entered the Royal Military College at Kingston.

The RMC was not going through its happiest period. A confidential supplement by the Adjutant General in the annual report stated that the Commandant, Major General Cameron, should be removed. Inspecting the College, General Gascoigne noted that the hospital was like a prison cell, and the ignorance displayed by the students in the French class was astounding. He recommended limiting the term of the commandant. Meantime, there had been a number of critical comments about the College in the Canadian and British press citing lack of discipline and cases of habitual drunkenness among cadets. Ignored by the critics was the high reputation earned by many former cadets.

A year after Hunter joined the College General Cameron, who was son-in-law of Sir Charles Tupper, left and was replaced by a man who would have a profound influence on Hunter's career choice. Lieutenant Colonel Gerald Kitson of the King's Royal Rifle Corps, an elite regiment of light infantry, would soon make changes in the College. They included expelling a number of cadets whose academic performance was mediocre; instruction in French was made mandatory; practical courses such as stable management and carpentry were introduced; and cadets were employed on reconnaissance and survey of the surrounding district.

Training then, as now in military colleges, emphasized sport and many cadets excelled. One former cadet won, in the year Kitson took command, the amateur golf championship of Canada. Hunter excelled at both sports and academic studies. In his second year he was top in his class in military studies. He won first prize in French. He became captain of the hockey team and was first in the Wheel Race. He was on the football team and in his final year not only won the long jump but did so with a leap of twenty-one feet ten inches, exceptionally good for that period and one which also broke the college record. Just as at the English public schools, at Sandhurst, at Woolwich, and among junior officers in their regiments - not permitted at that time to marry until in their thirties - sports and vigorous physical exercise were held to keep the minds of young men off sex. When they went to bed in their monastic quarters, exhaustion-induced sleep was instantaneous.

In his final year Hunter was promoted from Sergeant, of the year before, to Battalion Sergeant Major, senior cadet of the College. In that position he worked extensively helping Kitson wield the new broom. Probably more important is that as senior cadet he would have had many hours of conversations and occasional dinners during which Kitson had undoubtedly indulged himself in reminiscing. And Kitson, before coming to Canada, had served several years in India.

When Hunter graduated from the College on June 27th, 1898, he must have seemed to the others like one upon whom the sun always shone. Even years later, the summary in the College record of that year mentions only one cadet; "....a serving cadet, No 386 Sergeant Major F Fraser Hunter beat all previous records by obtaining every possible decoration during his College course, a wonderful example of versatility."[3] He had excelled in all he did and as a final distinction received the Governor General's Medal.[4]

He also received a military commission, not in those days automatically conferred on those who graduated. In Canada the situation was almost the reverse of the British. The Royal Military College at Sandhurst was never large enough to supply sufficient officers for the Regular Army. It was quite common for candidates who failed to pass the entrance examination - a difficult one with which Winston Churchill had considerable trouble - to enter the Militia and study for the equivalent of the Sandhurst final examination with a private military tutor (known as a "crammer"). If they passed this, they were eligible for commissions in the same way as if they had attended the college course as "gentlemen cadets". About one hundred and fifty commissions were given annually to militia officers. Robert (later Lord) Baden-Powell, a hero of Mafeking in the Boer War and later founder of the Boy Scout movement, twice failed examinations to enter Oxford, but received sufficiently high marks in the Army examination that he was granted an immediate commission in the 13th Hussars. He learned the craft of soldiering afterwards.

The purpose of the Royal Military College of Canada was to impart a military education so as to ensure that there would be in later years a number of men who, though engaged in civilian occupations, would be available for service in an emergency. The cost to Canada was about two thirds of the cost of cadet training - the balance paid by the cadets' families - which went on for four years. This was a long time. At Sandhurst, where young men were trained for the infantry and cavalry, the course was only a year and a half, while at the Royal Military Academy, Woolwich, where cadets were trained for the artillery and engineers, the course was for two years. The reason for the longer period at Kingston - it was soon reduced to three years - was that cadets were given considerable education in civil subjects, an area for which Sandhurst and Woolwich required a higher degree of proficiency before entry.

It was a difficult year for a cadet at Kingston to be granted a commission within Canada. On graduation there was no certainty of a military appointment and some graduates who failed to obtain commissions in Canada or Britain went to the United States. The top four graduates of each class - fourteen or so - were offered Imperial Commissions. Hunter was one of them.

Only six weeks after graduating Hunter wrote to the Prime Minister, Sir Wilfred Laurier, stating that he had graduated from the RMC, had received the Governor General's Silver Medal and had received also an Indian Staff Corps Commission - this Indian Staff Corps would soon be known as the Indian Army. He particularly wanted to be sent to the Bengal Presidency and posted to the Bengal cavalry. Its most famous regiment was the 10th Bengal Lancers, also called Hodgson's Horse. Because of this wish, wrote Hunter, he had refused a commission in the Royal Artillery, as well as in the British infantry and cavalry. Would the Prime Minister be good enough to write a letter of introduction and recommendation to Lord Lansdowne and Lord Strathcona? Lord Lansdowne had been both Governor-General of Canada and Viceroy of India and was at the time war secretary. Lord Strathcona had recently succeeded Sir Charles Tupper as Canadian High Commissioner in London.

Sir Wilfred did as he was asked and Hunter, armed with his two introductions, set off for London, age twenty-two and a second lieutenant on the unattached list. It was an exciting year in which to be sailing for England. It was the year in which Kitchener, inexorably advancing down the Nile, destroyed the Mahdi's army outside of Omdurman and where young Winston Churchill, just back from India himself, took part in what was probably the Empire's last cavalry charge. Hunter, like other Canadians, may have recalled the lines by William Wye Smith,

"O, East is but the West with the sun a little hotter;
And the pine becomes a palm, by the dark Egyptian water
And the Nile's like many a stream we knew that fills
its brimming cup.
We'll think it is the Ottawa, as we track the batteaux up."

It was a year in which the unabashed emotion of Victoria's Diamond Jubilee and all the colorful imperial trappings, were clearly remembered. This was that now almost forgotten period when Britain ruled an enormous Empire and when the word "imperial" did not have the unpleasant connotation it has, for some, since acquired. The British crown reigned over a major part of the world on which, quite literally, the sun never set. Included were Canada, Australia and New Zealand, large parts of Africa and islands circling the globe. It was a time when English-speaking Canadians thought of themselves as

British, part of a worldwide family. At Queen Victoria's Diamond Jubilee in 1897 there had been a glorious surge of pride at things imperial. Soon the decline in confidence would begin but now was the time in which the lines for young soldiers, "Now God be thanked who has matched us with his hour, and caught our youth, and wakened us from sleeping" would have been more appropriately written.

Problems faced him immediately. There were no vacancies in the Bengal cavalry. The army in India at that time was quite different from what it had been before the Mutiny and from what it would be after Kitchener's later reforms. The college at Addiscombe in England where future officers for the armies of the East India Company were trained had been closed in 1860 and direct appointments of British officers to local forces ceased in the following year. There were three Presidency Armies; Bengal, Madras and Bombay as well as the somewhat smaller Punjab Force. Each of these armies had several infantry battalions and cavalry regiments. The Bombay Presidency Army, for example, had following the Mutiny, thirty infantry battalions and seven cavalry regiments. After the Mutiny, the artillery became almost an exclusive preserve of British regiments stationed in India. A staff corps was formed in each presidency. The immediate command of troops and companies was the responsibility of Indian officers and there were only seven - later nine - British officers with each battalion of a regiment and they were principally concerned with overall staff work - hence the name Indian Staff Corps.

A number of additional changes had been made in the 1890s. The Presidency system was abolished - although names were retained initially - and the whole army was placed under one commander-in-chief. Most of the lower level structural changes affected the infantry rather than the cavalry and some of the Bengal and Bombay battalions were converted into units of Punjabis, Pathans and Gurkhas.

To a large extent the administration of the army in India mirrored the administration of civil India. Most of the senior posts were held by a small number of British. And it was a small number. In 1904 it was calculated that there were 6,500 British civil servants, including those in engineering, public works, forestry, telegraphs, education and police. These few administered a country of more than 300 million Indians. This meant that most of the administrative work was done by Indians. Subordinate courts, for example, were at the turn of the century almost entirely presided over by Indian judges. Provincial education services were recruited solely in India and there were four Indian engineering colleges.

So also in the army. While Hunter was seeking his appointment to the Bengal cavalry, the army in India numbered less than a quarter of a million of whom about seventy thousand were British regiments. The Indian army units numbered about 150,000 with fewer than two thousand British officers - there were in addition, the "princely states" with their own cavalry, infantry and transport troops. The Bengal Presidency, to which Hunter aspired, had nineteen cavalry regiments and each had only nine British officers. There would only be a vacancy when one of those officers either died or retired.

Hunter had shown considerable single-mindedness in refusing other offers of commissions. They were not offered lightly. Only those passing out near the top of their class at Sandhurst had much assurance of being commissioned into the regiments of their choice. And however highly they passed out, if they wanted to get into the Foot Guards, the King's Royal Rifle Corps - Kitson's regiment - the Rifle Brigade or the Household Cavalry, they had the added mandatory hurdle of personal nomination by the Colonel-in-Chief.

A British cavalry regiment might have appealed to Hunter, but they had the deserved reputation of being too expensive, too snobbish and too inactive. Even at the turn of the century a junior officer in a crack cavalry regiment could require a private income as high as five hundred pounds a year - more than Can$2,000. Household Cavalry regiments expected their officers to have double that amount. The snobbery aspect would probably not have mattered. All the subtleties of ranking the public school which the new officer had attended, who his family were, and the nuances of accent, would have mattered even less in a Canadian officer than they did in one from Scotland or Ireland. A Canadian officer would have been excused a hundred faults that might have been held against an English officer with flaws in his social credentials. But what would probably have irked Hunter the most was that when he was commissioned the opportunities for action were far fewer in a British regiment than an Indian - the Boer War had not yet begun. A wag in the British Civil Service had written, "We don't want to fight, but by jingo if we do, we'll stay at home and sing our songs, and send the mild Hindu." One British cavalry regiment, the 21st Lancers, saw no action at all until the Battle of Omdurman. Their unofficial motto, said some joker, was "Thou shalt not kill." Added to these deterrents to the British cavalry was that in those days its officers were thought to be "not too bright", possibly a result of the many appalling mistakes made in the Crimean War. Wealthy, socially charming they might be, but as someone, presumably a civilian, unfairly commented of one, "He was so stupid that even his fellow officers noticed it."

Living was less expensive in an Indian cavalry regiment than in a British one. At that time an officer in the Brigade of Guards, the Rifle Brigade or most cavalry regiments needed a substantial private income. Even in the less glamorous county regiments a young subaltern needed at least a hundred pounds a year to supplement his pay - which in those days was less than one hundred and fifty pounds a year. There was so much to buy; a whole array of uniforms, entertainment for guests, contributions to the band, even the upkeep of polo ponies or hunters.

This was not the case in India where officers in many infantry regiments did not feel that a private income was essential. Added to that, an officer's pay was about fifty percent higher than in the British Army stationed at home - in India their pay was increased but was still lower than that in the Indian Army. Although private means were not necessary in Indian infantry regiments, they were most helpful in the prestigious cavalry regiments such as the Bengal or Bombay Lancers.

Yet there was an overriding benefit to service in India. It was expressed by Winston Churchill who had become bored with life in the 3rd Hussars in southern India and managed to arrange an appointment as war correspondent in the Malakand campaign on the Frontier. Wrote Churchill, "For a young man who wants to enjoy himself, to spend a few years agreeably in military companionship.... the British cavalry will be suited...To the youth who means to make himself a professional soldier, and expert in war, a specialist in practical tactics, who desires a hard life of adventure and a true comradeship in arms, I would recommend the choice of some regiment on the frontier, like the fine ones I have seen, the Guides and the Bengal Lancers." Although the generalization is fraught with exceptions, militarily ambitious men, particularly those who could not afford expensive British regiments, went to India to learn their craft.

The official names of Indian regiments reflected their British organization. There was some logic to them. Grenadiers, for example, were originally men who threw grenades and were consequently long armed, tall men. Originally Rifle Regiments, such as the King's Royal Rifle Corps and the Rifle Brigade, carried rifles when other infantry carried muskets. Thus rifle regiments were something of an elite. They still are. Lancers were initially light cavalry armed with lances; dragoons were mounted infantry; hussars were also light cavalry. However, by the time Hunter arrived only the splendor of their uniforms would have distinguished one cavalry regiment from another. In India many British names carried over. But many were also known by the names of the men who had founded them; thus, Skinner's Yellowboys were the 1st Bengal Irregular Cavalry; the 10th Bengal Lancers was known as Hodson's Horse, and the senior regiment in India was Sam Browne's Own.

The men of the old Indian cavalry regiments were far more self-assured and individualistic than those in British regiments. And they had reason to be. Unlike British soldiers they were not simply hired men. They regarded themselves, after a tradition established in the old freebooter days, as shareholders in the regimental company. In the days of the East India Company recruits brought their own horses and equipment; they were independent men ready to fight. Later, because of the need to standardize the quality of horses and equipment, the recruits bought their way in with sufficient money to purchase a horse and equipment - costing in Hunter's day about fifty pounds. Naturally most young recruits could not afford this and were loaned the balance out of regimental funds. This loan was gradually repaid out of their pay. In a sense they were stockholders in a regimental company and the colonel was the managing director. This "company" supplied the Indian government, for a fee, with more than six hundred mounted and provisioned cavalrymen - the government supplied the weapons and ammunition. These cavalrymen, all shareholders in the family business, were responsible for their horses and equipment to a far greater extent than those in a British regiment. If the horse died they had to replace it. This added responsibility brought with it a greater sense of self-assurance and esteem. The men of these Indian regiments - at least until the Great War when so much changed - were gentlemen adventurers with a stake in their regiments' performance. They were treated as such.

The Indian cavalry regiments, such as the Bombay or Bengal Lancers, with their élan, their magnificent attire and chain mail epaulettes, and their distinctive traditions, had something extra as well. Wrote Philip Mason in <u>A Matter of Honour</u>, "You would find that Indian officers took more responsibility than was usual in the infantry, that officers and men shared a common interest in their horses (and) a feeling that the regiment was a family affair."

But Hunter could not yet enter that family. He had to wait for a vacancy.

Once the excitement of arrival in India had worn off, and that would have taken a few months, Hunter's stay with the Shropshire Light Infantry would have been frustrating. There was tension in the civilian areas. A few months before Hunter's arrival Moslem weavers began a riot during which several Europeans were murdered. Bubonic plague, and the measures taken to eliminate it, added to the consequences of a recent failure of the monsoon, and a resultant famine - to be soon repeated - kept tensions high. But from Hunter's personal standpoint, he simply did not want to stay with that particular regiment; it was just a way station on a journey to the Indian cavalry.

This was not unusual. Standards were high and vacancies rare. The future Field Marshall Montgomery, passing out of Sandhurst ten years later, had marks too low for him to enter the Indian Army. William Henry Irvine Shakespear, soon to be a close friend of Hunter, was born in India of a family that had served there for generations. He arrived in Bombay nine months earlier after graduating from Sandhurst and waited more than a year for a posting to the 17th Bengal Lancers.

British regiments were, and still are, family affairs. The regiment is the family; friendships begun there are close, often lasting for a lifetime. Officers of the Shropshires, seeing Hunter as a transient, would have been cordial but not close. Intimate friendships were generally reserved for those with whom they would spend their entire careers.

British India was also a society that deferred to age to a greater extent than was the case in England or Canada. Advancing years brought growing respect whether earned or not. Young men were kept in their place; promotion was slow; conversation in the Mess was dominated by the reflections or nostalgia of senior officers. Hunter might readily have accepted this, yet the problem of simply being young in a middle-aged world was exacerbated shortly after his arrival.

Lord Elgin, the Viceroy, was succeeded by George Nathanial Curzon. Lord Curzon was not only vigorous in his new measures, was full of ideas, knew what he was talking about and had a young and beautiful American wife, but he particularly disliked the administrations of Bombay and Bengal. Unlike other provinces, which were administered by the Indian Civil Service(ICS) through a Lieutenant-Governor, these Presidencies were under the administration of a Governor appointed by London. He ruled with a small Council and often ignored suggestions from the ICS. Curzon chided them and railed against them - and particularly against the administration of Bombay that seemed inadequate in the face of famine and disease.

Worst of all in the eyes of British officials - army as well as civil - Curzon was a young man, hardly forty. None of this would have had any direct affect on Hunter, very junior and far removed from circles in which such auspicious figures as Lieutenant-Governors, Governors and Viceroys moved. Curzon himself wrote in a letter to Lord George Hamilton, Secretary of State for India in London, "...I disturb and annoy these old fogies....picking out the flaws... urging decision.....detecting and protesting against delay. It is a new sensation which no man above fifty could relish."[6] It is quite possible that many, if not most of the old fogies would be irritated not just towards Curzon but by young men generally and would have expressed it by being additionally crabby to those thrust upon them.

Hunter could hardly have waited to move on. An Indian cavalry regiment had a commander - either an acting or substantive lieutenant colonel - four squadron commanders who were captains or majors, and four more squadron officers (on active service this number might be temporally increased) who were lieutenants and second lieutenants. In order for there to be a vacancy for Hunter one of the second lieutenants would have to be promoted to fill a vacancy higher up or seconded to extra-regimental duties.

Finally, slightly more than a year after Hunter arrived in Bombay, opportunity struck. He was offered an appointment to the Bombay Staff Corps, to be attached to the 1st Duke of Connaught's Own Bombay Lancers - a regiment with an unusual and distinctive feature; the regimental band, like the Household Cavalry's today, played while mounted on horseback. The Bombay Lancers were a distinguished regiment, with a history of action on the Frontier and beyond and they had stayed loyal to their officers during the Mutiny. They were also the senior regiment in the Bombay Presidency Army.

Hunter had wanted the Bengal Lancers. The Bengal regiments were seldom away from the Frontier for long, officers' careers were dramatic and dangerous and they learned their craft of soldiering from an opponent who used real bullets. Yet service in the Bombay Cavalry was certainly preferable to the third alternative, the Army of the Madras Presidency, regarded by officers who wanted action as a total backwater made still more tiresome by the enervating and unremitting heat. He accepted the offer of the Bombay Lancers. He would make his own arrangements for maximum action.

The Bombay Presidency was far more extensive than the city of Bombay. This vast Presidency stretched as far north as the deserts of Baluchistan, east to the Central Provinces and south to Madras and Mysore. It contained well over twenty five million inhabitants, most of whom were Hindus but there were also close to five million Moslems.

Years later, reminiscing to journalist Frederick Griffin of Toronto, Hunter recalled being invited with other young officers to go pig sticking by the Maharajah of Baroda. At the last minute the other officers could not go and young Hunter found himself the only westerner on a pig sticking expedition with 124 other riders. Admitting that all he knew about killing a pig was with a mallet on a Canadian farm he said,

"I was after a pig with my team of four when another pig chased by a different team came across my path and ripped my horse up under, which was too bad. A beautiful polo pony and the maharajah was none too pleased. However, he gave me another and I went chasing after the pig which ran into a clump of trees. I couldn't follow so like a fool I jumped off. They all started yelling at me 'Matjao" which means don't go, but I couldn't speak the language then so followed my pig carrying a nine-foot lance. But the pig was wounded and dangerous. It charged me and I managed to catch it on the nose. The lance broke and lifted the pig that went right over me. Just then a sowar (native trooper) ran in to help me but the pig charged and ripped him open."

Other sowars and dogs came in and finished off the pig that turned out to be a record breaker. It had two tusks 10 1/2 inches long. The Maharajah kept one and many years later Hunter had the other tusk mounted in the living room of his house in Durham.

Life as an Indian Lancer officer was luxurious, though probably not quite as replete with privilege as life as an officer in a British cavalry regiment stationed in India. Nonetheless, he had a bevy of personal servants to attend to his needs and had ample time to spend on the two most important pursuits in life - sport and soldiering. Days began before dawn when a servant carrying tea and hot water for shaving woke him. At 6am there was the early morning parade, an assembly of the troops, followed by some practice maneuvering and drill. Then a bath and breakfast, after which there was some time with the men and the horses. During the day time was spent at languages, studying initially the language of the men of his own squadron, Rajput, Sikh or Pathan, and then the languages of other squadrons. At 5pm sports began, particularly on horseback, although activities such as cricket and tennis were increasing in the army. This fitted nicely with Hunter's interest. He was wiry and kept his weight to around 140 pounds well into middle age and horses were an obsession throughout his life. He became a notable polo player and rider and, over the years rode over three hundred race winners. Eventually he took particular pride and pleasure in being a member of the executive committee of the Toronto Horse Show and well after retirement from service in India he still rode in races, points to point and hunted. Sport was a major interest but military action was what he yearned.

Action was unexpected but not long in coming. It was a result of events thousands of miles to the northeast. China, the "Sleeping Dragon" was waking up.

CHINA AND BACK

China's young emperor was gradually freeing himself from the malignant influence of his aunt, the reactionary Dowager Empress who resisted all attempts to modernize the country. The daughter of a Chinese army officer, she had been so beautiful as a young girl that in the 1840s she was selected, along with twenty-seven other Manchu girls, for the harem of the Emperor. Soon promoted to be a first grade concubine and the Emperor's favorite she had immense influence in court and was noted for her callous cruelties. It was an influence that continued for decades after the old emperor's death.

The failure of the Chinese in the 1895 war with Japan eroded her power and the new emperor, shaking off his aunt's influence, became an ardent advocate of liberal ideas. Two years before the end of the century the vermilion pencil of the court was giving imperial sanction to a flood of edicts, particularly those respecting education that would enable the Chinese to benefit from western ideas and science. It was even reported that in this passion for modernization an edict was contemplated that would do away with the queue, or pigtail. Originally this was imposed on the Chinese by their Manchu conquerors as a badge of subjugation. Instead it was adopted and cherished as a mark of national identity. The conservative mandarins, and others with vested interests, felt threatened by these foreign ideas and they were supported in their fears by all the forces of peasant superstition.

When China failed so dismally in her war with Japan - just one of the many foreign nations biting chunks from her territorial flanks - the emperor, having recently achieved his majority, gradually began to lead the country away from the influence of the so-called "petticoat government".

The old dowager-empress retired to the Summer Palace to await her opportunity. It was not long in coming. Resistance to the reform movement soon focused upon her and reactionaries in the army particularly supported her.

In the Fall of 1898 she pulled off a neat coup d'etat, imprisoning the emperor and having her own regency restored. Several reformers were summarily executed and the deposed emperor was reported as "gravely ill with his life despaired of". It was a condition from which he rapidly recovered when the British minister in China spoke of the dire consequences should he die. Nevertheless, the reactionaries were in the ascendancy; reformers fled, newspapers closed; an anti-foreign movement swept out of the northern province of Shantung into the metropolitan province of Chihli. A new movement, "the fist of righteous harmony", soon acquired the name of "Boxer" and gained thousands of supporters. Boxer banners were clear. "Exterminate the foreigners and save the dynasty."

China had a history of murdering missionaries and in June, 1900, Boxers killed two more and earlier destroyed a number of Chinese Christian villages and massacred the converts. They tore up rail lines and burned stations. Murder and carnage spread through the north. Instead of condemning it the dowager-empress was ambivalent and it was easy for lesser officials to see in that ambivalence tacit approval. Peking was soon in turmoil, despite the presence of some four hundred officers and men of various foreign naval detachments who had reached the city earlier to defend the legations.

Europeans and Christian Chinese took refuge in the British legation and prepared for attack. The chancellor of the Japanese legation was murdered. Hundreds of Chinese Christians were slaughtered in the city. Virtually all European property in Peking was destroyed. The German minister, Baron von Ketteler, was killed and Chinese troops opened fire on the foreign legations.

Unknown until later were the events of the interior where many of the killings were particularly savage. In one city a large number of Christians were butchered with the direct participation of the provincial governor. News of the slaughters provoked revulsion throughout the western world. During 1900 the Boxers killed about two hundred missionaries and fifty of their children, and many more Chinese.

Peking was cut off from the rest of the world from 14 July. An international force of two thousand left Tiensin for Peking. They did not get far. After suffering heavy casualties the force was driven back.

More troops were urgently needed. The only ones available - since the British Army was deeply embroiled in war in South Africa - were regiments in India.

Sending Indian troops to campaign outside India was not new but had Indian troops been sent to South Africa to fight the Boers, the entire Boer population would have risen in protest. China was another matter. Early in August a brigade from India under the command of Lieutenant-General Sir Alfred Gaselee reached Tiensin. Together with contingents from other nations a combined force numbering twenty thousand set off to battle their way through to the relief of the besieged legations. They were successful, although many of the contingents suffered terribly from the heat and the accompanying thirst. There was considerable competition for the kudos of victory, particularly from the Russians, and this early attempt at peace making was fraught with bickering. Nevertheless, largely because of the doggedness of the Japanese and the skill and tenacity of the Sikhs, the legations were relieved.

Before this had occurred the need for more cavalry had become clear. There were only the Bengal Lancers and a few Cossacks. The 6th United States Cavalry landed at Taku, but their horses had suffered so much from the voyage that the unit had to stay behind. Cavalry was important to the campaign and the Third Cavalry Brigade in India had been warned for duty as early as July 7, only a few days after General Gaselee had left for China. One of the units warned for duty with the Third Cavalry was the 3rd Queen's Own Bombay Light Cavalry. Although Hunter had been with his own unit for less than eight months, he immediately applied for a temporary transfer to them.

On 27 July the request by Hunter was approved, along with that of another officer of the 1st Bombay Lancers, a Lieutenant Lang. The two of them hurried off to Neemuch, a town in the state of Gwalior where the 3rd, under the command of Lieutenant Colonel Phayre, was preparing for embarkation.

The Brigade included with the Bombay Light Cavalry, the 14th Sikhs, two more regiments of the Bengal Lancers and a battery of Royal Horse Artillery. But the cholera that was ravaging India did not spare the army. A new regiment of artillery had to replace the one designated because cholera had so decimated its ranks, and the sailing orders of the 14th Sikhs had to be cancelled altogether. On 13 August the Cavalry Brigade sailed from Calcutta. The following day, as the ships of this reinforcement headed towards Singapore, further north, in China, General Gaselee's Rajputs and Sikhs, led by their British officers and followed by the Royal Welch Fusiliers, stormed into the legation compound at Peking. Russians, Americans, French and Japanese followed them in a victory attributable less to British military prowess than to Chinese incompetence.

Hunter had missed the relief of the Peking legations but he had a year in China ahead of him. In that year it is possible that he discovered that despite the Boxers, the violence was quite out of character with the people. A writer of the times remarked that "the Chinese are reserved, earnest and good natured; for the occasional outbursts of ferocious violence, notably against foreign settlements, are no index to the national character....and even strangers can travel through the country without meeting rudeness much less outrage... He is industrious but his industry is normally along lines marked out by authority and tradition. He is brave, but his courage does not naturally seek an outlet in war."[7]

While the Boxers and other peasants committed horrifying acts against foreigners and Christian Chinese other Chinese took immense risks helping Europeans escape and many hundreds of British and Americans owed their lives to lesser Chinese officials and peasants. In the Yangtsze Valley senior Chinese officials co-operated with British consuls and naval commanders, disregarding imperial edicts issued during the ascendancy of the Boxers.

The Third Cavalry Brigade, like the principal German force that was also on the high seas, missed the main actions. Peking had been relieved and the Taku forts, at the mouth of the Pei Ho River, had been captured by a brilliant and audacious naval action. One young naval officer there, Roger Keyes, as well as two others serving in north China at the same time, John Jellicoe and David Beatty, would all eventually become Admirals of the Fleet. It is possible that Hunter, who stayed with Beatty at his home in Brooksby in 1919, met him first in China.

The various other allied contingents, still bickering among themselves, had little fighting left to do and no government with which to negotiate - the dowager-empress had hastily fled south with her court. Many of the allied soldiers, senior officers to lowly privates, used their time to personal advantage by looting anything of value. The Russians were more brutish. When the Boxer movement was at its height in June Chinese authorities in Manchuria had unwisely declared war on the Russians, panicking the Russian administrations in the adjacent provinces. The Russians used terror to restore their prestige and power and there were many massacres; at one of them, Cossacks flung some five thousand Chinese - men, women and children - into the Amur River.

Hunter's Brigade arrived in northern China in September and was posted for the winter in the province of Chihli, where most of the fighting had been. The railway had to be repaired - much had been torn up by the Boxers. It linked Peking with Tiensin, followed the Pei Ho River almost to its mouth and the Taku Forts, then swung north, through the Great Wall after which it linked up the Russian Manchurian Railway. It had been financed by the British and controlled by British staff. During the fighting along much of its route - the allies used it in their attempts to reach Peking - Russians worked on the line as they were the only ones with trained railway men at hand. After the fighting the Russians wanted to keep it since, as an extension of their Siberian and Manchurian railways, it would have given them control over the whole line from Moscow to Peking. After many threats the Russians handed control to the Germans who in turn gave it back to the British. One of the British soldiers helping to administer the line was Lionel Dunsterville, who had been at Westward Ho School with Rudyard Kipling and was the person after whom the character "Stalky" was portrayed. Dunsterville would lead a force through Persia during the First World War and briefly occupy Baku. In his memoirs he speaks warmly of the assistance given him in China by a cavalry officer in the Indian Army named Hunter.

While many repair jobs were done and a peace treaty was debated and ultimately signed, there was constant argument over reparations - the Germans wanting far more than their belated contribution to the campaign could justify. All of them, with the exception of the Americans, wanted very substantial compensation. Serving with the Americans was Frank Irwin, a veteran of the Spanish War and formerly with Buffalo Bill's Circus. He too had been raised in Durham and years later, when Fraser Hunter had retired to Durham, Frank Irwin became mayor of the town.

In the early months of 1901 there were punitive expeditions into the interior in which, in all probability, more innocent Chinese coolies than Boxers were killed. The dowager-empress, who was so ready to impose death on others, went unpunished herself. She did, however, endeavour to expiate her offenses by instructing a number of her officials to commit suicide. They did so. The Germans finally caught the Chinese soldier who murdered Von Ketteler. He pleaded that he was only obeying the orders of his superior officers. The Germans, naturally oblivious of the historic irony, refused to accept this defense and he was executed.

Hunter must have been eventually thankful that although he had missed the fighting he could return to India, avoiding a second winter in the awful cold of north China. He had not wasted his time and in July, 1902, passed the Indian Army final examination in Chinese.[8] Most of the Bombay Light Cavalry left Taku at the end of October. By November 19 all of them were back in India. The campaign, for those arriving after the siege of the legations had ended, was a sorry one lacking the glamour that they probably hoped for. Hunter had nevertheless done his various tasks with competence and for this the American government gave him the Award of the Dragon.

A week after landing at Calcutta he rejoined the Duke of Connaught's Bombay Lancers, stationed now at Poona. It was a city that had suffered and was still suffering from bubonic plague, which remained at epidemic proportions throughout the Bombay Presidency.

During this period of his life Hunter became friendly with William Shakespear of the Bengal Lancers. This friendship lasted all of Shakespear's short life. Shakespear was with the 17th Bengal Lancers and had done a long stint of cholera duty with them while Hunter was in China. Shakespear was appointed an Assistant District Officer in Bombay in March, 1901, with the specific task of fighting the bubonic plague and had introduced some vigorous measures to rid the city of rats. He came from a family with long service in India and elsewhere in the Empire and the name crops up frequently in Indian Army history throughout the nineteenth century. A lieutenant Richmond Shakespear rode across Afghanistan and reached Khiva in June, 1840. He negotiated an agreement with the Khan of Khiva whereby the Khan agreed to surrender his Russian prisoners if the Russians would depart from Khivan lands - something which Delhi thought might reduce Russian pressure southwards.

Although familiar with cholera, a disease well known in India, plague challenged the ingenuity and resourcefulness of all directed to fight it.

Bombay was a thriving city of more than three quarters of a million people, but since September 1896, the city, along with much of the Presidency had been ravaged by plague, the same disease that had afflicted Europe in the fourteenth century and England during the Great Plague of the seventeenth century. Its origins were obscure but it was no stranger to Asia. In 1897 forty seven thousand people in Bombay died of the disease. By 1899, the entire region was afflicted. By the end of 1902, four hundred and fifty thousand had died and particularly hit were Karachi and Poona, a hundred or so miles south east of Bombay. Over the next two years another half million would die of the disease. The only really successful sanitary measure was migration but this was only practical in the villages. Segregation of the sick was also attempted but misunderstood by many Indians and there were riots against it. The city of Bombay became a world centre for the study of the disease and the army was active throughout the Presidency distributing clothing, food and medical supplies - and disposing of the dead. To add to the region's desperate situation the monsoon rains failed in 1896 and again in 1899 and the distress of the resulting famine was made still worse by yet another outbreak of cholera.

Not much was known about plague, but many of the doctors and army officers guessed there was some sort of a link between bubonic plague and the rats that infested the communities. Many army officers led campaigns against the rats and, armed with revolvers, knives, traps and clubs, killed thousands.

By the time Shakespear returned to his regiment, stationed in the north at Rawalpindi in April 1902 he and Hunter had met, perhaps because of their shared plague duties, or perhaps because of an introduction by Shakespear's uncle, Alex Shakespear, who was a member of the Bombay Motor Union. Hunter, a keen motorist, eventually helped Shakespear learn to drive, and it is probable that later on, they together both learned to fly. Later, in 1905, Hunter was almost certainly involved in the organization of the Delhi to

Bombay road race. Shakespear's Uncle Alex took part, driving a Darraacq and competing with the Humberettes, the De Dions, the Renaults, Fiats, Napiers, Lanchesters, Oldsmobiles, and Speedwells. In the preparations there had been considerable debate about whether steam-driven cars should be allowed extra time to take on water. Some thirty eight cars, driven by army officers, civil servants, an Italian count and three Indian aristocrats, finally set off on the race over nine hundred miles of rough road stopping at Agra and Gwalior on the way and with only one passable hotel on the route. Hunter and the other organizers gave the participants a tremendous ovation and a reception was held for them at the Taj Mahal Hotel in Bombay - a palatial hotel that had been completed only the year before.

It may be of no importance at all today that the road run was completed by twenty-one of the cars entered, with tire troubles the principal affliction of the competitors. It is still less important that a Darracq distinguished itself by not losing a single point or that both the Maharajah of Mysore's trophy and the Rajah of Kaputhala's Cup were won by De Dion cars, or even that the Maharajah of Gwalior's Cup went to a Speedwell. What is important is that change was in the air.

The British attitude towards the automobile was far less advanced than the attitudes in Canada or the United States. In Britain development of the car had been severely retarded by the Red Flag Act of 1865, which required any automobile on the highway to be preceded by a man carrying a red flag. It was not until this Act was repealed in 1896 that there was any real automobile development.

Today, looking back on those years before the First World War, it seems a time of tranquility and supreme self-confidence. Yet perhaps the confidence was not so assured. Perhaps it contained an element of bravado. The Boer War made an indelible impact, particularly on the junior officers, for the casualties exceeded those of all the colonial wars since Waterloo. In London the death of Victoria sounded the death knell of an era; the young Arthur Balfour had replaced Lord Salisbury, a man who epitomized conservatism, and the endless vista of prosperity was no longer so clear. There were cars on the roads and wireless waves in the air. Change was endemic. Even the Imperial challenge had undergone a perceptible change – at least for those whose sensibilities were finely tuned. The Imperial challenge was no longer to seize but to hold.

Thoughtful young army officers, and there were many in addition to Shakespear and Hunter despite today's tendency to caricature them all as blimpish buffoons, were far less concerned with swagger and far more concerned with being sensitive to change and its implications.

In 1904 Shakespear left the Bengal Lancers and joined the Indian Political Department. In 1905 Fraser Hunter, for the past two years a squadron commander and adjutant of his regiment, left the Bombay Lancers and joined the civil branch of the government of India; civil in that it was responsible to the Indian Department of Education, Health and Lands, yet military, in that virtually all its executive positions were held by army officers, who retained their military ranks and seniority and who continued in some respects to exercise a military function. This body, part civil, part military, was known as the Survey of India.

What made Hunter leave the Lancers? His career had been exceptional and he was already adjutant of his regiment. Most notably he was declared in 1905 "Best Man-at-Arms, Mounted and Dismounted in India".[9] Yet he still wanted to leave the army. Hunter made a confidential approach to the Commander-in-Chief early in

1905 asking for a transfer and the C in C had discouraged him. This was not unusual. Even quite recently it was usual to discourage young officers seeking extra-regimental employment and the view among senior officers was that young men should "stay with the regiment". But Hunter persisted. Whether the Lancers were too expensive and the higher pay in the Survey attracted him, or regimental life was too tedious away from "the frontier" or he saw no career future staying with the regiment is now unknown. Whatever the reason he was not going to take the C in C's advice and he wrote a formal letter to the Military Secretary to the Commander-in-Chief saying "After serious consideration, and for pressing reasons, I have concluded that I cannot afford to serve the Government in my present capacity. It is, however, still my hope that my services may be acceptable in another sphere for which my education, previous experience and strong inclination suit me. After consulting my commanding officer I venture to address you in the hope that His Excellency may be induced to permit me to accept - when it is offered - employment in the Civil Department of the Survey of India."

It may seem strange today that a young man in search of adventure should opt for surveying. But at the beginning of the twentieth century such a choice was far from odd. Most of the world was not properly mapped. When Hunter had been in China the maps were inadequate and it was only after the Boxer Rebellion that, between 1901 and 1905, maps of Chihli and Shantung were prepared from surveys made by Prussian officers. The use of the military in map making was widespread. Britain had its Ordinance Survey and Canada its surveyor-general attached to the Department of the Interior in Ottawa - although the intelligence branch of the department of military defense began publishing topographical maps in 1904. In most countries map making was the responsibility of the military.

The maps of India were of a particularly high standard and, unlike those of most Asian countries, had a survey that was equal to most European states. Although the mapping of India had been underway for more than a hundred years when Hunter joined, it had not been until 1903 that the first edition of the official one in one million scale map of India was published.

India's surveyors had a high international reputation and were often asked to contribute internationally. A former officer of the Indian Survey had organized the surveying of Siam[10]. Maps of the Yunnan Province of China and the Indo-China frontier owed much to the contributions of Indian Army officers. While Hunter was in China a Survey officer accompanied Sir Francis Younghusband's mission to Tibet. A British Army officer, Major P.H. Fawcett, surveyed the Brazilian-Bolivian boundary in 1906, (before he mysteriously vanished) and a Survey of India officer was assistant commissioner for the Argentine-Chile boundary commission.

What all the British in India knew was that the Survey of India was deeply involved in playing "the Great Game". When Rudyard Kipling's <u>Kim</u>, the story of the young boy, Kimball O'Hara, who managed, with his friend the Guru, to upset the Czar's sinister plots against India, was published in 1901, the covert role of the Survey was a frequent subject of speculation. It was said that many of the Anglo-English characters in the book were readily recognized. Colonel Creighton, Kim's mentor at the Survey, may not have been a deliberate portrait of Colonel Burrard, the actual Superintendent, yet Creighton's lifelong dream was to be elected a Fellow of the Royal Society. Wrote Kipling,

"No money and no preferment would have drawn Creighton from his work on the Indian Survey, but deep in his heart also lay the ambition to write 'F.R.S' after his name. Honours of a sort he knew could be obtained by ingenuity and the help of friends, but to the best of his belief, nothing save work - papers representing a life of it - took a man into the Society which he had bombarded for years with monographs on strange Asiatic cults and unknown customs... By all right and reason it was the Royal Geographical which should have appealed to him, but men are as chancy as children in their choice of playthings."

When Hunter joined the Survey Colonel Burrard, who was then superintendent of the Trigonometrical Branch at Dehra Dun, was the only Survey officer who had been recently elected a Fellow of the Royal Society. It was also true that most Survey officers gravitated towards the Royal Geographical Society - Hunter was elected a Fellow in 1903.

On 17 August 1905, 1st Lieutenant Fraser Hunter was posted to Simla as an assistant superintendent, 2nd grade, (on probation) attached to Number 18 Party. Eleven days later, under the command of Captain Maurice O'Connor Tandy, who was six years senior to Hunter, the party entered the so-called Northern Circle to continue the long task of mapping sixteen districts of the Punjab and North West Frontier province.

He was not there long. Shortly after normal surveying operations had begun in the high foothills of the Himalayas, the Survey received a special request. Lord Curzon, the Viceroy, had taken a tour of the Persian Gulf states in 1903 and seen how barren were existing maps. He also recognized, as did many others, that after Russia's disastrous defeat in a war with Japan and the attempts at revolution that were sweeping Russia, the pressing strategic threat from Russia had diminished while fears of Germany's intentions were growing. It was essential to improve knowledge of the lesser-known regions between India and the expansionist Germany and better documentation was seen as an essential pre-requisite.

J.C. Lorimer of the Political Department was instructed to prepare a gazetteer, to compile a record of the geographical, political, economic and ethnological facts. Hunter, using whatever information from any sources he could find, was to prepare a map to illustrate the gazetteer.

SURVEY OF INDIA

"But Kim did not suspect that Mahbud Ali,
known as one of the best horse dealers in the Punjab
....whose caravans penetrated far and far into the Back
of Beyond, was registered in one of the locked books of
the Indian Survey Department as C25.1B. Twice or
thrice yearly C25 would send a little story, badly
told but most interesting, and generally - it was
checked by statements of R17 and M4 - quite true.
It concerned all manner of out-of-the-way
principalities, explorers of nationalities
other than English, and the gun trade - was,
in brief, a small portion of that vast mass of
"information received" on which the Indian
Government acts."

Kipling.

Today, with high flying photographic surveillance aircraft and satellites in orbit keeping watch on the world, the role of MI.4 is no longer at the forefront of the imaginations of those interested in the secret services. Yet not so long ago, those who read the spy novels and knew that MI.5 was counter intelligence and MI.6, otherwise known as the Secret Intelligence Service, was responsible for espionage also knew the function of MI.4. This topographical section, MI.4, collated the vast minutiae of the countryside - not simply the contours and rivers, nor only the highways and byways, but detail such as the thickness of the tarmac on the roads, the width of bridges, the extent of roadside ditches, the availability of supplies and the people who would furnish them; in short, the ever changing geographical intelligence vital to the successful movement of armies. In British intelligence, that was the role of MI.4. In and immediately beyond the borders of India, it was the function of the Survey of India.

The Survey Department of the Government of India always attracted men who found the normal routines of soldiering insufficient a challenge. Nearly a hundred years earlier the tradition of mapping beyond the borders had been established when a veterinary surgeon named William Moorcroft had gone to Bengal to inspect the horses of the East India Company army. Using the excuse that the sturdy little horses of the Turkoman would improve the breed in Bengal, Moorcroft began his travels and explorations long before the Great Game had really begun. While mapping an ancient caravan route, he traveled to Kashmir, onto Jellalabad and Kabul and north to Bokhara, well inside Central Asia. It was even reported later that he did not die on his way back from Bokhara to India, as was first thought, but had instead made the journey to Lhasa where he lived for a dozen years. What is quite certain is that he produced a number of rough maps showing the caravan routes into Central Asia and that the route from Yarkand to Kashmir was the one by which the Russian could one day enter India.

The monumental task of mapping the entire sub-continent of India for many years occupied the surveyors. They were engaged in the Great Trigonometrical Survey as well as the detailed domestic map-making necessary for the complex business of administering so vast an area.

Then there was map-making necessary for the defense of India from outside aggression. India's mapmakers had included among their numbers great administrators such as George Everest, and writers like Richard Burton, as well as mountaineers and explorers. There can scarcely have been a department of government whose dry annual reports concealed more drama. The mapmakers might spend months without a break camping and trekking on the edges of the Himalayas; they might instead be vulnerable to disease in some fetid swamp; some could fall victim to attack by rogue elephant or tiger, while dacoits or fearful primitive tribesmen attacked others. Their territory ranged from Cape Comorin to the Himalayas, from the jungles of eastern Burma to the deserts of Baluchistan and their time spanned more than a century.

The designation, "Survey of India" began in 1877 by an amalgamation of the Topographical and Revenue branches of the Survey Department and the Great Trigonometrical Survey. Habit being what it is, the Survey of India was also frequently referred to as the Survey Department and the Trigonometrical Survey.

Many of the officers of the Survey of India were lead players in the Great Game and spent their lives assembling and assessing information about enemies, real or potential. However, Kipling's story of Kim and the activities of the Survey in thwarting the sinister designs of the Russians is almost certainly a delightful exaggeration. Espionage in Central Asian states was principally done by agents paid by Political Officers of the Foreign Department (themselves principally army officers) and, to a lesser extent, by agents of Army Intelligence. Nonetheless, for two reasons the Survey can be assumed to have had far more than a casual or incidental role.

As early as 1860 it has been decided that the Survey should gather information on ethnography and the flora and fauna as well as topography in areas examined. Secondly, the senior ranks of the Survey were almost exclusively held by army officers. There was something of an anomaly here that would affect Hunter much later. The Survey was part of the Home department of the Indian government and although civilians filled many positions most – but not all – senior positions were filled by army officers who retained their army rank. The Survey group often had attached an army officer from the Intelligence Department but at least in the early years of the century surveying was a civil function not a military one. However, most of them, like their contemporaries in military units and the Foreign Department, believed that covert Russian activities threatened India.

Assembling and assessing information about current or prospective enemies has for centuries been a concern of government. In England the man usually identified as the first great spymaster was Sir Francis Walsingham head of Tudor Queen Elizabeth's espionage system.

Despite this early start, three hundred years later the British had not evolved an intelligence gathering system as sophisticated as their early start might have allowed. Towards the end of the nineteenth century field intelligence gathering techniques had hardly changed since they were introduced by Wellington in the early part of that century. The poverty of the system soon became apparent. At the outbreak of the South African War the Intelligence Department contained eighteen officers, only two of whom were responsible for the Boer Republics. And the commanding general Buller - nicknamed "Blunder" - thought he did not need even them. When he received the Intelligence Manual on South Africa he sent it back unread on the grounds that he already knew everything there was to know about the country.

Yet changes were evolving and accelerating. Goaded by the disasters of the Crimean War the British had established the Military Intelligence Branch in 1873. Only forty-one years later, at the outbreak of the First World War progress had been such that the Special Intelligence Bureau, forerunner of MI.5, wiped out the entire German espionage system in England immediately war was declared and by the end of August 1914 fifty intelligence specialists were with the British Expeditionary Force. It is significant that these intelligence agents - university professors, travelers, adventurers - who had been secretly listed before the war, initially had no commanding officer to take them to France and organize their activities. The man selected to lead them - a Major Torrie - was an Indian Army officer home on leave when war began, for despite progress, Britain in those days had no equivalent of the Indian Army field intelligence specialists such as the Intelligence Corps in Peshawar or the Corps of Guides.

Yet Britain had come a long way since the Crimea. This immense progress was made even though many thought that Britain, splendidly isolated by the sea from direct military or naval threats, did not need it. In India and the Middle East the threats were more obvious and the need for detailed intelligence far greater. Lord Ellenborough, supervising the East India Company as head of the Board of Control in London, formally requested government agencies to assemble information on the routes by which the Russians might attack India as early as 1829.

Anxiety about Russian intentions reached crisis levels in 1885. A committee was established in London to facilitate the exchange of naval and military information. This Colonial Defense Committee was the forerunner of the Imperial Defense Committee. The most advanced field intelligence gathering work had been done in India, where the danger was closest and had been seen for the longest.

India, with its own government acting in many respects independently of London, could not afford that detachment from danger that the sea and the Royal Navy allowed England. Consequently subversive and overt gathering of intelligence was most advanced there, though not centrally organized until later than in England.

Military and political officers assembled information from the Frontier and beyond and the Survey of India department, that earlier began the Great Trigonometrical Survey of India, mapped the routes by which the enemy might come. One military group whose importance should not be under estimated was the Corps of Guides, which had from its inception been involved in map making and intelligence gathering. The men of this corps were of an incredibly high standard and may, in some ways, have set the standards upon which the modern Special Air Service was founded. They involved themselves in countless daring exploits, sometimes working as individuals out of uniform, well beyond the borders of India.

The Survey served a military and political as well as a geographical function since for tactical as well as strategic and logistical reasons, knowledge of geography is essential to the successful prosecution of war. All campaigns needed their surveyors to keep the commanding general thoroughly familiar with the topography. The British were not the only ones to realize this, of course, and they would later have their MI.4, also known as the Geographical Section of the General Staff (GSGS). Similarly the Survey of India was represented on British military campaigns on the borders of India. In 1878 the

Survey had seventy-seven army officers and a long list of "native agents" gathering intelligence.

Some of the surveyors' work was speculative but by triangulation and experience a topographer could, with the aid of a few fixed points and supplementary information, sketch out with some degree of certainty territory in advance of his own position. Triangulation was the extension of a base line from which a skeleton could be formed as a first step to a complete map. The basis for surveys across Afghanistan and Baluchistan to the Oxus and Persia was founded by triangulation.

The work of the Survey of India contained two principal functions. The first was the need to act as any survey office - that is, making and issuing maps of territory under its own government's jurisdiction. The second was an intelligence gathering function beyond the borders of India. Maps produced by the Survey generally had attached the designation SI. When maps were made for the Army or the Foreign Office, they were designated IB (Intelligence Bureau). The only way today of knowing who was doing what is to check the reports listing "officers on special duty" and to conjecture from "miscellaneous funds allocated".

Military intelligence gathering in India was the responsibility of the Quartermaster General(QMG) who, in the 1870's was Frederick Roberts. Roberts, like virtually all other military men in India, was concerned about the Russian advance southwards and what would happen should the Russians cross the Oxus and press into Afghanistan. His planning for this contingency was frustrated by lack of detailed information about what was happening beyond the Himalayas. The Intelligence Branch, which became the QMG's responsibility, was formed to gather, collate and analyze all the vast amount of information obtained by individual army units, the Survey of India and officers of the Political Department.

General Roberts, "Bobs" as he was known to his men, took part in the Second Afghan War and, as a result of his spectacular march from Kabul to Kandahar, became a popular hero in England. He was later appointed Commander in Chief, India and in 1895 a Field Marshall. Less well known, he had established a formal intelligence agency in India as part of the Quartermaster General's department.

There were two forms of intelligence gathering in India, Political Intelligence and Military Intelligence. The dominant theme of both was the protection of India from foreign and internal threats to security.

The Great Game, a chimera to some but in the eyes of many a response to real dangers, was countering the threat to India from Russia as it advanced inexorably southwards towards Tibet, Afghanistan and Persia and information from those countries was gathered assiduously. In Rudyard Kipling's "Kim" intelligence gathering is portrayed as a centralized enterprise dominated the Survey of India. The reality was far more complex. Consular posts in Persia were divided between the Indian Political Service and His Majesty's Levant Consular Service. Political intelligence was gleaned in the chaotic nation of Persia by a permanent British legation in Teheran and by Consuls-General in Bushire, Isfahan and Meshed and Consulates in smaller towns throughout the country. The legation in Teheran and larger Consulates, for example, Shiraz and Resht, was staffed by and reported to the Foreign Office in London and the smaller consulates, such as Meshed and Ahwaz, by the Indian Civil Service or Indian Army officers in the Political Service.

The consulate-general's office in Meshed was the intelligence centre for a network of agents working in Central Asia as far northeast as Samarkand; the Indo-Persian Telegraph Office at Jask, on the Gulf, housed those responsible for the Persian Gulf and was particularly concerned with combating gun running from the Arab emirates to tribes like the Kashgai in Persia. Far to the northeast, the consulate at Kashgar was the "listening post" for events eastward into China. All these consulates had secret service funds.

Internal communications within and between the various services was unwieldy. Not only were most reports at the time handwritten but messages from Indian Army staffed consulates in Persia were sent first to Delhi, then copied to the Indian Office in London and from there onto the Foreign Office.

At the latter part of the nineteenth century there had been some duplication by the army intelligence service of the work of the Survey of India. Following Roberts as Quartermaster General was Major General Charles MacGregor and he sought to limit the duplication of efforts by the Survey and the Army with greater integration but his hope of consolidating intelligence gathering completely by including the Foreign Service Officers (FSO) of the Political Department was frustrated. MacGregor had an acerbic opinion of these FSO's, who apparently did not always cooperate with him.

While the Political Department – in essence India's Foreign Office - remained sovereign duplication of Survey and Army intelligence gathering was finally ended in 1911. In July of that year a memorandum" authorized the transfer of officers from the Intelligence Section Drawing Room of the General Staff to the Survey of India Drawing Office then at Simla and stated that from then on the combined staff, military and survey, would be under the command of an officer of the Survey of India who would report exclusively to the Surveyor General. Only the costs of purchasing the maps from the survey department would then be on the estimates of the army and foreign departments.

Consequently in India the Survey acted much like MI 4 in Britain, while officers of the Political Department in the foreign consulates acted like MI 6, the Secret Intelligence Service, and departments of the Army and Indian Police as MI 5, the domestic intelligence-gathering agency[12]. Intelligence gathering on and beyond the frontiers of India, far from being a vast monolith dominated by the Survey was in reality collection of agencies that resulted inevitably in much duplication.

The territorial "reach" of British and Indian intelligence gathering in Asia had been defined in 1878. London would be responsible for Russia in Asia, Turkey in Asia, Egypt, Africa, China, Siam and Japan. The Indian government would be responsible for information gathering in Arabia, Persia, Baluchistan, Afghanistan, India, Kashmir, Nepal, Burma, Malaya, Ceylon, Dutch Colonies and Foreign colonies in India. Both London and Simla would involve themselves in Central Asia - the political vacuum between the Oxus River and the advancing Russians.

The manner in which information was gathered changed over the years, particularly within the Survey of India and the methods of both the Survey and the army changed with the evolution of new technologies. The "pundit" era of espionage on and beyond the Indian frontier dominated the Survey during the mid and late nineteenth century. In 1864 the Survey of India established a special school at Dehra Dun - conveniently close to the northern border - to train native agents as surveyors. These agents, known as "pundits", were used in areas inaccessible to Europeans. They traveled disguised as traders or holy men and were taught some medicine to make them welcome in remote communities. Their instruments were hidden in paraphernalia that would normally be carried for more innocent purposes.

The Buddhists had prayer wheels and rosaries, the Moslems compasses pointing to the most sacred places of Islam. They were identified in the Survey of India files by numbers or letters, such as AK, who was Kisham Singh and who made several surveys across Tibet and Chinese Turkestan. MH or Number 9 was Hari Ram who concentrated on the Everest region. Sarat Chandra Das, in addition to surveying and espionage, undertook diplomatic missions for the British. There were Mohammedan pundits as well. One, Mirza Shuja, was finally murdered by his guides during his second survey mission in the direction of Bokhara. Another, Ata Mohammed, known as the Mullah, traced the then unknown course of the Oxus. The Survey employed a Chinese who was to find out if the Tsangpo River ran into the Brahmaputra. He quickly deserted and sold his assistant, a Sikkimese named Kinthrup, as a slave to a Tibetan village. Kinthrup managed to escape, made it to a Tibetan monastery where he became a novice monk but finally got to Lhasa from where he managed to send a letter to the Survey of India. From Lhasa he struggled across the Himalayas to Darjeeling. So impressed was the Surveyor General that he took him personally to meet the Viceroy.

Nain Singh, the most distinguished of all the pundits, was made a Companion of the Indian Empire after journeying more than a thousand miles along the southern trade routes of Tibet to Lhasa, mapping and measuring all the way. After that the use of pundits declined - although Hunter attempted to use the same techniques to assemble information about the Hijaz railway when he was compiling the map of Arabia.

The passion for sport had overtaken the English and the methods for acquiring information about the routes by which the Russians might attack India were heavily influenced by the new passion.

The Alpine Club had been formed in London in 1854 and so enthusiastic were the early climbers that they soon conquered all the Alpine peaks. So they moved on to the mountains of the Caucasus. After that their attention turned to the highest peaks of all - those in the Himalayas.

Native agents had frequently reported sighting parties of Russians on the northern approaches to the Himalayas and even the occasional squadron of Cossacks there. It would have been all too easy for a party of mountaineers to make an error in its movements and wander into territory claimed by the Russians. For despite the definition of the Afghan - Russian border in 1885 it was still unclear where much of the border was in the Himalayas. In order for the frontier to be delineated it would first have to be mapped.

Francis Younghusband, as a young lieutenant of Dragoons had, in 1887 crossed China and the Gobi Desert to Yarkand and from there crossed the Karakoram range to Kashmir and became the first European to see the mountain later called K2. Two years later Younghusband made another significant discovery. With a party of Ghurkas way up in the mountains of the Hunza facing the Pamirs, Younghusband came into contact with the Russian soldier-explorer Captain Grombchevski accompanied by a German naturalist and a troop of Cossacks. The meeting was friendly but soldiers of British India had finally come eyeball to eyeball with the Cossacks in an unnamed mountain pass.

More had to be known about this territory and from that time on the Survey of India and various climbing parties worked hand in hand.

What was probably the supreme moment came as late as May of 1913. Colonel Kenneth Mason of the Survey, with six Ghurkas and two assistants, was working in the mountains of northern Kashmir. Mason peered through the telescope on his theodolite. On a distant ridge of the nearer Pamirs he saw a pyramid of poles. They supported the vertical masts of the Russian survey station. The two frontiers had finally met.

Still more information was needed to fill in the many blank areas on the map and expeditions quite innocent of subterfuge were a means of improving maps. In 1913 Major Wood of the Survey, who went on to make observations at Tashkent, joined the Italian Scientific Expedition. Two surveyors accompanied Sir Aurel Stein's archeological expedition to Central Asia. At the same time Captain FM Bailey - soon to excel as a British secret agent in Soviet Turkestan from where he barely escaped with his life - accompanied by Captain Moreshead of the Survey spent six months exploring the unknown portion of the Upper Brahmaputra. Eight years later, shortly after Bailey made his daring escape from Turkestan, Moreshead, by then a major with a DSO, accompanied a newly joined member of the Survey, Major Oliver Wheeler MC, on the very first expedition, one of reconnaissance, to Mount Everest. One of the climbers, George Leigh Mallory, would in three years time die on Everest. Oliver Wheeler, a Canadian born in Ottawa, whose father had founded the Alpine Club of Canada, became Surveyor General of India and eventually retired to Vernon, BC.

The files of the Survey of India are replete with examples of extraordinary adventures. Colonel Mason, for example, after making contact with the Russian surveyors, went north through Russian territory to the summits on the Chinese frontier so that he could link them with the Great Trigonometrical Survey. The same year

Captain Noel, disguised as a Mohammedan Indian and accompanied by three Himalayan tribesmen, crossed the high passes of Sikkim to the Tibetan plateau and then went westward to Everest. Although driven out by border guards he made the first confirmation that Mount Everest was approachable from the north.

Information available for the army or the foreign department from the Survey of India was extensive. In 1906, for example, there were reports on the preparation of three Tibetan maps, a map of Sikkim, another of Bhutan, a map of Persia and "a special map for the Foreign Department prepared under the direction of Lieutenant FF Hunter."

Consequently the intelligence reports had titles as diverse as, "Who's Who in Central Asia", "Strategical Routes in Russian Central Asia", "Routes in Tibet" and "Strategical Routes on and Beyond the NW Frontier."

The consuls in Persia and the Gulf States were generally army officers of the Indian Political Service. Captain Percy Sykes – soon to be Hunter's boss - was consul in Kerman before being transferred to Siestan and later the Meshed. Captain Percy Cox - later Shakespear's chief as Resident of the Persian Gulf and also, after the war a strong promoter of Fraser Hunter - was earlier at Muscat. Shakespear served in Bandar Abbass and later Kuwait, while Captain Lorimer, author of the Gazetteer of Arabia and the Gulf who worked with Fraser Hunter on the map of Arabia and the Gulf, became Resident in the Persian Gulf after Cox.

In India the Quartermaster General's department supervised the Indian Intelligence Department that was divided into four sections each manned by a deputy assistant quartermaster general. One of the four, Section W, watched Russia in Asia, Persia, China on the Russian Frontier, Province of Baghdad and, jointly with War Office

Intelligence, Turkey in Asia. Section T was responsible for the native states in India, maps and the topographical section.

The Survey of India had five surveying branches - or circles as those with a geographical area of responsibility were called - and the Geodetic Branch and Map Publications Branch. Headquartered in Calcutta was the Map Publications Branch that contained the Number One Drawing Office, the Engraving Office, the Mathematical Instruments Office, the Photo-Litho Office and the Map Record and Issue Office. Hunter served at various times in three of these four offices and eventually became head of the whole branch as had a predecessor of his, Colonel(later Sir) W Coote-Hedley, who left India just before the Great War to head up MI.4 in England.

Rudyard Kipling had summed up earlier fears of Russian encroachment with his verse:

"Listen to the north, my boys, there's trouble in the wind;
Tramp o' Cossacks hooves in front, grey greatcoats behind,
Trouble on the Frontier of a most amazin' kind,
Trouble on the waters of the Oxus."

Times change and the danger with them. The trouble in the wind, a trouble soon to reach storm force was no longer blowing from the north, at least, not with the same intensity.

After the humiliating defeat of the Russians by the Japanese and the internal turmoil that resulted from it, the new Liberal government in England deemed the time ripe for a treaty that would end close to a century of mutual distrust. The Treaty of 1907 in which both sides agreed to keep out of Tibet and not interfere in Afghanistan, also divided Persia into zones of influence – divisions made without discussion with the Persian government. Despite the unease of the "forward school" in Britain - and Curzon was one of this group – the perception was that the immediate trouble was blowing now from the West, from Berlin, stirred feverishly by Kaiser Wilhelm, across the Anatolean Highlands of Turkey.

The trouble on the waters of the Oxus was no longer as feared as the potential for trouble on the waters of the Persian Gulf, the Euphrates and on the Caspian. The trouble feared was not from the Cossacks and the grey great-coated masses behind them but from a newly active Germany, its Drang Nach Osten policy, and its meteoric Kaiser. The noise in the wind was of hammers driving the spikes on the German-financed Baghdad Railway, pressing eastward. Clearly, while the menace of Russia to the north should not be permanently ignored, the threat to India from German expansion through the Ottoman Empire and Arabia was far more immediate.

HUNTER'S MAP

Hunter had become deeply involved in new strategies through his work with the Survey of India - though such was the secretive nature of his employers that the map he produced, a map of the Persian Gulf, Oman and Arabia, a supplement of John Gordon Lorimer's gazetteer of the area, remained on the secret list for years.

Lorimer and Hunter, along with a draftsman, spent the winter of 1905-06 in the Foreign Office building at Simla, the summer resort of the Indian Government.[13] Naturally the buildings at this summer station were not designed, heated or insulated for winter use. Simla, more than well over two thousand metres metres above sea level and in the lower slopes of the Himalayas, could be bitterly cold, especially when the wind swept down from the mountains. The three of them, working ten to fourteen hours a day in overcoats and mittens, frequently found that their ink froze and that the quality of the work was far from being as high as any of them would have wished. Nevertheless, by the spring of 1906 the first copies were available and photographic reductions and reproductions were being prepared at Dehra Dun.

Spelling of names prompted considerable acrimonious challenge from "authorities" who knew the various places on the map. For example, would it be Bahrein or Bahrain? Mecca or Makka? Masquat or Musquat? Bushehr or Bushire? The disputes about place names were only finally resolved by inquiry through local authorities and political officers and were ultimately published as a supplement to Lorimer's gazetteer.

For the sake of accuracy and completeness Hunter sought out all possible sources. They included the Bible and the fifteen hundred year-old works of the Arab scholar, Hamdani. The sextant sightings of the explorer Niebuhr in south western Arabia were found to be particularly accurate and a much greater contribution to geographical knowledge than, according to Hunter, the sightings of Sir Richard Burton whose reputation was far greater - and whose name is far more widely known today, though largely because of his translation of the Kamasutra and the movie, "Mountains of the Moon". Special surveys of the interior were commissioned and the navy made numerous sightings along the coast.

The search for detail led to a remarkable discovery. Hunter discovered that the Sheik of Dhufar was the descendant of a shipwrecked American sailor who had married the daughter of a former chief and whose children then succeeded to the sheikdom. In 1904, the Russian fleet left St Petersburg on its way to give the Japanese a pounding. It was a long voyage that went wrong from the very beginning. In the mists of the Dogger Bank in the North Sea, the voyage scarcely begun, the Russians fired on some English fishing boats believing them to be Japanese torpedo boats. It brought Britain and Russia to the brink of war. But the Russian fleet pressed on, lost to a world so anxious to know of its progress - how, for example could these coal-burning vessels refuel before they reached the Sea of Japan?

Hunter, speaking to the Royal Geographical Society in London in 1919, reported that the part-American offspring of the shipwrecked sailor helped solve the Russian problem. The Sheik, demonstrating that there was true-blue Yankee ingenuity in his genes, stockpiled coal of Murbat, bringing it there with hundreds of rowboats and sailing dhows from Kuwait and other ports along the Gulf and on the Arabian shore.[14] The Russian fleet refueled and prepared for its rendezvous with the Japanese fleet and, soon after, the bottom of the sea.

Hunter's surveyors did more than listen to intriguing tales or make careful measurements. In Oman one of his surveyors was frequently shot at by tribesmen gathered a safe distance away - they hit his plane table several times. Finally they came in close enough to verbally threaten his life. He allegedly told them, "Why don't you go home and learn how to shoot before you try to kill a man you can't hit?", or words to that effect. They left him alone.

There were delays in map publication of a type not normally met with by a cartographer. For example, in 1906 a valuable pearl was found at the end of Musamdam Island. The Sheik of Bahrain claimed it since it came from waters over which he had sovereignty. But the Sheik of Qatar said that he should have the right to dispose of it since it had been found by one of his people. The man who found the pearl claimed to have come from a village no one had heard of - although Colonel Cox, the British Resident at that time, found that the man came from the Rub al Khali, the terrible "Empty Quarter" and while pursuing his investigation - during which time the Sheik of Qatar was murdered - found sufficient information to fill in many empty spaces on the map.

There were many other incidents to give colour and warm Hunter's enthusiasm, if not his fingers, during the days at Dehra Dun map making. He realized that a number of small islands at the entrance to the Persian Gulf could, if fortified, control the shipping lanes. At that time the islands belonged to the sheik of Abu Dhabi - a close ally of the British. However, a neighboring sheik, not an anglophile, wanted to control them himself and invited the Sheik of Abu Dhabi to a party. When Colonel Cox called by on a routine visit he found the sheik's family desperately concerned that all might not be well. "He was being entertained in the desert," they said with obvious concern. This was so unusual that Cox investigated by gate-crashing the party. He found the Sheik of Abu Dhabi pegged out in the sand and several of his finger nails had been pulled off with red hot pincers in an effort to persuade him to hand over ownership of the islands. Colonel Cox's arrival not only assured the sheik's release but added a few more details to Hunter's map.

The production of this map constituted a major advance over anything else which had been produced up to that time and Hunter employed some of the established skills of the old pundits of the Survey of India. One of Hunter's surveyors, Khan Bahadur Abdur Rahmim, decided to make a pilgrimage to Mecca. Hunter supplied him with a small pocket sextant, a compass and other instruments and a photographically reduced list of questions about the territory around Taif, near Mecca, and the road between Mecca and Medina, as well as a reduced handkerchief copy of a map of the area. Unfortunately, other Moslem employees of the Survey of India heard of Khan Bahadur's intentions and one of them informed the Turkish Consul-General in Bombay.

When Khan Bahadur arrived in Ottoman territory the Turks were waiting and all his instruments were confiscated. Not, however, the map that was assumed to be an innocuous handkerchief. With this map the Khan was able to correct many details concerning the projected Hijaz railway and pass the information to Hunter. Hunter also obtained, though he does not say how, a copy of the complete line of the Turkish Hijaz Railway, something that during Lawrence of Arabia's campaign against the Turks during the Arab Revolt, was probably most useful.

Hunter's map, though far from perfect, was the best available at that time. All previous traveler's map had been simply compass traverses. Hunter was able to add much detail and to consolidate information of the area from sources ranging from ancient holy books to the substantial detail available in Dr David Hogarth's Penetration of Arabia. Both Hogarth and the explorer Captain St John Philby praised Hunter's contribution to knowledge of the area. In fact Philby later told Hunter that the relative positions of the places were accurate and he was able to corroborate for the first time the existence of most of the places marked on the map.

But the map did something else. It stimulated Hunter's desire to get to Arabia and to see for himself.

Making the map of Arabia and the Gulf for the Indian Foreign Service had certainly heightened Hunter's reputation within the Survey Department - although that service contained many remarkable officers whose careers spanned half of Asia and are still remembered by armchair travelers. But it did more than that. The bug of the desert bit Hunter. He became a victim of the obsession that had afflicted so many English men and women. As Walter de la Mare wrote, "He is crazed with the spell of far Arabia."

There were many others like him and, like him, British and in the government service. They were enormously confident; fond of the strange people they found themselves with, energetic and resourceful. They were children of their parents' imperial glow and they breezily traveled in some of the world's most fearful places with self-assurance and aplomb. They are as unreal to us today as are those "adventurers" who people the novels of the day, novels such as King Soloman's Mines. In later life they would retire to the leathered armchairs of the Royal Geographical Society and reminisce about guns and game. Today it is easy to find their style patronizing and their enthusiasms a bore. But that is because the world has changed. The mud of Flanders, the concentration camps of Germany, destroyed the certainties and the self-assurance forever.

QUEST FOR ARABIA

Years later, Hunter stated that he had been influential in establishing order in Persia in 1908 and 1909. Given the secrecy that necessarily surrounded such efforts during the so called "Persian Revolution" it is not possible today to be certain as to what that influence was, particularly since Persia was, at least technically, a neutral and sovereign country. However Hunter's earlier map-making experience assembling information about Arabia and the Persian Gulf and his interests, soon to be widely known, in traveling in Arabia, are sure clues to what that influence was.

The Indian government was deeply concerned at gun running from the Arabian states skirting the Persian Gulf to Persia and then onto Afghanistan and the Pushtun border areas. There these guns were used against Indian Army outposts. In the past the tribesmen on the India-Afghan border had used the old jezail – muzzle-loading smooth bore muskets that were locally made. But a decade earlier it was discovered that breech-loading Martini-Henry rifles were on sale in the Kurrum Valley adjacent to the Afghan border. Where had they come from? Possibly the Amir of Afghanistan had supplied them or they had been taken from Indian Army sepoys killed in border skirmishes. But the Political Resident in Bushire, Percy Cox, believed they had been purchased in Muscat, smuggled into Persia and then onto the tribal border.

By 1907 military intelligence estimated that more than a quarter of the belligerent tribesmen had acquired these weapons. A German enterprise, the Wonkhaus Company initially operating from Lingeh on the Persian side of the Gulf, but later pressured Sheik Mubarak of Kuwait to open there, may have been the conduit for the smuggling. Certainly many believed that it was involved in espionage and furthering Germany's expansionist goals as a private business while the German government was openly encouraging the development of the railway to Baghdad. In light of later knowledge, this accusation, though widespread, was probably unfair. It is likely that it was simply a business whose success was attributed to secret German funding rather than business prowess.

The real threat to the security of the Northwest Frontier and Persian tranquility came from gun running by hundreds of dhows from Muscat to the Persian-Baluchistan coastline. It was reported that as many as a quarter of a million rifles were stored in Muscat. From the Baluchi coastline camel caravans carried tens of thousands of rifles and ammunition across the desert to the Afghan border then onwards north along the Helmand valley to Gereshk and Kandahar. The volume of traffic was so great the local gunsmiths suffered a major decline in trade.[15] The danger to the Persian government stemmed from the heavily armed and largely autonomous tribesmen who escorted the caravans and frightened off the poorly armed and badly trained Persian military.

In the first half dozen years of the century Royal Navy patrols tried to intercept gunrunners and the Indo-Telegraph office in Jask supplied the navy with information, as did secret agents at both ends of the trade. Percy Cox in Bushire tried unsuccessfully to have contingents of the Indian Army enter Persia. In 1908 the intelligence department of the Indian Army became more actively involved particularly with the recruitment of Pushtun secret agents posing as arms traders and initiating what would now be known as "sting operations". Hunter used native agents to gather information while working with J G Lorimer on the map and gazetteer of the Persian Gulf and his immense knowledge of the Gulf States was undoubtedly utilized.

Much of Hunter's work was academic in that he analyzed reports of agents and made suggestions for action. Now he looked for fresh stimulus. A man of action, he needed physical as well as mental stimulation. His daily preoccupation with Arabia had led him to some theoretical conclusions. Now, though he had not been there, he wanted to validate them. But before he could tackle that challenge he had to spend time in the Survey doing some of the more routine, less glamorous, tasks of map-making in India.

The Number 19 Party of the Survey had been employed on forest surveys in Madras for the past twenty years and was in 1907 mapping in the Malabar Hills and the Nilgiris, the so-called Blue Mountains of southern India. The area included abandoned gold workings in dense jungle clearings as well as a great many coffee plantations. The survey party found the most pleasant area to be the long belt of land between the sea and the Ghats - the string of hills parallel to the shore where local people lived in comfortable though modest huts and had their own gardens where they grew vegetables, peppers and betal and coconuts. Unfortunately, they could not confine their activities to the more pleasant parts and the party of forty- eight surveyors under the command of Hunter from the summer of 1907 until the Spring of 1908, spent a considerable amount of the second year in the Wynaad area.

The health of the party deteriorated; fever spread among them and two of the surveyors died. Added to their difficulties was the problem of finding labour that had to be brought in from further afield since the jungle tribes would not work with and actively impeded the work of the surveyors.

There were compensations. The French Governor of Pondicherry gave Hunter permission to survey Mahe, then a decaying French settlement on the coast, southwest of Bangalore. Hunter reported that nothing could have exceeded the hospitality of the French officials there who gave them much help in carrying out their work. Despite this, the entire party was relieved to get back to Bangalore, and Hunter had added relief in the knowledge that long awaited leave was due and a return to the contrasting climate of Canada was imminent. A further compensation was that Hunter was promoted to the rank of Captain.

Two seasons surveying in the jungles of southern India had heightened the appetite created in mapping Arabia. Hunter was now more anxious than ever to travel to the desert and he was able to rationalize this yearning with some academic objectives.

Colonel Cox's discovery of some villages in an area previously considered part of the infamous Rub al Khali, the Sea of Death, led Hunter to conclude that their water came from a number of subterranean flows which appeared at the sea's edge near Bahrain, and that other outflows might, in their hinterlands, support additional populations. He believed that several potentially fertile tracts might exist between the Trucial Oman and the Hadramaut.

He managed to arrange leave for a year and three months - later extended still further - and headed off to New York. On his way he organized radio contact points at Mokalla and Abu Dhabi for his proposed expedition and met with Sir Richmond Ritchie in London to garner additional information on Arabia.

Sir Richmond, William Makepeace Thackery's son-in-law, was senior under-secretary at the India Office - and he was interested to hear Hunter's views about Arabia and the Gulf since Hunter, though he had not been there, had gathered a substantial volume of detailed information when he had been preparing his map and could well be regarded as an authority on this increasingly strategic area.

In New York Hunter raised five thousand pounds sterling for his expedition - no mean feat for a young Ontarian who had spent the past several years in the East. He also met in New York the Reverend Samuel Marinus Zwemer originally from Michigan. Zwemer was nine years older than Hunter and had made a modest name for himself as an authority on the Arabian Peninsula. A missionary, he had trained at Hope College at Holland, Michigan, and represented the Reformed Church in America at Basra, Bahrein and other outposts in Arabia. In 1892 he had published <u>Arabia, the Cradle of Islam</u>, which gave a substantial amount of information about the peninsula and its tribes and outspokenly supported the extension of British power in the region. His brother, Peter Zwemer, had also made a number of exploratory journeys in Oman before dying of fever in 1898.

Samuel Zwemer had traveled to Sana, an ancient city now capital of Yemen, to distribute New Testaments in Hebrew to the large population of Jews who lived there at that time. He wanted to continue on across the Wadi Danasir but his journey coincided with an Arab revolt and he was robbed of all his money and imprisoned by the Turks. His travels in the area were extensive. He crossed the Oman Peninsula, visited Sana twice, the second time in 1904, and although largely forgotten today he was one of the very few Europeans of his time to have penetrated the Rub al Khali.

In 1906, while Hunter was working on his map of Arabia, Zwemer organized and chaired the Mohammedan Missionary Conference in Cairo. He then returned to North America and Hunter met him in New York while Zwemer was working on his doctorate at Rutgers University in New Brunswick, New Jersey.

Zwemer supported Hunter's plans for a trans-Arabian expedition. More than that, he wanted to go along as well[16].

Hunter's time in New York was fruitful. He not only raised money and the support of Zwemmer, but also discovered that a number of Jewish businessmen in the city had contacts in Arabia - particularly with the chief of the Dam tribe in Wadi Dawasir, and with tribes in Wadi Saba whom they contacted by way of Jeddah and Taif. These businessmen not only knew of chiefs and of communities which appeared on no maps, but were willing to arrange financing for Hunter by way of drafts drawn on these communities in southern Arabia.

Zwemer gave him tips on how to handle actual cash. Gold was accepted throughout the Middle East and in the interior the Maria Theresa dollar[17] had long been preferred. The British gold sovereign was widely accepted and because of trade from India in British ships throughout the Gulf and along the Arabian coast the Rupee was perfectly acceptable as well. The Bedouin of the interior, the men of the desert whom Hunter would meet, had little preference between the "abu bint" (the Indian Rupee with a girl's head) and the "abu tair" (the father of a bird - the eagle on the reverse of Austro-Hungarian dollar.)

Gold coins could be very easily stolen and a money belt was seen as a challenge to a thief's ingenuity. However, throughout Arabia a European, any European, was regarded as a physician adept at curing most illnesses; their medical supplies were rarely tampered with. The gold coins could therefore be concealed in the powdered quinine and could be extracted even when Arabs were present simply by pouring out some of the quinine for medical purposes.

Hunter did not get all the support he hoped for. The American Geographical Society supported the concept but the Royal Geographical Society in London did not.[18] The Royal felt that the use of a car was impractical - yes, Hunter did not plan a typical expedition at all, he wanted the car to be shown as the vehicle of future desert travel. His friend Shakespear had returned to England that way. Hunter had driven Shakespear to Karachi in 1907 where Shakespear had taken delivery of an 8 hp Rover for a mere 250 Pounds. He could not even drive, but after a few weeks of tinkering with the engine and lessons from Hunter he shipped it to Bushire in the Gulf - thus avoiding the hazards of crossing Baluchistan - and set out on his escapade. The idea was not quite as bizarre as it seems now and some other adventurers at this time were proposing to drive their cars from Peking to Paris. So Shakespear set off with a supply of gasoline and spares and sufficient whiskey to nourish him through the cold desert nights, through the mountains and desert that Hunter would soon come to know so well. Eventually, after numerous flat tires and exhaustion he arrived home completing a journey remarkable for the times. His success encouraged Hunter but, in light of present knowledge, had Hunter and Zwemmer set off on their trans-Arabian adventure in a car of 1908 vintage they would probably have soon died.

The government of India supported Hunter's plan. The original letters to the Foreign Office from India are no longer available but a telegram from the Viceroy's office on 15th March, 1910 was categorical. "Desire of Captain Hunter, Survey of India Department to travel across Arabia from Medina to coast of Persian Gulf and thence to Mokalla. Government of India considers that if he can arrange matters with Turkish government, it is not necessary to stop him."

Despite India's support, Sir Gerald Lowther, the Ambassador in Constantinople, had a month earlier cautioned against the expedition - with the fall of Abdul Hamid and the rise of the Young Turks the core of the Ottoman Empire was in turmoil and Turkish control of the outlying desert areas was not secure. Wrote Lowther,

> "It appears to me that considering the state of unrest which continues to prevail throughout the country and in view of the suspicions which might be aroused in the minds of Turkish officials by the fact of a British officer traveling through it just now, it would be inadvisable for Captain Hunter to undertake the journey at present time and I would suggest that he be recommended to postpone his project, at any rate for another year."

Nevertheless, the Viceroy continued to be supportive and wrote reinforcing the earlier telegram to the Foreign Office.

> "Captain Fraser Hunter of the Survey of India
>
> Department at present on leave, desires to travel in a powerful motor car, at his own expense and entirely as a private person, from Medina across the mainland of Arabia to Abu Thabi(sic) on Trucial Coast of Persian Gulf and thence across the Rub al Khali to Mokalla. He reports that he has the official support of the Royal and American Geographical Societies. (As it turned out, he did not have the support of the Royal.) Surveyor General warmly supports the proposal as Hunter is eminently fitted, having compiled maps of Arabia, and anticipates most valuable geographical results. He

could also let him have a Mohammedan volunteer assistant surveyor, purely as a private person, and with no claims to compensation and no authority from government. I propose to inform Hunter that government cannot be responsible for his journey in any way as country is dangerous, but that if he can arrange matters with the Turkish government I do not think it necessary to stop him. I have no objection to a surveyor going with him as a private volunteer."[19]

Despite this support, London continued to oppose and there was a flurry of correspondence involving such distinguished officials as Foreign Secretary Sir Edward Grey and Louis Mallet, his right hand man at the Foreign Office who would soon replace Lowther as Ambassador in Constantinople, as well as Lord Morely, Secretary of State for India. The correspondence illustrates the struggle for ascendancy over the Viceroy's government in India by the India Office and the Foreign Office in London - particularly in respect of Middle Eastern affairs. Hunter, now staying on Spadina Avenue in Toronto, may have got wind of the arguments flying and would have been aware of the chaos in the Ottoman Empire caused by the revolt of the "Young Turks" for on April 6th he sent a letter to the Surveyor-General's office modifying his original plan. He wrote:

"Owing to information as to the political situation....I have decided to alter my plan for exploration to the following.

1. All contact with Turkey to be avoided and no attempt to explore territory under Turkish control to be made.
2. The journey to begin at Abu Dhabi in Trucial Oman and then have as its chief object the crossing and exploration of the great unknown desert called the Ruba al Khali. With this object in view and in search of the best methods of crossing the desert, its edges to be skirted via Jabrim Oasis and Aflaj, as far as Dam, the

capital of the Wadi Dawassir country. The crossing of the desert to be made to Wadi Hadhrammaut and thence that great line of drainage to be followed to its mouth the sea....

3. The government of India to be asked for a general letter of introduction to the Persian Gulf Arab sheiks, somewhat along the following lines:- 'That the traveler, a scholar with no political motives, wished to cross the Ruba al Khali in search of inscriptions and of knowledge of that unknown tract, that the government accepted no responsibility for the traveler but believed his motives to be sincere and worthy and would be obliged if he could be helped in his quest.

4. The cost to be arranged for by myself.

5. The above is my present idea of exploration but the chief object of the exploration being to explore southern Arabia, I am prepared and willing to alter the details to suit circumstances.

6. It will be seen that the territory to be explored is under the control of independent Arab chieftains or within the British sphere of influence and none of it is within Turkish control.

The above plan cuts out all idea of entering Arabia by the Hijaz Railway and avoids all approaches to the Holy Places."

The same day that Hunter sent off this substantially amended plan from Spadina Avenue, he also wrote at length to Sir Richmond Ritchie at the India Office in London reminding him of their meeting when Hunter had passed through London eighteen months earlier on his way to New York.[20] What Hunter wanted to know and what he asked Sir Richmond to do for him was to ask the Secretary of State for India just what the position was and at the same time he gave Sir Richmond details of the amended plan so that he could argue on Hunter's behalf. As he pointed out, the new plan differed from the original but the differences were all in favor of India lending assistance and the practicability of the exploration.[21]

Hunter, pressed now for time, was not waiting for India to submit his new application to London but was going direct to where the final decision would be made. But it was no good. In fact, unknown to Hunter, Sir Richmond had earlier spiked the original request. Writing on behalf of Lord Morley he noted that while the object of the journey appeared harmless, "it is possible on the one hand that an assumed obligation to protect Major Hunter might serve the Porte as a pretence for asserting or (word illegible) claims in portions of Arabia where HMG do not admit them; and on the other hand that the journey if successful might act as an encouragement to other travelers with less (word illegible) objects in view."

The responsibility for the ultimate decision was pushed upwards to Sir Edward Grey. "Lord Morley, in the circumstances, would not press the proposal of the government of India, if Sir Edward Grey sees any objection." Clearly Sir Edward did.

An unsigned Minute from the Foreign Office notes that Hunter's new plan is very much like a plan submitted by a Mr. Bury in 1908 for which permission was refused. (Much later, in a speech to the Royal Geographical Society, Hunter said that Bury's work in the Hadhramaut was of much value "not withstanding the official prejudice against him at the time.") This Minute states that although the objections to the new plan are not as strong as those to the old, "they are still significant. It is impossible, in fact, for H.M.G. to disassociate themselves from responsibility for Captain Hunter's safety and it is not desirable to encourage travelers."

Hunter's application was finally and formally turned down in a telegram sent to him in Toronto on 26 April 1910. A personal letter of regret followed this from Sir Richmond Ritchie - the man whose comments had so lucidly made the case against Hunter's application.

Years later Hunter attributed the rejection of his plan to those who thought that people like him were similar to those who wanted to go over Niagara Falls in a barrel. Hunter thought he had been labeled a lunatic and probably never became aware of the voluminous correspondence his application had evoked nor the lack of support from Sir Richmond Ritchie - the man he thought his ally.

He was also unaware of the final ironic episode - prompted no doubt by the activity of German agents in the Gulf. On December 23 1913, nearly three years after the rejection of his application, the Under-Secretary of State at the Foreign Office wrote "in view of the alteration the situation has undergone in the last few years, the Maquis of Crewe feels that the objections suggested by his predecessor to Captain Hunter's proposed journey....no longer have the same force. (We) would be glad if the Government of India's request could be complied with."

Hunter would have burned with anger at the rejection of his application. Gerald Leachman, reporting back to the War Office in London, traveled in the first four months of 1910 south from Baghdad although his plans for a 1911 expedition were rejected. Shakespear left Basra and headed through Kuwait in January and February of 1910. The case would have been that Leachman was doing a job for the War Office and that Shakespear, as Political Agent in Kuwait, was occupied in the duties of that position. Nevertheless, the rejection would have rankled with Hunter particularly since two years later Barclay Raunkiaer, a Dane sponsored by the Danish Royal Geographical Society, traveled through Turkish territory to Kuwait

- where he met Shakespear - then cut across Arabia to Riyadh and then due east to the Gulf.

Hunter's application may have been rejected as part of a British effort to prevent the Danish expedition from penetrating Arabia. Sir Edward Grey was trying to stop all incursions so that the Danish expedition could be included under the same blanket refusal. The Danish expedition, sponsored by their geographical society, was under the patronage of its president, Admiral de Richleau. The admiral's interests were not exclusively naval. The admiral had invested in eastern railways and was particularly interested in the German-financed Baghdad Railway. This made him suspect in the eyes of British Intelligence. The British successfully blocked the Hunter's expedition but they were unable to prevent Barclay Raunkiaer from taking off on his own.

The Ruba al Khali, "the Empty Quarter" which so fascinated Hunter as it has many before and since, was eventually crossed. Bertram Thomas, traveling by camel and accompanied by bedou tribesmen, crossed the sands in 1931. The following year and by a longer route the Empty Quarter was crossed once more, this time by St John Philby, the explorer who thought so well of Hunter's map. The most extensive crossings followed the Second World War and were done by a man whose desert travels make him at least an equal to all earlier explorers of Arabia - Wilfred Thesiger.

It is difficult to state with assurance today the extent to which Hunter would have been aware of the scheming and planning to protect India from real or imagined threats. He would, however, have been aware of some of the undercurrents of activity - particularly since, like so many of those stirring of the undercurrents - he was a Fellow of the Royal Geographical Society where ideas and strategies were discussed with animation by Foreign Office officials, senior academics, and Indian and Colonial officials home on leave.

One important change in responsibilities occurred in 1912. The Indian Intelligence Department's Section E, which was responsible for gathering information over an immense area extending from Japan, through China to Arabia and Abyssinia, had its responsibilities for Arabia modified. Thereafter they were confined to the area south of a line extending from Aquaba, at the head of the Red Sea, to Basra, at the head of the Persian Gulf, that is, the greater part of the Arabian Peninsula - although excluded from India's authority would be the Hijaz and Yemen where an Arab revolt had been long smoldering. Intelligence gathering in the Arabian Peninsula north of that line – now containing Iraq (formerly Mesopotania) Syria, Jordan, Lebanon and Israel - would be the responsibility of MO 2 in London.

In Britain MO 2 (then responsible for foreign intelligence from countries in the Middle East, Europe and the Americas) was then under the direction of Colonel William Robertson, soon to be Chief of the Imperial General Staff and the only man to rise from private to Field Marshall. One of its first tasks was to prepare a report on Syria and this was compiled under the direction of the British Military Attaché in Constantinople, Colonel Francis Maunsell who had assisting him two so-called "honourary attaches", Mark Sykes, later to achieve prominence as co-author of the Sykes-Picot Agreement, and Aubrey Herbert, after whom John Buchan had modeled Sandy Arbuthnot in Greenmantle and a man who would soon be a key figure in Dr David Hogarth's Arab Bureau. South of the line from Aquaba to Basra intelligence gathering was India's responsibility - although London never really surrendered its paramountcy - and

John Lorimer and Fraser Hunter had just recently prepared the report on much of that area.

There were strong linkages between the world of military intelligence and the world of the academic. The clearest contact was in the person of Dr. David Hogarth, later Lieutenant Commander Dr. David Hogarth, RNVR. David Hogarth was said to be so much the self-assured academic that he was both pedantic and autocratic at the same time. He was a writer - he authored several books including, The Penetration of Arabia in 1904 - and an archeologist and had been on several "digs" in Greece, Crete, and the Middle East. In 1897 he was appointed Director of the British School in Athens and in 1909 returned to England to head the Ashmoleun Museum at Oxford. One of his Assistant Keepers was a medievalist, Leonard Wooley, who befriended a bright Jesus College student also interested in medieval history - particularly the Crusades to the Middle East - Thomas Edward Lawrence.

When Abdul Hamid of Turkey ordered an extension of the Euphrates Branch of the Baghdad Railway this extension would cross the Euphrates by a bridge near a site where, as chance would have it, the British Museum had a lease. In 1911 Dr. David Hogarth headed an archeological expedition to explore this lease. They began their work on this site at practically the same time that German engineers across the river began building the bridge over the Euphrates.

The links between British and Indian intelligence were well oiled even though relations between the India Office in London and the government in India were often crotchety. When the responsibilities of various intelligence departments touched upon each other they appeared to work together easily enough. For example, when Naval Intelligence was working out of the Royal Geographical Society offices in 1916 one of their tasks was to add flesh to an idea developed by David Hogarth, Mark Sykes and Hunter's friend Shakespear for an invasion into Syria from the south by car.

Working out of India, Hunter's co-worker on the Arabian map, Captain Lorimer, became Resident in the Persian Gulf. He died soon afterwards of gunshot wounds but prior to that he tipped off Intelligence about the movements of a German expedition to Afghanistan led by Otto von Niedermayer - thus confirming, or adding substance to reports the British would have received from their agents in Constantinople.

Unofficial linkages between the espionage system, the military and the academic world were then numerous, though not today able to always be established with complete certainty since the "old boy network" was sometimes used. A year after Hunter joined the Survey, an older man, Major Walter Coote-Hedley from the Royal Engineers joined as well and from November 1906 to July 1908 was in charge of the Photographic and Lithographic Office - at that time the principal section of the Map Publications Branch. He left to become head of MO4 in London. Hunter first became part of the Map Publications Branch in August, 1911 - four weeks after the Drawing Office, a section of Map Publications, became responsible for intelligence gathering tasks which had previously been the task of Section T, Military Intelligence. Previous directors of Map Publications generally rose to high ranks in the Survey and Fraser Hunter's career followed the path of predecessors be being ultimately appointed, in 1928, Director of Map Publications and Deputy Surveyor General of India. That however was all ahead of him.

When Hunter got back to India, in May 1911, he was appointed an Assistant Superintendent and attached to the Southern Circle. Since the heat of summer was already upon them and mapping in the field was done from the Fall to the Spring, it is probable that Hunter, in fact, spent that summer in the government of India's summer quarters at Simla. Whatever happened that summer, come the Fall he was appointed Deputy Superintendent in charge of the Surveyor General's Office and the Mathematical Instruments Office - part of Map Publications - and so was close to the centre of the activities concerned with topographical intelligence.

What happened next is quite unclear. Although he had been only back from "home leave" for a few months, twenty five days after this new posting he vanished for a year in a combination of what was ambiguously described as "special leave" and "extraordinary leave". We know for certain that while on this remarkable leave his rank of Deputy Superintendent was made substantive and also that he was out of India since records show that he landed back in Bombay at the end of August, 1913 and was immediately put in charge of the Number 1 Drawing Office at Musoorie - the heart of all the Survey's intelligence gathering.

DRANG NACH OSTEN

Almost exactly a year after Hunter went to Musoorie war erupted in Europe and quickly spread. Turkey became involved and oil supplies had to be secured to feed the Royal Navy. Still later revolution convulsed Russia and the eastern front collapsed, and the United States entered the war.

Hunter returned to the Bombay Lancers as part of mobilization and his first war posting was to the Afghan border. Soon after he was embroiled in Persia countering the activities of German agents. Still later he was in Petrograd when the Bolsheviks took the government.

Yet well before war began, the Liberal Party in England, and particularly the Foreign Secretary, Sir Edward Grey, felt that it was important to accommodate Russia in matters important to her - such as Persia - in exchange for good relations that would hopefully offset increasing German power in the region.

In the first few years of the century Russian efforts to dominate Persia had accelerated. Russian doctors, well escorted by Cossacks, had established plague stations on the Indian and Afghan frontiers. Russian surveyors charted the shores of the Persian Gulf and a Russian gunboat patrolled there. Russians mapped the routes through Persia and consulates were opened where she had no commercial interests.

But the humiliating defeat of her army and navy by the Japanese - followed by an abortive revolution in 1905 - made the Russians reconsider the realism of their ambitions. They consequently proposed to abandon their long held aim of reaching the Gulf, and make an agreement with Britain turning Persia - whose "integrity" they guaranteed - into a buffer state with British and Russian spheres of influence. It was not long before Russian troops were acting in north Persia as if it were simply an extension of their own country. Yet in the short-lived euphoria that followed the signing of the 1907 Convention, it was hoped that the Great Game was finally concluded.

But although the treaty of 1907 may have temporarily allayed fears of Russian encroachment of India, they were very rapidly replaced by fears of German expansion.

Turkey, "the sick man of Europe", was slowly disintegrating - had been for a long time - and the process of disintegration was helped along by Christians of the Ottoman Empire agitating for independence. Russia championed these freedom fighters, partly out of a desire to assist fellow Christians and partly motivated by a spirit of pan-Slavism. As a result of these interventions Greece, Serbia and Bulgaria became independent and Russia made some territorial gains in the Caucasus - fueling British anxiety still further.

England would rather have a weak Turkey controlling the Bosphorus than a strong Russia. Because of this Britain was frequently guilty of permitting the Turks to ignore reforms required in Macedonia and Armenia. Turkish atrocities were a contributory cause of the Balkans Wars of 1912-13 which in their turn led to an assassination in Sarajevo and the First World War - which brought about the Russian Revolution and all the changes of the old order that have occurred since.

While British policy towards Turkey may have been at times ambivalent, German policy certainly was not. Like the British, Germany wanted to keep the Russians away from the Bosphorous and out of the Mediterranean. But Germany wanted to be the primary influence in Turkey and, by the use of a railway, the so-called Baghdad Railway, extend its influence from Berlin through the Austro-Hungarian and Ottoman Empires to Baghdad, Basra and the Persian Gulf.

The uncontrollable Kaiser Wilhelm made his contribution. As a part of his Drang nach Osten policy - the Drive to the East - he made a pilgrimage to Jerusalem. He used the occasion as a flamboyant gesture of support for the Ottomans. In addition to Jerusalem the Kaiser visited Constantinople and Beirut and in Damascus laid a wreath on the tomb of Saladin. He proclaimed eternal friendship with the Sultan-Caliph of Turkey and all those Moslems who venerated him - a piece of theatre which did not go unnoticed in London or Delhi where they were well aware that the Sultan-Caliph was venerated among Moslems of India and the people of Afghanistan.

The Kaiser's tactic bore immediate fruit. German officers would train and modernize the Ottoman Army: Britain and France lost influence at the Sublime Porte; Germans received concessions to build the Baghdad Railway. There were even Germans who, reflecting their envy of British control of Egypt, referred to Turkey as "Germany's Egypt" and hoped that Mesopotamia would soon become "Germany's India".

Although some in London saw the German railway project as a check on Russian expansion, most were concerned and began soon to refer to it as the Berlin-Baghdad line. The original intention was that this line would be 1255 miles long and a single track of standard gauge. The two concessionaries organized to construct the railway were both German and both were controlled by the Deutsche Bank. Initial progress was slow and Ottoman government bonds did not sell well. There were long gaps between sections of the line. The rugged countryside and the barrier of the mountains suggested tunneling but the costs would have been exorbitant. By the time the First World War began fewer than nine hundred miles had been completed.

German policy received a major setback when the Turkish Sultan, Abdul Hamid was overthrown by the Young Turks but Berlin was not slow in reasserting itself. By the time war began the need to speed work on the railway was clearly understood, particularly since the man who trained the Turkish Army, German General von der Goltz, was enthusiastic about its strategic potential. Von der Goltz reasoned that fear of German intentions would force the British to the conference table as the line continued to press towards India. He was quite sure that a march to the Indian sub-continent was a real option. After all, Alexander the Great had done it. British supremacy, thought von der Goltz, was based on their control of India. Even if German troops were simply within striking distance of India it would have a profound effect on British strategic thinking.

As it turned out it was suspicion of the Germans by the Turks that was a constant impediment to the Turkish war effort and the Baghdad Railway failed to be the major menace that von der Goltz hoped for. It is a sad irony of the war that one of the reasons the railway was not constructed on schedule was the shortage of manpower. By 1915 one of the reasons for this lack of railway labour was the massacre of Armenians by the Turks.

Yet however unrealistic the hopes of von der Goltz may have been - or, for that matter, the Drang Nach Osten policy of the Kaiser - it was little wonder that the British, relieved of their fear of the Russians by the treaty of 1907, should turn their attention to Turkey and to German penetration of Turkish territory in Mesopotamia and Arabia. Espionage activities, similar to those in Persia, Afghanistan and Turkestan in previous years now focused on the Ottoman Empire. Thus it was that Robert Baden Powell, in the guise of a tourist, examined new guns in the Turkish fortifications on the Bosphorous and pretended to fish while sketching these guns and their embrasures. For very much the same reason did Lord Curzon have Fraser Hunter labor to produce maps of Arabia and the Persian Gulf.

In one sense the new threat in the east was more ominous than the old. Russia, campaigning its way south in the nineteenth century, was Christian. And so, of course, was Germany. But Turkey, as an ally to Germany, changed the complexion of the Game. The participation of Turkey in the Great Game was particularly menacing not only because Turkey was Moslem, but its Sultan, gross and decadent though he was, was also the caliph. The Ottoman Empire was a religious as well as a political entity. The Sultan-Caliph, whose Empire still included the holy places of Jerusalem with its Golden Dome, and Medina and Mecca, commanded the spiritual allegiance of the Moslem world. Seventy million of those Moslems lived in British India. The possibility that they might side with Turkey if the Sultan declared a Holy War was terrifying - there was still a Sultan even after Abdul Hamid was exiled, although the Young Turks controlled most of the political activity. Little wonder that Britain endeavored to keep Turkey as an ally. The wonder is that she did not try even harder. This would have been one of the reasons that Britain did not protest too vigorously Turkish failure to carry through with promised reforms in Armenia.

Germany, on the other hand, had few concerns about expressing support for Abdul Hamid or later, the Young Turks, even though there were constant strains on the German-Turkish alliance. Assistance was initially channeled through their ambassador to the Sublime Porte,

Hans von Wagenheim, a man whom the American Ambassador, Henry Morgenthau regarded as the perfect embodiment of Prussian militarism - and a womanizer to boot.

Von Wagenheim's immense energy won considerable support for numerous enterprises and Germany came to be admired by Turks because of his efforts. Just prior to the war, for example, thousands of young Turks, Enver Pasha among them, seeking an urbane and sophisticated image, sported the upturned mustache favored by the Kaiser.

Von Wagenheim believed that Germany was missing an opportunity to win the support of the Armenians in the eastern areas of the country. While Germans generally disparaged them as "the Jews of the Orient" the Russians, by spending a little money on propaganda, had generated superficial support. This support would have been even greater had not the Armenians remembered the notorious Russification programs of thirty years earlier. This period is principally remembered for harsh measures against the Jews. But treatment of other minorities, including the Armenians, was at least as repressive, and the Armenians had neither forgiven nor forgotten. Nonetheless given a choice between Russian or Turk the Armenian chose the Russian. Germany might have succeeded in establishing some sort of protectorate in Armenia - something that von Wagenheim sought - but the German Foreign Ministry wanted to avoid antagonizing either the Turks or the Russians.

The Turkish Army was pro-German, although the Germans had grave reservations about Turkish military competence. The Prussian General, Colmar von der Goltz, had overseen the training of many of their officers but they were nonetheless, soundly defeated in the first Balkan War when Bulgaria, Greece, Serbia and Montenegro attacked. Later, General Otto Linman von Sanders, immediately prior to the Great War managed to achieve considerable control over the Turkish Army with a special supervisory mission.

The key figure in Turkey immediately prior to the war, one of the triumvirate ruling the country, was Enver Pasha, unquestionably pro-German and soon to be Minister of War. But Enver, though pro-German was pro-Turk first. It is also worth noting that while the Germans had influence in the Turkish Army, the British, through their naval training mission in Constantinople, had considerable influence in the Turkish Navy. This advantage quickly evaporated in 1914 through the insensitivity of the British to Turkish nationalism when they abruptly commandeered two Turkish warships constructed in England with subscriptions raised by popular appeal. The Young Turks might be pro-German but they, like virtually all Turks in the heady days of nationalism then sweeping the country, were pro-Turk before all else.

The Ottoman Empire had once been a vast concern extending over three continents - Europe, Africa and Asia - and had once even reached the gates of Vienna. But the nineteenth century explosion of new technology brought growing confidence into western Europe resulting in reversals right across Ottoman territory. Britain occupied Egypt; Austria-Hungary annexed Bosnia and Herzogovina; other Balkan provinces broke away; France seized Tunisia and Algeria; Italy took Libya; Bulgaria battled south towards Constantinople. The Ottomans were used to it. In its six hundred-year history not one year had passed in which they were not fighting to expand, preserve or protect the Empire. As it crumbled various western powers reassessed their relationships with the Turks and between themselves. Britain particularly had a problem because the tens of millions of Moslems in India looked to Ottoman Empire with particular respect as the home of the Sultan-Caliph, head of the Moslem world.

The three-man dictatorship ruling the remnants of the Ottoman Empire sought to preserve what was left. As it happened, their action of entering the war against the Entente brought about the final destruction of the Ottoman Empire.

Before the war had begun the Turks had suggested that a few Germans participate in a mission to Afghanistan to persuade the Amir Habibullah, to come in on their side - at the appropriate time. It was as clear to Turkey as it was to Germany that a threat from Afghanistan against India would compel India to keep so many troops on the Frontier that participation on other fronts would be substantially reduced.

The British recognized the threat as well and the Amir's nephew, Nasrullah, had for years been seeking a Jihad against the British. The Viceroy had written to the Amir, seeking assurances that there would be peace - he pointed out that he was obligated by treaty to be absolutely neutral. The Amir reassured the Viceroy. He and a great many Afghans clearly recognized that by being neutral they were in fact acting against Turkey's interests by allowing Indian troops, so many of them Moslem, to fight Turkey or her allies. The neutrality of Afghanistan permitted the free movement of almost the entire Indian Army. (Some troops would always be needed in case of the usual trouble on the Frontier) Small wonder that the British sought to preserve and the Germans to break that neutrality.

Even before war had begun a party of twenty-five Germans had set off for the East. They pretended for reasons of security in the Balkans to be part of a traveling circus. But they soon had trouble with Customs, though their radio aerials escaped detection by being described as tent poles. However, the Rumanian Customs post found machine guns and ammunition and, presumably finding this inappropriate baggage for a circus, confiscated them.

They arrived in Constantinople in September of 1914, before Turkey had committed itself to the war and perhaps for this reason Enver, who had initially been so enthusiastic about the project, was having some doubts. His principal concern was that twenty-five Germans were simply too many. What he had envisioned was Turkish Mission preaching pan-Turanianism and Islamic solidarity, with a few Germans along to signify the international support that this Turkish mission was receiving. He was also soured, as were many other Turks, by the behavior of the Germans while they were in Constantinople. He complained that they were loud, lazy and constantly drunk and had to be physically ejected from public cafes where they were openly contemptuous of Turkey. Apparently they were even more insulting than earlier Germans who had been involved in the training of the Turkish Army and had given Turkey the nickname "louseland". Added to the generally offensive behavior of this new mission was the additional problem that their security was abominable. They openly boasted of what they were up to and some had even registered in a hotel there as "Members of an expedition to A----------".

That Enver did not support this German expedition undoubtedly limited its potential. But it contained two men who were to plague the British for years. Both knew Persia well. Both were leaders - joint leaders - of the expedition. Oscar von Niedermayer was a geologist; Wilhelm Wassmuss, who would soon be the focus of Hunter's activities, was the former German Consul to the Persian Gulf town of Bushire. Neither happily accepted the leadership of the other and neither would accept the leadership of a Turk. Since von Niedermayer and Wassmuss could not work together Wassmuss left the expedition and headed for his old territory along the Persian Gulf shore where he planned to incite the tribes against the British.

He succeeded. The British failed to capture him, but they came so close to it on one occasion that he lost most of his baggage before heading into the mountains to join his tribal allies. That loss, or more likely the seizure - illegally done - of German diplomatic papers in Bushire, caused immense consequences for the German war effort. Despite this, Wassmuss soon became something of a legend, later to be described as "Germany's Lawrence of Arabia". Within a short while he would be the prime concern of Fraser Hunter

Enver Pasha, despite his low view of the expedition, thought that some good might come of it and had some British oil refineries at Abadan blown up and ordered that the expedition be commanded by a Turkish hero of the Turco-Italian war, Colonel Rauf Bey.

Von Niedermayer had no intention of serving under a Turk and to avoid the dilemma created by this appointment moved eastward and well clear of Enver's authority. He carried with him sufficient money to effectively bribe the pro-German officers of the Swedish gendarmerie in Persia and their support would not only facilitate travel but could result in the Swedes influencing the Persian government to side with Germany in the war.

Another group had formed at the suggestion of the Indian Committee in Berlin and its purpose was to make contact with Indian revolutionaries in Afghanistan and ensure that anti-British propaganda crossed the border into India. This expedition was also jointly led. The Indian revolutionary Mahendra Pratap sharing leadership with German Lieutenant Otto von Hentig.

The parties of von Niedermayer and Hentig and Pratap joined forces and traveled to Afghanistan together - to be followed by still another group led by Ferdinand Seiler bringing along the radio equipment. Seiler had once been dragoman at the German Embassy in Constantinople - a dragoman is an interpreter for travelers in the east - and would later be implicated in the murder of the Russian bank manager in Isfahan in May, 1915. He left Baghdad at the head of the so-called Jihad Mission. Although the Niedermayer-Hentig group eventually reached Kabul, Seiler's party was effectively prevented from doing so by British border patrols.

Von Niedermayer had never been particularly confident that he could persuade the Amir of Afghanistan to attack India or that there would be a spontaneous rising of Indians against the British. He later wrote in Under the Burning Sun "I was extremely suspicious of the numerous rumours of disturbances in India and of the opinions spread by revolutionary Indians all over the world that the people of India would rise. It was in the Spring of 1914 that I returned from India where I became convinced that there was no question of any danger to British rule.....in fact, I considered it doubtful that serious revolt would occur even were a hostile force to appear on the frontier of India.....I must admit that my various scruples were finally overcome by the spirit of adventure which had once more been aroused in me."

It is possible that von Niedermayer had foreseen his mission in the coming war. In 1913 he spent several weeks as the guest of the British Consul in Meshed - Percy Sykes, who as head of the South Persia Rifles in 1916, 1917, and 1918 would chase German agents, like von Niedermayer, in Persia.

It is also possible that much more would have come of the Niedermayer-Hentig missions if there had been greater secrecy. The British, who had a whole network of agents covering the territory from Turkestan to the Persian Gulf, knew a considerable amount about enemy plans. Even as early as September, 1914, almost as soon as the "traveling circus" crossed over from Rumania into Turkey, the British knew a mission on its way to Afghanistan to agitate for a

Holy War - Hunter's former co-worker, JG Lorimer, picked up news of the mission while he was the Resident of the Gulf stationed in Bushire.

Much earlier, as a result of the Kaiser's enthusiasm for things Moslem, his journey to Jerusalem and his pilgrimage to Saladin's tomb, there were frequent allusions to the Kaiser having become a Moslem. The more sophisticated Turks, Arabs, and Persians may have talked this with their tongues planted firmly in their cheeks. But it was not long before the less sophisticated believed it. Rumours of the Kaiser's profession of a new faith were spreading fast - speeded along by German agents who saw distinct advantages to such a belief. It was soon said in the bazaars of Afghanistan that the Kaiser had indeed embraced the Moslem faith, had made a pilgrimage to Mecca and was now known as Hadji Guillaume.

The Niedermayer-Hentig missions slipped across the frontier into Afghanistan despite the British knowing they were on their way and despite regular border patrolling by the Russians from the north and the British from the south. They were welcomed in many towns and felt optimistic about the reception they would receive in Kabul. And they did receive a good reception - but not, after the initial reception of the general public from whom they were then kept isolated, but from Turkish employees of the Amir. At first the "King", Amir Habibullah simply refused to receive them and it was only after they went on a hunger strike to press their claim for an audience that the Amir relented.

Niedermayer made his request. Would the Amir follow the call made by the Ottoman Sultan for a Jihad against the British? Could Turkish troops cross Afghanistan to attack India? Would Afghanistan break off diplomatic relations with the British?

The Amir's response was cool. He believed he could win greater benefits from the British by remaining neutral while appearing to be listening to the proposals and blandishments of the Germans. Many Afghans were certain that Habibullah was missing a heaven sent opportunity to score one against the British and finally rid their country of its influence. However, the Amir shrewdly realized that apart from a handful of gifts - the bulk had been lost in Persia - all the Germans had to offer him was "something later".

The Niedermayer-Hentig missions though not successful, were accompanied by others, which caused the British continuing anxiety. Indian nationalists, Mohendra Pratap and Barakat Ullah, were both preaching active rebellion. There was also a further group of Indian revolutionaries under the leadership of a Turk named Maulvi Obeidullah, who proclaimed himself Turkey's ambassador to Afghanistan. With a small band of students he formed "the Army of God" and planned a provisional government of India in Kabul. Although the Amir had them jailed for a couple of weeks, his nephew, Nasrullah, and the war party in Afghanistan supported them.

Von Niedermayer quickly realized that his earlier expectations of the expedition were correct. The Indian revolutionaries appeared to have no great success and his own efforts to win over the Amir looked as if they would fail. A treaty was signed but the terms were such that only if Turkey and Germany were totally successful would anything come of it. Despite the failure of the enterprise to achieve many of its objectives it did cause considerable worry to the British and the Russians. Von Hentig stayed on in Kabul as German representative there and, more important, the Indian revolutionaries and Turkish agents stayed on as well. They were able to continually stoke the resentment of the border tribes for the British and this eventually resulted in 1917 in a general uprising of the Pathan Mahsuds on the Northwest Frontier.

British fears that should the Turks succeed in reaching Afghanistan in force then the whole country would rise, sweep Habibullah aside and swing south to take on the British, was realistic. The Afghan Army, reinforced by the Pathan tribes along the border could have stormed into India when the bulk of the Indian Army was either in Mesopotamia fighting the Turks or in Europe fighting the Germans. To bring the Indian Army home could have mortally wounded the Allied effort. Everything depended on keeping Afghanistan neutral, insulating it from enemy agents and preventing the Turkish Army from reaching its borders.

That task, far from easy in the early years of the war, was clear and the methods understandable. With the Russians holding the Turks in eastern Anatolia and the British holding them in Mesopotamia it was a relatively straightforward undertaking. When the Russian Army collapsed following the Revolution in 1917 the danger of a Turkish advance eastward became intense. The vacuum created by the Russian Army disintegration and later the separate peace made by Lenin's emissaries, signaled immense danger for India and, consequently, allied efforts on the Western Front. The breach caused by this Russian disintegration had to be shored up.

PERSIA AT WAR

When war began in Europe a major British concern was to secure the oil supplies from the Persian Gulf. Since the Royal Navy was now dependent upon oil, the oil had to be protected. Persia was not then a major oil producer. The United States in 1913 produced 140 times more oil than did Persia. However, that oil had to cross the Atlantic, harried by German submarines, and alternative sources needed to be secured.

By the end of October, 1914 an Indian Army brigade, to known as "Force D", had reached Bahrein and the British government authorized it to advance to the city of Basra which would be its base. The city was taken on November 22 after some hard fighting with the Turks and Percy Cox, who was Political Officer with the force, read, in Arabic and Kurdish, a proclamation referring to Britain's long friendship with Turkey. Britain, he said, although now at war with Turkey because Germany had tricked the Turks into numerous intrigues and acts of hostility against British interests, bore no ill-feeling against the population which would now enjoy the benefits of British liberty and justice.

Within days Force D was moving north again, although with no clear ultimate destination in mind. It had received orders to take Kut el Amarah, seventy miles up the Tigris. It had also been instructed to take Nasiriya, to the northwest and on the Euphrates and also, to the northeast, Ahwaz, in Persia and starting point of the oil pipeline to Abadan. The Force was expanded with more troops and supporting artillery and placed under the command of General Sir John Nixon. Major General Townsend was to advance still further north up the Tigris and seize Kut al-Amara, while Major General Gorringe was to take Ahwaz, which he succeeded in doing and drove the Turks permanently from the oilfields.

Taking Ahwaz made considerable strategic sense. Taking Kut may not have been necessary. Moving still further north proved to be a major disaster. Ironically, a factor in the decision to advance beyond Kut was the desire of the British government to retrieve popular support lost as a result of the fiasco at Gallipoli. The Viceroy of India was told by the British cabinet, "Nixon may march on Baghdad if he is satisfied the force he had available is sufficient for the operation." Part of the Mesopotamian force continued advancing northwards towards Baghdad suffering casualties from bullets, heat and disease all the way until they reached Ctesiphon, only twenty miles southeast of Baghdad. The assault on that fortified position cost the Indian Army a third of the force in casualties and the sick and wounded were evacuated as 1915 ended down river back to Kut, which Townsend figured he could hold against the Turks. He was wrong.

Townsend was soon besieged. It was a siege in which the Turks, commanded at this point by the veteran German General von der Goltz, would be soon victorious and many thousands of British and Indian troops would either die or spend the remainder of the war in primitive prison camps after a savage march into captivity. The siege of Kut and its surrender at the end of April proved to be one of the worst disasters suffered by the army. Control of the Mesopotamian campaign was taken from India by the War Office and eventually, in March, 1917, British and Indian troops marched into Baghdad.

Persia was technically neutral, though its Parliament tended to vacillate in its sympathies depending on the progress of the war elsewhere. This was not surprising. The country had hardly developed a strong sense of national identity and the political leaders in the major cities were accustomed to using foreign political connections to advance their own interests. Furthermore, Persia had no armed forces with which she could defend her neutrality. The British had moved into Persia early on, moving up to the oilfields at Ahwaz even before the end of 1914. However, one of the first breaches of Persian neutrality was by Turks who sent a raiding force against the pipeline to Abadan. If the Turks were going to raid and try to destroy Britain's source of oil in Persia, it was incumbent on Britain to defend it. Sir Percy Sykes stated the allied position with simplicity when he wrote "Persian neutrality could only be maintained by the un-neutral presence of British and Russian troops on Persian territory. So long as these troops remained passive the Persian government would never declare war on the Allies. The aim of the Germans was to provoke the British and Russians to abandon their passivity."

There was hardly a single goal shared by all Persians. This was partly due to the diversity of the people. In addition to the substantial urban population large tribes of nomads dominated the countryside. In the region in which Fraser Hunter operated there were - and still are - three main tribes. They are not all impoverished drifters and some of the families were exceedingly wealthy, their children were educated in Europe and their wives shopped on the boulevards of Paris.

The Bakhtiaris from the area west-southwest of Isfahan were probably the most powerful. They were pro-British. But they were also anti-Russian and so some Bakhtiari would align themselves with the Turks resisting Russian General Baratov's efforts to reach the beleaguered British at Kut. Others were brigands interested in loot wherever it was. But for the most part the Bakhtiaris allied themselves to British interests during the war years and received financial subsidies from the Anglo-Persian Oil Company. They were extremely independent and resented any attempts at control by the government in Teheran.

In Fars Province - beautiful Shiraz is the capital - are the tribes of the Khamseh confederation. In reality this confederation is composed of five tribes - the name Khamseh derives from the Arabic word for five - and because they were less unified than the others they were less dangerous. They were also spread over a very large area with their summer and winter grazing areas as much as 350 miles apart. Their leader, at that time, was the Kavam-u-Mulk. He was twenty-nine years old in 1916 when the South Persia Rifles reached his area, was educated, spoke English well and was a keen shot. He was even more keen about women and wine, both of which he pursued diligently. He was not as wealthy as some of the chiefs partly because he had five sisters who received equal shares of their father's estate. The Kavam later knew Hunter well and Hunter was able to exert some influence over him. Unfortunately, his brother-in-law, the Nazim-u-Mulk who had been educated at the well-known English public school, Bedford College, also considerably influenced him. A memorandum of the time dryly notes that "The Nazim-u-Mulk is not a satisfactory product of English education, being a bosom friend of Mirza Mustafha Khan,....... who was removed by us from Shiraz as his influence over the Kavam-u-Mulk was apparently exerted against us." The Kamseh tribal confederation was not technically led by the Kavam; the Kavam was instead the Confederation's representative with the Governor-General of Fars in Shiraz. Generally they were on good terms with the British but on bad terms with the most powerful tribe in Fars - the Kashgai.

The Kashgai were anti-British - indeed, it could be argued that they were anti-everyone. They cherished their independence and were prepared to fight to maintain it. Nomadic, their flocks wintered in the Firuzabad region and then moved two hundred miles to mountain pastures over the summer. Legend has it that the Kashgai had originated from the region of Kashgar in what is now western Singkiang, and then followed the train of Ghengis Khan, first to Azerbaijan, then to Khalajistan, then south to Fars Province. The closeness of the name Kashgai to that of Kashgar superficially suggests the association. Some maintain that many of the Kashgai used only horses with a white blaze on their foreheads. In the Turkish language the word "Kashgai" means a horse with a white blaze on its head. Wherever these mounted nomads originated, they were feared wherever they went. Picturesque they might be but in the early part of this century they were pitiless fighters, living independently and bearing allegiance to little but their own code of honour. The chief of the Kashgai at the beginning of the war was Solat-u-Dola. According to a British intelligence note of the time he was vindictive, unreliable and unstable, totally opposed to any law and order save that he imposed. He is believed to have incited the local chieftain near the town of Kazerun - straddling the road between Bushire and Shiraz - to seize the garrison there. On the purely personal level he was quite amiable towards British army officers but had no room at all for Farman Farma, a prince of the Kajar dynasty and soon to be Governor-General of Fars. Nor did he and the Kavam-u-Mult get along well together.

The tribes were well armed, and the Kashgai better than any other. Just about all the tribal bands of southern Fars province, including the Tangistanis who occupied the area immediately adjacent to the Gulf, were heavily involved in gun running, principally from the Arabian side of the Gulf.

On August 8 1915, the British seized Bushire, the coastal port connected to Shiraz by a steep mountain road by way of Kazerun. They felt compelled to do so because of evidence of a vast espionage network controlled by the German Ambassador in Teheran. Enemy agents were active throughout Persia, particularly the elusive Wassmuss in Fars Province, along the Bushire, Kazerun, Shiraz road and south into Tangistan. An intelligence summary in May, 1916, reported that on the route between Shiraz and Bushire Sykes and Hunter would have to contend not just with Wilhelm Wassmuss and his native supporters but with as many as eighty six Germans or Austrians plus four other Caucasians or "fanatics". The report also estimated that as many as seventy-two Germans had reached Afghanistan and that up to twenty-five were working in the Kerman area.

Bushire was a critical link in the communication line between London and India. Germans must not dominate it. It was also a major centre for the German Wonkhous Company, ostensibly a commercial enterprise initially established to buy and sell seashells, but probably a front for German espionage throughout the Gulf States and in southern Persia once war had begun. Before the war both Cox and Shakespear, headquartered at Bandar Lingah across the Gulf from Oman, warned the Political and Secret Department of the India Office of the possible subversive activities of the Wonkhaus Company. In February 1915, the British consular guard in Bushire "arrested" the German consul, Herr Listermann, and his wife, and also the Germans working for the Wonckhaus Company, who were all deported, first of all to Basra and then on to India. It was at this time that Wassmuss' possessions were seized, an event that soon had grave consequences for the German war plans.

However, British action gave Wassmuss an excellent propaganda opportunity. He was not slow to use it and was soon inciting tribes to attack British interests.

The seizure of Bushire had not gone smoothly. Martial law had to be imposed and the weapons of the gendarmerie confiscated. Anyone entering or leaving the town was required to produce a pass and there were a number of arrests, including that of the local newspaper editor and the son of one of the khans. An embargo was placed on grain going to the tribes of Tangistan. Four days after the seizure of Bushire sailors from HMS Juno and some Indian sepoys stormed a nearby hostile fort and burned down the village. The operation went badly. HMS Juno accidentally opened fire on its own men who in the confusion, fired back; nine sailors, including the commander of the ship, were killed and seventeen wounded. The Indian troops suffered fifty casualties.

The tribes had won the day and Wassmuss encouraged them to attack Bushire. Bushire is an island connected to the mainland by a mud causeway and in the early hours of September 9, many tribal khans and their followers massed along the ravines at the edge of the causeway. It was a confused battle with casualties heavy on both sides, but the tribesmen were convinced that the victory was theirs, even though they failed to secure the town. Morale soared.

Bushire was soon handed back to Persian authority - once they had installed a governor compatible with British interests - but the territory between the town and Shiraz as well as southwards into Tangistan continued throughout the war to be dominated by tribes hostile to the British and led by Wassmuss.

While German influence among the tribes was considerable at the outbreak of war, the allies had not been idle. In the northern section of the country, in the Russian zone of influence, Russian dominance was indisputable. But even outside of the Russian zone allied interests had been pursued, albeit with a less heavy hand. Percy Cox had negotiated a treaty with the Sheik of Mohammerah guaranteeing the safe passage of oil across Khuzestan to Abadan. The British dominated the ports on both sides of the Gulf and were influential among the tribes of Siestan. Indian Army officers, serving in the Political Branch, continued to man consulates across Persia.

By mid-1915 both British and German agents were widely spread over Persia, each side struggling to dominate the neutral Persians. The Germans had an initial and major advantage. The Swedish officered Gendarmerie was openly pro-German and assisted in supplying guns to the tribesmen. In September the British consul in Isfahan was wounded in an assassination attempt and his Indian orderly killed. A week later the British vice-consul in Shiraz was shot and died the next day and a few weeks later an employee at the consulate was murdered. Russian and British colonies were being driven from the main towns and British banks looted. When the British and Russian consuls tried to return to Kermanshah after the Turks evacuated it they were blocked by a German-led band of two hundred local tribesmen.

In Shiraz the Kavam seemed quite incapable of controlling the city. Shiraz, once known as the city of wine, roses, poets and lovers, was controlled by pro-German tribal levies. On the morning of November 10 the British consulate was surrounded by armed gendarmes - their Swedish officers had left town on some pretext the day before. A letter delivered to the staff and signed by the

National Committee for Persian Independence, ordered them to leave as prisoners in three hours.

The consul, William Frederick Travers O'Connor, burned his correspondence, deposited with a neighbor some two thousand pounds sterling which had been saved from his budget, and surrendered. Eleven members of the British community were taken, four women and seven men. The party was marched south, accompanied by Wassmuss for much of the way, through the town of Kazerun. They were then split into two groups, men and women. The women were taken onto Bushire and handed over to British authorities. The men were taken to a mountain tribal fort at Ahran where the Tangistanis held them for eleven months before being exchanged for fourteen Persian prisoners held by the British.

To The Afghan Frontier

While the efforts of Wassmuss were gaining momentum in the Persian mountains parallel to the Gulf and German agents and their local armed levies were dominating much of the Persian countryside, Fraser Hunter was hundreds of miles further east, patrolling among the Pathans of the North West Frontier.

Since 1842, when tribesmen on the Frontier wiped out the Army of the Indus retreating from Kabul to Jellalabad, British and Indian soldiers have had a healthy respect for the Pathans. With good reason. The tribesmen who inhabit the mountains of the Afghan border are fiercely independent, truculent of authority - often including that of their own chiefs - know the forbidding countryside intimately, and are unsurpassed guerrilla fighters who neither give nor expect quarter. It has been said of them that they only feel at peace when at war.

Although the actual frontier of India stretched over a vast distance from the Gulf of Oman to Burma, when Anglo-Indians referred to "the Frontier" they meant the North-West Frontier, a rugged line of mountains reaching from Baluchistan to the Pamirs and inhabited by tribes, then called Pathan but now more generally referred to as Pushtun. More precisely they meant the territory between the Durand Line, which was the agreed frontier between Afghanistan and India, and the administrative frontier, which in the northwest was not always the same as the political frontier. Between the administrative frontier and the Afghan frontier were the highly volatile tribal lands, the agencies such as Malakand, Wana, Tochi, Kurram and Khyber, where life was too often bloody and short.

The Pathans who live there were fierce, arrogant and cruel; they were easily and frequently inflamed by religious passions and when their own barren mountains failed to provide what they needed or wanted they were always ready to raid into the fertile valleys and plains of the administered area.

The Pathans are divided into a number of tribes, which in turn, are divided into clans. All of them are ruled by a code of honor, Pathanwali, and spent their lives involved in blood feuds that had their roots in some breaching of this code. The code of Pathanwali imposes three obligations. Fugitives must be offered protection; hospitality must be extended to all who seek it; insults must be avenged. Offend a neighbor's guest and the resulting feud could continue for years. Any insult, no matter how small, had to be avenged no matter how long it took. Small wonder that each village was fortified and its watchtower always manned.

The various tribes had their own peculiarities. The largest tribe, the Afridis of the Khyber, were said to spend so much time feuding among themselves that they had little time left to quarrel with their neighbors. The "Bar" or "Hill" Mohmands were seen as the most belligerent, the Orakzais as particularly fanatical; the graceful-looking Mahsuds were outstanding guerrilla fighters and were regarded, along with the Waziris, as the most formidable of all the Frontier tribes. In the Kurrum Valley were also the Turis who, being Shiah Moslems, were disliked by their neighbours who, with the exception of some of the Orakzais, are Sunnis.

So independent of authority are the Pathans that within the tribes the power of the chief is limited and decisions are reached by democratic process at a council or "jirga". Only the mullahs exercised real authority and the Pathans were quick to respond to the call for "jihad" or a holy war, putting aside, at least temporarily, the local blood feuds to kill and die instead in battle with the infidel.

The Frontier was the scene of a seemingly endless series of campaigns – forty-five of them between 1849 and 1900 alone - and of almost constant skirmishing and raids. Even after the British had gone the Pathans came raiding out of their mountains with awful ferocity into Peshawar, where in 1947 they killed ten thousand and into Kashmir where they were incited by the prospect of loot, rape, murder, and of saving their co-religionists from being absorbed into the new state of India. Sir Olaf Caroe, last British Governor on the Frontier and author of the classic <u>The Pathans</u> described them with English understatement as "a prickly and untrimmed hedge between Rawalpindi and Kabul".

At the turn of the century the Frontier was settling again after the great Pathan Revolt of 1897 which took sixty thousand troops six months to quell and part of which was eloquently described in the dispatches of the correspondent for the Daily Telegraph, Lieutenant Winston S Churchill.

Lord Curzon, appointed Viceroy in 1899, removed responsibility for the Frontier from the Government of the Punjab and created the North-West Frontier Province that would report directly to the government of India. Previously commissioners of tribal territories reported to the government of the Punjab that in turn reported to the Indian government - a clumsy and time consuming process.

Much of Curzon's subsequent unpopularity with the army may have been rooted in his related reform. Curzon believed that the administration and policing of the Frontier in the tribal areas was inefficient and wasteful of money and life. The small British-occupied forts, threatening the long-standing independence of the tribes, were goads that incited the violence they were intended to eliminate. Small and undermanned, yet alien and antagonistic, they invited attack.

The new Frontier policy would be to hold substantial bodies of troops back from the tribal lands in major garrisons in the settled areas, which could move in quickly in force should the need arise. Instead of small units of Indian or British Army regiments scattered through the tribal areas, these lands would instead be policed by levies raised from among the tribes themselves. The army did not like it. The generals wanted bigger and more forts. The subalterns wanted to be where the action was. But Curzon prevailed and units of Militia - later to be called Scouts - were raised in the Kurrum, the Zhob, and in North and South Waziristan. These militia were controlled by the Political Agents and were stationed in the small forts and in advanced posts of platoon strength. When fighting was heavier than they could manage they could call on regular troops based at Kohat, Bannu, Peshawar and Malakand.

Associated with the unpopularity of the reorganization that kept young officers distant from frequent action, was the social life of the larger garrisons. The social life of India reeked of snobbery and while an Indian Army cavalry officer would have been socially very acceptable, the whole climate of petty jealousies and the nuances of the social order would have been alien to someone from Toronto. Toronto, of course, had its snobbery as well, but it was a far larger community than the British community in, say Bannu, or for that matter, in Bombay and would not have been so pervasive and inescapable.

Fate had decreed for Hunter that no sooner had he come back from China, prospects for action in India had been considerably reduced by events which he could neither have influenced nor foreseen - Curzon's reorganization of British forces on the Frontier. Perhaps this was a contributing factor in Hunter's decision to join the Survey of India. But the war changed even the disposition of troops on the Frontier. When he went back to the army at the outbreak of war he was posted straight to the Kurrum Valley and the heart of the tribal territory.

The other reason for Curzon's unpopularity was far less laudable.

Curzon was not only an energetic Viceroy. He had a clear sense of duty and law. His concept recognized no racial difference. Before the law all should be equal. This did not always sit well with the British Army in India. Curzon's conviction that the law had to be both paramount and color-blind was put to test shortly after he arrived in India. Twenty British soldiers of the West Kent Regiment raped an elderly Burmese woman. Curzon heard vague reports about it and on inquiry it was apparent to him that army authorities were trying to hush up the whole affair. When the accused were finally brought to court they were found, on a technicality, "Not Guilty". Curzon, believing that blind justice was the greatest contribution Britain could to make to India, acted somewhat imperiously, punishing the innocent as well as the guilty. The culprits were thrown out of the army; the colonel and the sergeant-major were compulsorily retired, and the regiment was posted to Aden - regarded as the worst possible station in the Empire - for two years without leave. The army felt the punishment Draconian and deeply resented Curzon for it.

Yet Curzon had cause for alarm at the double legal standard that existed. There had been a number of cases in which British soldiers had killed Indians - sometimes accidentally but too often deliberately - and got away with it. In the previous twenty years eighty-four Indians had been killed but since the Mutiny only two Europeans had been hanged for murder. Curzon attempted to understand the causes. He knew that because of differences in temperament there would inevitably be clashes between the two races. But they had to be kept in check and "check is only possible, not by crushing the aspirations of the native, which is destined to grow, but by controlling the temper of the European.....the English may be in danger of losing their command of India because they have not learned to command themselves."

Although today Curzon's attitude seems perfectly reasonable - and some of his punishments of British regiments high-handed - the animosity of the English in India sometimes depressed him: not often though, he was too much the aristocrat to bother for long about what others thought of him. He was convinced that just about everybody in the army detested him and he was probably right.

By the time the First World War began Curzon had long gone from India. A dispute with Kitchener, Army C-in-C India, over the status of the Military Member in the Viceroy's Council had begun a train of events that ended in his resignation in 1905. But his reforms had a profound effect on the Frontier.

Kitchener too had his impact on India before he left in 1909. Like Curzon, Kitchener believed that the function of the army was not to protect the British against the Indians but to protect the subcontinent form external aggressors. Both were deeply concerned at Russia's seemingly inexorable advance southwards and the possibility of Afghanistan or Tibet falling under Russian domination. Kitchener re-positioned the army to protect the north.

The Frontier had remained relatively tranquil in large part due to the military and administrative reforms. But "relatively tranquil" on the Frontier was a long way from being peaceful. In the first decade of the century a fanatical mullah named Powindah - labelled by Kitchener "the Pestilential Priest" - incited the Mahsuds into a series of raids into the administered areas and ambush and murder continued until his death in 1913. Even on his deathbed the mullah urged the Mahsuds to fight on against the infidels. Further to the north it had required a division of infantry in 1908 to end a rising of the Zakha Kel, a sub-tribe of the Afridis, and no sooner were they quiet than the Mohmands rose. These difficulties were compounded by raiding Pathans from across the Afghan border in the area of the Khyber Pass.

The moment war was declared in Europe the Viceroy, Lord Hardinge, mobilized three infantry divisions and a cavalry brigade to watch over the more turbulent border tribes. The Amir of Afghanistan, Habibullah, assured the Viceroy of his country's neutrality but the antipathy of his younger brother Nasrullah towards the British, combined with the fanaticism of the mullahs and the urging of Turkish agents, raised fears that tribal risings could quickly develop into a full scale border war. There were strong reasons for concern. The Mahsuds had murdered the British Political Agent for South Waziristan in April of 1914 and since then, following the deathbed wish of the Mullah, Powindah, had made no effort to conceal their hostility to the government. Roos-Keppel, the Chief Commissioner wrote, "no village is safe, and the Mahsuds raid from their hills right down to the banks of the Indus and kill, entrap and abduct Hindus."

It was essential that border fighting not escalate into war - and the British were well aware, from Lorimer's reports, that a German-Turkish Mission was heading for Kabul. A war on the Frontier would have prevented India from sending troops to Europe, Mesopotamia and the other theatres. That India was able to contribute some seven hundred thousand men to the allied cause was because peace - or at least "relative tranquility" - was maintained on the North-West Frontier.

The strategy was to keep the Afridi Pathans quiet. If this could be done - principally with increased financial incentives - then no rising, either to the north or the south of them, would spread into a general conflagration.

This strategy was largely successful and generalizations about the tribes should not conceal the lack of unanimity among them. At the outbreak of war, for example, although the Mahsuds continued their murderous forays, tribes in the Swat, Chitral and Khyber Agencies and the Waziris of the Tochi Valley offered their services to the British and the North Waziristan Militia and the Khyber Rifles actually volunteered for active service. The Moslems in India made a massive contribution to the war effort. Although only one fifth of the population, they furnished a third of the seven hundred thousand soldiers sent by India. The Moslems of the Punjab, less than four percent of the population of India, supplied twenty five percent of India's total. Some of the Pathan tribes, the Khattacks for example who are noted for their music and dancing, supplied large numbers to the Indian Army, and remained loyal throughout the war. This was not the case in the tribal areas among the trans-border Pathans, those who migrated too and fro across the Durand Line. For example, at the beginning of the war five thousand trans-border Pathans were serving in the Indian Army, half of them Afridis. Less than a year later six hundred had deserted and all recruiting of trans-border Pathans was stopped. Local raiding did not end. In 1915, urged on by the mullahs, trans-border Pathans attacked into the Frontier area and were repulsed by Pathans of the North Waziristan Militia and the Bannu Brigade, and there were at least five attacks in the Peshawar district by the Mohmands and other Pathans. Clearly, Hunter's destination on the Frontier was no backwater.

In February 1913, the Bombay Lancers moved eastward from Thal thirty miles to Kohat, just outside the tribal area, and established their headquarters there. Detachments patrolled the Kurrum Valley watching the Turis, the more belligerent Orakzais and the tribesmen coming across the border from Afghanistan. Kohat at that time was linked to Peshawar, twenty-eight miles away, by a narrow cart track through the Kohat Pass.

On the 26 November 1914, Hunter, the Superintendent in charge of the Number 3 Party surveying the Northern Circuit, put on once again the uniform of the Duke of Connaught's Bombay Lancers and hurried to rejoin his regiment at Kohat. He was immediately placed in charge of a special force, which he romantically called "the Upper Kurrum Column" the same name given by Lord Roberts' to his Force of 1879. Roberts had advanced through the valley, one of the prettiest of the Frontier, to the pass at Peiwar Kotal during the Second Afghan War. Here his numerically smaller force had outflanked the Afghan Army and won a victory which had given birth to Robert's reputation as a field commander. Later, two years before Hunter arrived in India, there occurred an event that stirred boys and men through the English-speaking world - including the young men at Upper Canada College and the RMC Kingston. Between Kohat and the Peiwar Kotal Pass into Afghanistan, a little to the north of the Kurrum River is the Samana Range of hills on the southside of which are the Dargai Heights. The Orakzais and Afridis Pathans made their stand there against Roberts. The Tirah Field Force, which included the Peshawar and Kurrum Columns advanced from Kohat and there was bitter fighting first to capture and later to regain the heights. The Gordon Highlanders advanced up the steep incline despite continuous fire from the tribesmen on the Heights. Then, with bayonets fixed, they surged towards the Afridi Pathans, led by the bagpipe playing Piper Findlater and followed by the Gurkhas, the Dorsets and Derbys. Piper Findlater was shot through both ankles but, propped against a rock carried on playing "Cock o' the North" as the green kilted Highlanders charged. The Afridis fled. Both the Colonel and Piper Findlater were awarded the Victoria Cross.

Hunter would have known this story and been aware as he rode westward out of Kohat that reputations could be made - or lost - in the Tirah and the Kurrum and in the hills beyond them. He was probably also aware of Kipling's lines, from "Arithmetic of the Frontier":

> A scrimmage in a border station–
> A canter down some dark defile–
> Two thousand pounds of education
> Drops to a ten-rupee jezail–
> The Crammer's boast, the Squadron's pride,
> Shot like a rabbit in a ride.
>
> One sword-knot stolen from the camp
> Will pay for all the school expenses
> Of any Kurrum Valley scamp
> Who knows no word of moods and tenses
> But, being blessed with perfect sight
> Picks off our mess-mates left and right.

While three squadrons of the Duke of Connaught's remained at Kohat, Hunter led the remaining squadron of cavalry an approximate fifty miles past numerous small fortified villages to the larger village of Parachinar. Parachinar lies in the shadow of Mount Sikaram that at 15,600 feet is the highest peak in the Safed Koh range and was the headquarters of the Kurrum Militia. This force totaling 1,400 contained only four British officers and occupied an additional thirteen small forts commanded by Subadars (Company Officers), Jemadars (Junior Officers) and Halvidars (Sergeants). Also in Parachinar at that time were two companies of the 2-4th Gurkha Rifles and a section of mountain artillery. Hunter, soon to be promoted to the rank of major, had his squadron of Lancers and the combined force was to hold the western end of the Kurrum Valley. The area itself was pleasant enough with apple and pear orchards, rice paddies, wheat and corn fields. But the land rose rapidly to the Safed Koh range and a few miles to the west of the village the old trade route to the Afghan town of Gardez crosses the Peiwar Pass at an altitude of more than 8,500 feet. It is possible that Hunter crossed the border into Afghanistan at around this point in "hot pursuit" of some raiding trans-border Pathans.

Tensions were running high in 1915. British agents knew that von Niedermayer's German-Turkish Mission was nearing Kabul, that the mullahs from southern Afghanistan had joined the border mullahs, but that because of the demands for troops in Mesopotamia the army in India was weak. At one period in 1915 the total British garrison in India numbered less than fifteen thousand men.

Added to fears of tribal uprisings was the concern that German agents would be able to stir into militant action the revolutionary movement inside India. Attached to the German-Turkish Mission to Kabul were the Indian revolutionaries Mahendra Partab and Barkat Ullah. They were carrying letters signed by Bethmann Hollweg, the German Chancellor, to the princes of India urging their support in the Kaiser's cause. These letters never reached their destination and had they done so they would probably not received the reception the Kaiser hoped for. There was also some alarm at what came to be known as "the Silk Letter Plot", a far-reaching, pan-Islamic conspiracy with the aim of uniting all the forces of Islam against the British.

Some Indian Moslems had gone to Arabia in an attempt to win the Sharif of Mecca to the pan-Islamic cause but the Arab Revolt against Turkey in 1916 prevented any growth to that plot. British agents succeeded in obtaining some of the documents which had been written in Kabul by the Indian revolutionary Obeid Ullah and which contained the names of some of the conspirators. The document was written on yellow silk and hence the name given to the conspiracy. Planned was a provisional government of India with authority divided between the Moslem Barkat Ullah and the Hindu, Mahendra Partab. According to Sir Michael O'Dwyer, Lieutenant Governor of the Punjab, a British officer passing himself off as a revolutionary Hindu in Bokhara in 1920, met with Mahendra Partab who confided to him that one of the reasons for failure was that the Hindu revolutionary party balked at the idea of establishing Moslem dominance in India. While that may have been an excuse for failure, the revolt in Arabia against the Turks, the loyalty to the government of so many Indians, and the determination of the Amir of Afghanistan to remain neutral probably doomed the revolutionary movement. It was only after the war that a groundswell of disillusion with the government began to stir in great numbers of Indians.

Major Fraser Hunter, with his Lancers, the Kurrum Militia, and with the Gurkhas patrolled the border of Afghanistan throughout 1915 aware always, through intelligence reports, of the frenzy of the mullahs and of events in Kabul only seventy miles to the north.

Then came an event that was to profoundly influence Hunter's career. The South Persia Military Police, soon to be called the South Persia Rifles, was to act to restore order and to rescue consular officials kidnapped by tribes in southern Persia. Hunter left the Kurrum headed for military headquarters at Simla.

SOUTH PERSIA RIFLES

When Hunter reached army headquarters he found official thinking about Persia despondent. Persia, long regarded as the sentry at the gateway to India was, to say the best, unreliable. Mauraudering bands of tribesmen, led by German officers, dominated the southern part of the country. The German guerrilla leader, Wilhelm Wassmuss, roamed at will through much of the south and in the towns and villages, where the Swedish-officered Gendarmerie should have been keeping the peace and some semblance of neutrality, the Swedes openly sided with the Germans. Consul O'Connor had been captured and was imprisoned in a remote tribal fort.

British officials were hardly surprised that such a situation existed. For a long time Persia's decline had been all too apparent and official India saw Persia as simply a feudal society of tribes bound together only by a common religion. Many had feared, up to the 1907 Treaty, that Persia would soon be a Russian province - in fact, many in India feared that the Treaty would even accelerate the advent of that dismal possibility, rather than limit the extent of the Russian advance, which was the hope of London. The Persian army was an ill-armed, undisciplined mob. When a delegation arrived from London to present the Shah with the Order of the Garter - an honour that Edward VII had been most reluctant to confer - the sentry at the palace was said to have presented arms with a broken table leg. He had no rifle and unconsciously symbolized Persia as sentry to the gateway of India.

Persian officials systematically looted the public purse. Payment of soldiers and officials was always in arrears and they took whatever recourse was open to them to redress the balance. Bribery was endemic, corruption widespread. The only order reliably maintained was by the Persian Cossack Brigade, a force of eight thousand Persians officered by Russians with headquarters at Teheran and detachments at Tabriz, Kasvin, Hamadan and other major centres.

Despite the chaotic conditions - perhaps even because of them - Persia was important to the British. Not all recognized that. Lord Hardinge, who would be Viceroy of India from 1910 until 1916, lamented earlier that "everybody regards Persia as an unmitigated bore ...no wonder the Russians always beat us; they are in earnest and we are not". But Curzon knew that like Afghanistan and Tibet it was a country that separated India from the advancing Russians and now from the Germans and Turks. Most British were convinced that treaties with Russians were of little lasting value since the Russians simply ignored them when it suited them. Just as Russia would have liked access to the oceans of the world by way of Constantinople and the Bosphorous, so a similar opportunity for its fleet existed through Persia to the Gulf. British interest in the country was not to acquire more territory or influence, but to prevent the Russians from doing so. Aside from this, British interests were commercial.

The Province of Siestan had been the principal area of concern. The alternative to Herat and Afghanistan as an invasion route for the Russians was through Siestan, and Russian dominance of that province would allow their agents to supply guns to the ever-turbulent tribes along India's North-West Frontier. So worried was the Indian government about Siestan that Curzon had wanted the province as security for a loan being considered for Persia. In the first decade of the century British agents worked with the tribes to ensure that, should the central government collapse Britain's positions along the shores of the Gulf and trade along the roads would be protected by friendly tribesmen. There had been talk of creating militias among the tribes, similar to those on the North-West Frontier, but it had come to nothing because the central government in Teheran would have seen it as weakening its authority and encouraging an even greater independence among the tribesmen than existed already. In addition, the British courted the mullahs, who had immense influence in the countryside, and bribed them from secret service funds.

Britain was weak at the beginning of the century. Army prestige suffered as a result of defeats in South Africa and the army in India was only big enough to defend its own borders. Perhaps the best way to keep the Russians from getting too close to the Indian border was to acknowledge their closeness as irreversible by dividing the country into zones. In that way Britain would at least be able to concentrate on those areas that were vital to her interests. The 1907 Treaty gave the Russians a zone of influence in the north, the British one in the southeast, and a central buffer zone under the control of the government in Teheran. Both the Russians and the British paid lip service to the territorial integrity and independence of Persia but understandably virtually all Persians found in this "partition" as they saw it, an intolerable affront to their national integrity. It ensured that both Russians and British were suspect in the country - Russians for what they did, British for suspected sinister designs. The only ones happy with the arrangement were the Russians. The Russian line started at the Persian border west of Hamadan, crossed to Isfahan and Yedz and then ran northeast to where the Russian and Afghan borders intersect. The British line, encompassing a far smaller area, and that principally desert, started at the Afghan border east of Birjand, ran from Birjand to Kerman and down to Bandar Abbas on the Gulf coast. The neutral zone in the centre kept the two zones apart - although when war came Russia accepted Britain's predominance in the neutral zone in exchange for Britain's acknowledging theirs in the Bosphorous.

Far earlier, some aspects of the treaty had been rendered obsolete by the discovery and growing importance of Persian oil and a concession granted to the Englishman, William Knox D'Arcy that covered all Persia except the five northern provinces. In 1914 the British government, at the time of the Royal Navy's conversion from coal to oil, became the major stockholder in the Anglo-Persian Oil Company.

The treaty did not end factional disputes in Persia. The countryside remained chaotic and by the end of 1907 was in a state of revolution - Royalists versus Nationalists - the Russians supporting the Royalists, the British sympathetic of the Nationalists. All over Persia there was violence. Kurdish raiders sacked villages near Tabriz; Persian bandits attacked Russian border guards and the Russians, to reinforce their demands for compensation, burned several villages to the ground. Bakhtiari chiefs near Isfahan joined the Nationalists, deposed the royal governor and marched on Teheran where, after severe fighting, the Persian Cossacks deserted to the rebels and the Shah fled to the Russian Embassy. This was seen as abdication and his thirteen-year-old son, who ruled through a regent, replaced him.

In the north, Russian influence was heavy handed - barbarous even - while in the south the British pursued commercial interests and sought friendly relations with the chieftains. Percy Sykes, for example, stationed as agent in Meshed in the Russian zone, became a personal friend of Prince Farman Farma, a member of the royal house, an ex-minister of war and at one time Governor-General of

Arabistan, the west of Fars Province. Farman Farma was anxious that his son go to either the Royal Military College, Sandhurst, or the Royal Military Academy, Woolwich, in England and Sykes supported the application. British policy was to a large extent, based on favorably influencing key figures in the country by the careful use of money and favors. The British felt, and events frequently proved them right, that so great was the vanity of official Persians that the favors that elevated their prestige were the most influential. It was in pursuit of this policy that the reluctance of Edward VII was finally overcome and the Order of the Garter was conferred on the Shah back in 1903. Within a week a new commercial treaty was signed between Persia and Britain.

Yet the British made a mistake. In the north Russian influence was exercised through the Russian-led Persian Cossacks. But in the south the British had no equivalent force. Instead there was throughout the country the gendarmerie, a police force officered by Swedes, chosen because of their neutrality, but which at the beginning of the war was already actively pro-German and a major ally of Wassmuss and his tribesmen. The British "mistake" was a consequence of their trying to be neutral in what became known as the Stokes Affair. Back in 1910 the Persian government had asked the Americans to provide them with someone who would endeavour to put their chaotic finances in some sort of order. The Americans sent their financial wizard, W. Morgan Shuster, who soon realized that unless there was some means to compel the payment of taxes the revenue of which Persia was capable would never materialize. He proposed the creation of a Treasury Gendarmerie.

The British Military Attaché in Teheran was a Major Claude Bayfield Stokes, an enthusiastic supporter of the Persian Nationalists - and later probably a friend of Fraser Hunter - who had gone as far as to join secret societies of politically nationalist groups. Shuster was taken with Stokes and, since his appointment as military attaché was near an end, suggested that he might head the Treasury Gendarmerie. The Russians strongly opposed his appointment and, after some initial ambivalence, the British agreed that for a British officer to lead a Persian force in the Russian sphere of influence was not consistent with the spirit of the Anglo-Russian Convention.

Equally, the British would have strongly opposed the appointment of a Russian army officer to the Persian-Indian frontier. Stokes was told to leave Teheran and return to London. Instead of meekly obeying these instructions, Stokes moved into Shuster's home, began helping him with the organization of the gendarmerie, and, to overcome the hurdle of being a British officer in north Persia, simply tendered his resignation. The Russians saw it as a sinister English plot and were convinced that Stokes would be a British agent in their midst - his resignation simply a theatrical gesture to legalize his intrusion. The British thought the Russians had a fair point. Consequently London refused to accept Stokes resignation calling it "detrimental to British interests" and ordered him to return to India immediately - or face the consequences of disobeying a legal order given to a serving officer.

Shuster, who felt the British behavior reprehensible, had nonetheless, no alternative but to have his gendarmes trained by others and eventually Swedish officers came to Persia. They were supposed to be neutral but when war began, such was Swedish antipathy for Russia that these Swedish officers openly sympathized with the German cause. In fairness to the Swedes, many of the original officers of the force returned home in 1915 when it was clear that their "neutrality" was compromised.

When war began it was immediately seen as essential that Persia, if it could not be persuaded to become an ally, must at least remain neutral so that oil from the British leases continue to flow the 70 miles to Ahwaz and on to Abadan. The oilfields were in the heart of Bakhtiari country and the tribesmen - who were inclined to sympathize with the Germans because their allies, the Turks, were their co-religionists - were kept neutral by the payment of oil dividends which would obviously cease should British control of the oilfields end.

The German Minister in Teheran, Prince Henry of Reuss, had been active in propaganda work - he not only knew the Persians but was familiar with the ways of the British as well since he had been Consul-General in Calcutta before the war. In large part because of his activities much of western Persia was in turmoil and actively anti-British by 1915. The British had felt compelled to seize Bushire - a critical link in their telegraph line from Europe to India - and had arrested the Germans there. Wassmuss managed to escape, made a daring dash to Shiraz where he organized the Germans and friendly tribesmen, and arrested the entire British colony, including the Consul, O'Connor.

When Hunter arrived at Army H.Q. to receive his instructions, Sir Percy Sykes was there - he had just come down from a mission to Tashkent via Moscow where he had met the Czar - and had been appointed head of the mission by the Viceroy on January 20 1916. A telegram had been received in Delhi, unusually cryptic for the times. "Send Sykes to Bandar Abbas for restoration of order and the liberation of O'Connor." Events soon showed that Sykes' initial instructions were far too cryptic.

While India and London were to remain critical of him throughout the war, he could, with justification, reply that the goals of the South Persia Rifles (SPR) were too often changed. Initially they were to restore order and rescue O'Connor; then he had to raise a force to counterbalance Russian influence; at another time the priority was hunting down German agents: at yet another he was to raise a force to support Persian authority.

Sir Charles Marling, the British Minister in Teheran, in a testy letter to Sykes some time later tried to clarify the role he should play. "The main object of the Governments of Great Britain and Russia in the formation of the South Persia Rifles and the Cossack Division was to ensure the maintenance of tranquility in their parts of Persia – the Persian Government being incapable. And to entrust the training etc of these forces to officers supplied by themselves to ensure that they will not be used against their interests as was the case with the Gendarmerie under Swedish officers." The Persian government however, nervous of its position as a neutral state, always delayed giving official recognition to the SPR, even though it had been formed with their consent.

There was also the question of the suitability of Sykes to command such a force. Admittedly the Indian Army at that time was hard pressed for senior staff because of its campaign in Mesopotania. But Sykes' experience had been largely as a political officer. In his early days, before service in the Boer War he had taken part in the Persian Baluchistan Boundary Commission in 1895, but after his South African experience – as an intelligence officer who saw some action with Territorials he had trained – he was part of the Indian government's Foreign and Political Service. From 1905 to 1913 he was agent for the government of India in Khorasan and consul in Meshed where he had met and become friendly with Farman Farma. Sykes was an intrepid traveler and later wrote extensively on Persia and Afghanistan and their history. He had, as early as 1905, advocated the formation of a British-officered mounted force to bring some order into south Persia. Yet his experience in managing large numbers of troops and local untrained levees on active service was negligible.

The War Office in London said that it was desirable that six or seven officers who had special knowledge of Persia and could speak the Persian language be appointed to assist Sykes. Hunter was to be his chief of staff and organizational work and travel arrangements must have been completed quickly because in March, 1916, Sykes and his party were seen ashore by a Guard of Honour of Australian bluejackets at Bandar Abbas - a town of about ten thousand and principally noted for its poor climate and worse water. Its use to the British had been as a trading post and once a week a steamer of the British India Steam Navigation Company called there. It was also a key link on the telegraph line between India and Europe.

William Frederick Travers O'Connor, whom Sykes was instructed to liberate, was an Indian Army officer in the Political Service who, along with the rest of the British colony in Shiraz, had been captured by German-led tribesmen. His career had been dramatic. Like Hunter he too had patrolled the Kurrum Valley but during the violent Tirah campaign of 1898. Later he had been part of the Tibet invasion force - called a mission - and although severely wounded joined the march on Lhasa - since he could speak Tibetan he went as an interpreter. He became Consul for Siestan in 1909 - when Sykes was up in Meshed - and went to Shiraz in 1912. Later, in New York, he and Hunter would become good friends. Now he languished in a tribal jail and efforts by Cox, British agent in Bushire, to have him released had developed an almost comic side.

Cox had offered a prisoner exchange as a way of having the British from Shiraz released. Late in February O'Connor's jailer, Zair Khidar Khan, responded.[22]

"I have received your kind letter offering the exchange of Major O'Connor for a prisoner with a fractured leg. I find that Major O'Connor is comparatively too fat and that he eats five fowls a day. We have all the best Khawis sweet limes specially reserved for him and he eats these every day. He is also allowed every morning and evening to go for his constitutional walk. So we cannot exchange him for a poor fellow with a broken leg. He has been detained here for the damage done to the properties of the poor by the British. What do you profit by keeping in prison a poor man with his leg damaged and should he happen too die while with you, I fear you might experience greater difficulties. So I think it is better that you might release him so that he may die in his own house."

The British were not amused. Rescuing O'Connor was not the only task. Law and order had to be restored throughout southern Persia – the Russians were to take care of the north with their Cossack Brigade – where German and Turkish agents were wrecking havoc on British institutions such as the banks consulates and telegraph offices. The Persian government was to be paid an annual subsidy to accept the British creation of the South Persia Rifles. They had little choice but to accept, much to the anger of Persian nationalists and democrats who were heartily sick of foreign interference.

Sykes and Hunter worked hard throughout the spring of 1916 in Bandar Abbass to build up a force able to restore order throughout South Persia preparatory to their march to rescue O'Connor. It was no easy task. The whole countryside was demoralized by anarchy and dominated by predatory tribesmen. And the task was made infinitely harder by the successes further west of Wilhelm Wassmuss. Eliminating Wassmuss was Sykes' prime concern – as it had been for Cox in Bushire. Cox had even issued a proclamation – it appalled the Foreign Office in London – in which he offered a reward for Wassmuss "dead or alive". This was quite contrary to London's style of doing things and they ordered the immediate withdrawal of the proclamation. Said the Foreign Office "His Majesty's Ministers viewed his methods with abhorrence and detestation". Later that year the Foreign Office sent a message to Cox asking him just what could be done about Wassmuss. Replied Cox, "Fear of exciting the abhorrence and detestation of His Majesty's Ministers precludes me from making any suggestion." Wassmuss' successes were to plague Sykes just as they had plagued Cox in Bushire.

Wassmuss remained the principal concern of British efforts against German agents in Persia during the war. But not their only concern. German agents had penetrated all regions of Persia and operated from the northwest to the southeast.

April 1916 was a terrible month for the British. For Sykes and Hunter it began badly when the Governor of Lingah's bodyguard murdered the British agent there and his two brothers and then killed or wounded most of their Indian sepoy guard. In the nearby province a tribesman acting on behalf of German agents murdered two young British lieutenants before being killed himself by Indian sepoys. Sykes's difficulties were made worse by a disaster that devastated British prestige throughout the East – the fall of Kut el Amara in Mesopotania.

In the highlands and along the coast of south Persia Sir Percy countered the setbacks by stoically ignoring them. Recruiting went far better than expected. The Indian Foreign Department had been pessimistic of his chances of being able to raise much of a force at all. As it was, within twenty-four hours of arrival he had recruited fifty-three men. There was an instant setback because of strong pro-German sentiments in the town and the following morning the new recruits were anxious to give back their advance of pay on the grounds that they did not wish to fight the Germans. Tact, isolation from the rest of the town, and Hunter's infinite patience managed to gradually overcome that problem and within two weeks of arrival a force capable of some type of military action was organized. A small mission was sent to the borders of Baluchistan to counter the activities of German agents there.

It was then that Sykes had a morale-boosting success. The Germans in Kerman decided - when the local Bakhtiari tribesmen disarmed the Swedish gendarmerie there - that the tide of events had turned against them. One German party containing the agent Dr Zugmayer left Bam and fled to Sirjan. On the way they were attacked by Bakhtiari who took some of them prisoner and made off with most of the party's money. Bakhtiaris attacked another group of Germans, as well. Most of that party - which contained sixty Germans and Austrians, a dozen Turks and some Afghans (who turned out to be deserters from the Indian Army) were captured and imprisoned at the fort in Shiraz. They had a difficult time. They bitterly complained of their treatment by the British who, when they arrived there, turned them over to the Russians. The Russians marched them north and they spent the remainder of the war on an island, the so-called "island of death" in the Caspian off Baku.

German influence in Kerman was declining fast. More and more nomad chiefs contacted Sykes and asked him to move into their areas - where, of course, he could continue recruiting for the South Persia Rifles. However, much of the success was probably the result of Fraser Hunter's energy. Later in the year an Englishman, Clarmont

Skrine was appointed vice-consul in Kerman where he was well positioned to see and comment upon the activities of the SPR. In an acerbic letter home he wrote, "Everyone knows that Sykes is an utter humbug, a man of shallow judgement and capacity, combined with inordinate vanity, who has only got his position because of a good Press at home ...I heard some pretty strong language about Sykes in Simla and opinion here in Persia, alike among Europeans and Persian partisans of the British, is even stronger about him than at HQ. Everyone knows that his chief Staff Officer, Major Hunter, a most brilliant man, who has kept the general safe and secured (up to date) the success of the mission. In nearly everything he twists the general around his finger and it is only when..the General goes against Hunter, that there's bad trouble."[23]

In late April additional Indian Army troops reached Bandar Abbas from Bushire and then began a journey that may still constitute a record for distance marched by a single military unit – claimed to amount to five thousand miles over the next three years.

The initial success of this column, undoubtedly the result of Hunter's staff work, encouraged Sykes. Arrangements were made for the next stage, the march on Kerman. Camels were hired - no easy task since the hot weather was upon them and the desert to be crossed harsh - and a large number of donkeys were purchased or leased. The division of the camels among the various units was complex - particularly since the camelmen were unreliable and frequently deserted back to their villages - and Sykes attributed the prompt start of the march to Fraser Hunter and a Mr. Wittkugel of the Indo-European Telegraph Department. Hunter and Wittkugel worked unremittingly for several days apportioning loads among the camels and overcoming the truculence of the camelmen. Because of these efforts the column was able to start on May 17, two days earlier than initially anticipated. Wrote Sykes "Owing to the scarcity of water and to lack of space at some watering places it was necessary to have two echelons. Major Fraser Hunter, Staff Officer, was the mainspring of the two echelons and whatever credit may be considered to be due is mainly his."

Fraser Hunter with fellow cadets at Royal Military College (Hunter on far right.)

Fraser Hunter graduates from Royal Military College

David Newton

Officers of Duke of Connaught's Bombay Lancers.
(Hunter far left)

Hunter with Persian officers.

- 133 -

South Persian Rifles officers. Hunter on left next to Sir Percy Sykes.

Map of Persian Gulf during Hunter's time.

Particularly important, Sykes sent agents ahead of him to explain to the villagers that the South Persia Rifles were their friends and that the general leading them sincerely hoped that peace would return and they could resume their normal patterns of trade. The public relations exercise worked. Despite the weather - up to 110F - during the day and cold at night - the march quickly became a triumphal progression. By the time they crossed the bracing uplands on their way to Kerman their own spirits were high and the population with every appearance of genuine relief greeted them in Kerman. The Germans had left weeks before and the criminal element in the town, which had been terrorizing the community, fled shortly before the SPR marched in.

The next destination would be Shiraz – three hundred miles to the west - and dominated by the Germans and their levies. As importantly, it was the capital of the two hundred thousand strong Kashgai tribe, pro-German, anti-British and used to a freebooting way of life. The most direct route there had disadvantages. There was, for example, no telegraph line and so Sykes could not be sure of the security of any supplies that he might put along the route. Particularly disadvantageous was that this route crossed the summer pastures of the Baharlus Arabs - nomads who had furnished the Germans with levies - and Sykes feared that the owners of his hired transport could be easily intimidated into desertion.

Consequently, instead of the direct route, the other two sides of the triangle were decided upon - north along the telegraph line to Yedz, then across to the Ishfahan and then southwest to Shiraz. It was a longer route but it was far more secure. Others felt differently.

Clairmont Skrine who became British vice-consul in Kerman, again in a letter to his mother wrote, "I tell you, everyone, the Govt of India, the SPR, Political elite, is thoroughly sick of Sykes. The universal opinion is that neither the SPR nor the peace of southern Persia has a proper chance to get established until he's outed. He's literally nothing but a man of words and d...d dull words at that. He's never done a thing in his life except write a few inferior books, nor has he an idea in his head beyond flattering and getting popular with the Persians and advertising himself."

"Why did Sykes insist on going to Isfahan, right out of the way? Simply swank; he wanted to have a triumphal entry into the ancient capital of Persia: he wanted to pow-wow with the Russians there and get an Order or two out of the Russian government (this he succeeded in doing). For this purpose he delayed his arrival at Shiraz – the most important thing to be done – for several weeks and shirked marching through the rougher and more dangerous country of Laristan and Fars."[24]

The column set out on July 28, avoiding the heat of the day by lying up in the shade in the pistachio orchards. Two and a half weeks later they were welcomed into Yedz by a jubilant and recently returned British colony.

Despite the elation bad news awaited them. The Russians to the north had reached Isfahan, but with a small force - a mere six hundred Cossacks and a couple of field guns. Opposing them and preparing to attack was a large force of tribesmen, led by German officers and reinforced by Turkish regulars and a battery of field artillery. The Armenians in the town, terrified by the approach of the Turks, were ready to beat a fast retreat along the bandit-infested road to Yedz. They would have risked death from the bandits along this road but death would have been certain if the Turks had captured Isfahan.

The Russian commander, Colonel Bielomestonow, head of a force of Kuban Cossacks, appealed to Sykes for help and Sykes, arguing that his own position in Shiraz would be untenable if Isfahan was held by the Turks, agreed to march to his aid.

Word of the progress of the South Persia Rifles sped ahead of them - every mile embellished the size of the approaching force. When the Turks heard of Sykes' approach the force was reported to number ten thousand. Sykes discretely halted far enough away so that his actual numbers could not be ascertained. As an additional precaution he sent Fraser Hunter ahead to make contact with the Cossacks and the British Consul. The following day Hunter and the consul rode out to meet Sykes and led the South Persia Rifles in a triumphal entry into the town. The Turks had quietly withdrawn to Hamadan.

While there Sykes and Hunter learned something of administrative methods and the predatory nature of the Cossacks. Time was to show that Sykes was ruthless enough himself in his relations with the Persians but in Isfahan he was shocked to discover that the Russians simply took whatever they wanted - horses, money, jewelry, furniture and carpets. Houses and land they simply declared "Crown Property of H.M. The Tsar."

While in Isfahan Sykes coped with another irritant. The route southwest to the British forces guarding the oil installations at Ahwaz ran through Bakhtiari country. The Bakhtiari were generally pro-British and most of the route was open to traffic but a notorious brigand, Jafar Kuli, dominated the last fifty miles before Isfahan and consequently a mountain of trade goods was accumulating just fifty miles short of its destination. A British column marching across Jafar Kuli's land, escorting three thousand camels and mules loaded with supplies, broke the bottleneck.

Fraser Hunter had a close call with Jafer Kuli while he was reconnoitering west of Isfahan with a couple of cavalrymen. They were hidden and not noticed by a group of tribesmen passing along the track. Hunter thought they were road guards – they were unusually well dressed for nomads – but he was mistaken. Jafer Kuli led the party of six and moments after Hunter realized this ten more tribesmen joined them. Hunter was outnumbered. After he sent one of his men to tell Sykes what was happening the sixteen tribesmen quickly saw the two of them. They immediately came under heavy fire from two hundred yards range.

Within minutes Jafer Kuli's party had increased to forty and Hunter, armed only with a rifle, saw signals being sent to someone apparently just below his position. Firing off five rapid rounds caused sufficient commotion in Kuli's force for Hunter to make a quick getaway and the two quickly galloped back to Sykes' position.

Hunter, who spoke Russian, had no time for a pause. He was urgently needed with the force of Russian Cossacks so that he could act as interpreter and relay messages to Sykes. The rest of the day he spent with a laconically cool Cossack named 2nd Lieutenant Gregory Nikevforovitch Paschcoff. Hunter was impressed. Not only were these Cossacks officers cool, they were efficient, and Paschcoff was intelligent. They were all frequently under heavy and sustained fire at relatively close range. The slightest exposure prompted a fuselage of fire from the brigands. Nevertheless, the Russians, accompanied by Hunter, advanced on horseback to within two hundred yards of the enemy.

At this point the artillery came into action, their shells landing among the brigands hidden among the rocks of the hillside. Paschcoff attacked and in the face of the charging Cossacks the brigands fled. Many of the enemy were seen escaping with their horses and Paschcoff again charged despite heavy enfilading fire from the nullahs. Hunter kept in radio contact with the artillery and they were able to add to the chaos among the tribesmen. Skirmishes continued all day long. Reported Hunter to Sykes, "...the hottest fire of all was directed against this small Russian detachment who were first into and almost last out of the action. Under the greatest disadvantages as to ground and under heavy fire in a most difficult situation, Lieutenant Paschcoff led his men with great coolness and ability - the Cossacks were almost careless in their cool behavior."

Sykes could now begin the 326-mile march to Shiraz.

This trek through the Province of Fars was accomplished without great difficulty although many of the inhabitants of the town of Abadeh, principally those of the Bahai faith and also the so-called Persian "Democrats", were unfriendly and it was in this town that Sykes would eventually cope with a full-scale mutiny. He reached Shiraz on November 11 and found that his old friend from pre-war days, Prince Farman Farma, had arrived ahead of him as the new governor and was there to greet his entry. Sykes' little "army" had marched a thousand miles.

The most pressing task was the reorganization of the gendarmerie, the force that had been organized in 1911. A year earlier raiding tribesmen had effectively brought an end to traffic on the Bushire-Shiraz-Isfahan caravan route; there were riots in Shiraz and a number of Jewish businessmen and their families were robbed and murdered. Because of the importance of trade the British sent a small force of cavalry from the Central India Horse to pacify the countryside, at the same time supporting the Persian government's view that there should be a gendarmerie with Swedish officers - whose motives were not at that time suspect in any eyes - to permanently police the countryside.

Twenty Swedes reached Persia in 1911 and began the difficult task of bringing some order to the countryside. They were supported by British consular officials who knew that trade would only flourish if there was some semblance of peace and that without it all Persia might disintegrate into a number of small tribal provinces, all dominated by bandits.

The gendarmerie had some successes. But in the south a major disaster struck them and devastated what little prestige they had when a substantial body of under-trained police surrendered to an attacking body of Kashgai near Shiraz and were all disarmed. The Swedes, who had little experience of coping with banditry - nor knowledge of the language and countryside - built large and small forts at four and five-mile intervals along the routes they wished to protect and manned them with half a dozen or so poorly trained gendarmes. It was relatively easy for the tribesmen to seize these little outposts and disarm their occupants, particularly since they knew that the Swedish officers at the larger forts had no mobile columns with which to pursue them.

When Sykes reached Shiraz the gendarmerie numbered about three thousand in that area. They were spread over a huge area and all but a small handful of their former officers had returned to Sweden when war began. The three who remained kept clear of the British and were well known for their pro-German activities. Their attitude was understandable since many detested the Russians and at that time the British and Russians were allies.

Sykes had a dilemma. Since the Persian government had not authorized him to take over the gendarmerie, neither could Prince Farman Farma. To add to his difficulties, many of the Persian officers with the force were also pro-German and had been involved in the seizure of O'Connor and the British colony at Shiraz the year before. But if Sykes did not take them over then they would probably disintegrate into a number of small bands, either becoming brigands themselves or join the pro-German levies in the countryside.

Sykes decided on a compromise. Fraser Hunter, his acting Chief of Staff, was given the task of reorganizing and commanding the gendarmerie in and around Shiraz and converting it into what would be called the Fars Brigade, a mobile column and part of the South Persia Rifles. Hunter would command the Fars Brigade. From this point on a split began between Sykes and Hunter, Sykes seeing the Persians as part of a British force, Hunter seeing them instead as a Persian body which, while British trained and paid, was an extension of the authority of the government in Teheran - not India. The split would grow and irreparably sour their relationship.

WASSMUSS

Hunter's task beginning in mid-November, 1916 was a monumental one. He was acting Chief of Staff for the entire South Persia Rifles, which although primarily in Fars Province also had a strong force in Kerman; he had received instruction to take over the gendarmerie and incorporate it as the "Fars Brigade" into the South Persia Rifles. In addition to all this he was responsible for intelligence gathering in the tribal area - particularly among the hostile Kashgai. The intelligence function might have gone unrecorded by history had not Sykes constantly referred to Hunter as his "Chief Political Assistant". This was something that annoyed the British Resident, Sir Charles Marling, in Teheran - from whom Sykes was supposed to accept direction.

Marling was sensitive to the interpretations that the Persian put on words. He was, for example, concerned that the force was called the "South Persia Rifles" since this name was repugnant to many Persians who saw in it British acceptance of a partition of Persia. "Chief Political Assistant" also inferred interference in the political affairs of Persia by British officers - Sykes and Hunter - in what was officially a Persian force. Said Marling, "Participation by (Sykes) in political questions cannot but confirm the existing suspicion that our real aim is to create a force to be employed by its British officers in British political interests......And in this connection I would strongly urge that some other name than that of Political Officer be given to the officer (Hunter) at the head of your intelligence service...the title of Political Officer can easily be seized upon by Persians as proof of the political character of your mission and it seems to me the expression 'Intelligence Officer' is not only free from objection but also more correctly describes the functions to be discharged."

Training the men of the gendarmerie was essential if they were to an effective part of the South Persia Rifles. They had been poorly trained, were frequently unpaid, poorly equipped and badly armed. Their morale was low and most were not sure if their new function was sanctioned by their own government. The officers shared many of these problems, but most of them were Teheranis, sophisticated and urbane, and less influenced by local or tribal loyalties within Fars Province.

Hunter's intelligence function was an onerous one. The SPR were in most respects - with their Indian Army units and British officers - understandably viewed as a foreign force occupying part of neutral Persia. If Hunter was to be successful in detecting the threats to the force and to the tranquility – such as it was - of the countryside then naturally he would try to impress upon his Persian friends that the SPR was not a British force occupying Fars Province but an arm of the Persian government, keeping the peace for Persians. This understanding of the role of the SPR not only correctly reflected the attitude of the Foreign Office in London, but was also one to which Hunter personally adhered. Unfortunately Sykes did not endorse it.

The intelligence function was not easy, particularly since Hunter was operating in hostile country. Most of the inhabitants of Fars Province resented the presence of the SPR. It was not that they did not welcome a peacekeeping force. The particulars of their resentments depended upon who they were. If they had any sense of national identity they were humiliated by the need for foreign control. Many probably believed that the British had previously sold them out to the Russians with the earlier partition, and trusted the Germans more than any other participant in the war. If they were either Kashgai tribesmen or members of the Khamseh confederation of tribes, they resented any interference in their freebooting ways. Urban Persians strongly objected to the earlier British occupation of Bushire.

The Khamseh tribes - sometimes contemptuously called "the Arabs", although only one of the five tribes was Arab - numbered about thirty thousand families and while their leader, Qasam-u-Mulk, generally appeared to be pro-British, his authority was not as extensive as that of other tribal leaders. He was the hereditary mayor of Shiraz, lived near the city in an opulent palace, and was more of a political spokesman for the tribes he represented with the Governor-General than a tribal chief. The Qasam was of Persian descent, not a member of one of the five tribes, which had grouped themselves in order to present a united front to their old antagonists, the Kashgai.

The Kashgai, double the strength of the Khamseh and better armed, were as independent of authority as the Pathans of the Northwest Frontier. When they moved from summer to winter pastures and back again they dominated the countryside accepting orders from none except their hereditary chief, the Saulat-u-Dowla. Though considerably diminished in numbers from earlier years, they covered an immense area when they moved at the end of the winter from the warm fringes of the Persian Gulf to their summer haunts in the highland pastures. They would leave behind a handful of followers in the coastal areas who reaped their fields and stored their grain in pits while the mass of tribesmen, driving their great flocks of sheep and goats ahead of them, traveled by night to the mountains between Isfahan and Shiraz.

With them, and contemptuous of palaces in Shiraz, rode Saulat-u-Dowla happy to sleep at night in the black goats'-hair tents of his people - although a different tent each night as he feared assassination. The Saulat was not trusted by the SPR and he was careful not to commit irrevocably to any side until the summer of 1918, when it looked as if the Germans would win the war, when he declared war on the SPR. By then Hunter was long gone.

It is reasonable to conjecture that it was Hunter's sensitivity to Persian feelings and tribal loyalties that kept the antipathy of the countryside from increasing. What is beyond doubt is that after Hunter left the SPR relations between British officers and Persians - tribal and urban - deteriorated and almost resulted in the destruction of the SPR.

The beautiful city of Shiraz was the headquarters of Hunter's Fars Brigade. The hereditary mayor of the city, Qavam-u-Maulk, Chief of the Khamseh confederation, was answerable to the governor-general of the Province, Prince Farman Farma. He was consistently pro-British. He was also adept at enriching himself. It is said that when he approached Shiraz ahead of Sykes to take over as new governor-general, he deliberately delayed the occupation of the town by demanding a huge cash payment from the Saulat-u-Daula, chief of the Kashgai in return for recognizing that leadership.

Farman Farma had replaced the former governor-general of Fars Province, Mukbar-i-Sultanah - educated in Berlin and ardently pro-German. Now without a job he lived in embittered unemployment until 1917 when he was appointed Minister of the Interior. From this powerful position in Teheran he is said to have engineered the rising of the Kashgai against the British in 1918.

Sykes' column had landed at Bandar Abbas, marched north to Kerman, on to Yedz and after a diversion to Isfahan, south again to Shiraz. But to complete their journey they needed to push on southwest and join the British garrison in Bushire.

The original urgency of the mission had evaporated with the liberation of O'Connor. O'Connor and the British at the Shiraz consulate had been arrested by pro-German Persians in October, 1915 while Wassmuss was at Ahram, a town of about eight hundred in the hills of the district of Tangistan. It will be recalled that Wassmuss had been German Consul in Bushire, had joined Niedermayer's expedition to Afghanistan, but had parted from it in Baghdad and headed down to Bushire. There he had been almost captured by a British agent, Captain Noel, but had escaped less his baggage, and disappeared into the tribal lands of Tangistan – "Country of the Passes". The Sheik of Ahram, also known as "the cock of Tangistan", was Zair Khidair Khan. He was a consistent ally of Wassmuss until almost the end, and it was Zair Khidair to whom Wassmuss entrusted the prisoners of Shiraz. They had a poor time of it.

Wassmuss, who was later to be compared with Lawrence of Arabia, owed much of his considerable success in southwest Persia to his knowledge of the area, his ability to speak both Persian and Tangistani, that he wore Tangistani clothing and allegedly had become a Moslem. He told his hosts that he was a Moslem but also that he was in direct contact with the Kaiser who was also now a Moslem and was committed to protect all Islamic society; Wassmuss was to lead the Tangistanis on a holy war, a jihad, against the British and Russians. Added to that, the Tangistanis were bitter towards the British who had interfered with their main enterprise – arms smuggling.

Zair Khidair's prisoners were Major O'Connor, a Mr. Ayrton and Mr. and Mrs. Fergusson of the Imperial Bank of Persia, a Mr. Smith and his clerk who were telegraph operators on line to India, Mrs. Smith, a merchant named Livingstone, Mr. and Mrs. Pettigrew, a Mr. and Mrs. Christmas and a Ceylonese clerk, and finally on the dismal procession, the captured and disarmed Indian cavalry consular guard. Hundreds, possibly thousands, of jeering and triumphant tribesmen, surrounded them. Mrs. Smith, who was in poor health, collapsed and died on the journey, but the other women finally reached Bushire and were handed over to the British. The men were sent to Ahram, and lived for almost a year in a squalid mud fortress - though they later reported that Zair Khidair had treated them for the most part courteously and with chivalry. Wassmuss demanded the release of Persian and German prisoners and the British evacuation of Bushire in exchange for his prisoners.

The British had no intention of leaving Bushire as they feared that if they did so, all the tribes of the south - including the Bakhtiari - would rise against them and it would be impossible to hold onto the oil wells and refineries that supplied fuel to the fleet. The prisoners managed to secretly communicate with Bushire - adding messages in invisible ink to otherwise innocuous letters - and reported in 1916 that Wassmuss seemed to be losing his grip on the sheiks of Tangistan. Consequently the British tried a rescue mission, lead by Captain Noel, but Zair Khidair dragged out all the prisoners, had them lined up against a wall, and opposite them a firing squad. He told Noel that the first shot from the British would be the signal for his own men to execute the prisoners. Noel acknowledged a checkmate and withdrew to Bushire but the stress of facing a firing squad for well over an hour had been extreme. Pettigrew had a heart attack and died. Finally, in the summer of 1916, in exchange for sixteen Tangistanis, O'Connor and his remaining companions were released.

The territory between Shiraz and Bushire remained throughout the war, implacably opposed to the British. This was in part because the sheiks of Tangistan and the townspeople of Kazerum, angered by the British occupation of Bushire, committed to the German side. It was also because Wassmuss was able throughout the war to travel among them, convincing them of the ultimate success of the German war effort. It was through this territory that the South Persia Rifles would have to travel if they were to complete their march through Persia to Bushire. The road - it was called that although it was scarcely more than a track made by generations of livestock and human travel - ran across the line of mountains that are parallel to the Persian Gulf. The key town on the route from Shiraz to Bushire was Kazerun. The headman of the town, Nasr Diwan, was a close ally of Wassmuss.

Sykes had sent a small detachment to Kazerun after Farman Farma and Qavam-u-Mulk had assured him that Nasr Diwan might accept them. However, after the British officer had left the Kazerunis rose up against the detachment of former gendarmerie, stripped them of their arms and all other possessions and drove them beyond the walls of the town. In reply Sykes then sent Major Bruce and some men of the Lancers to reinforce the isolated detachment still at the small community of Khan-i-Zinian, high in the hills, approximately half way between Shiraz and Kazerun. Then, on December 21 he ordered Lt. Colonel Twigg to take a further detachment, pick up Bruce's party and go on to Dasht-i-Arjan - beyond Khan-i-Zinian, towards Kazerun. There he would reconnoiter the Pir Zan, "Pass of the Old Woman" and report back Sykes by telegraph for further instructions.

Colonel Twigg's force was substantial. It consisted of a section of mountain artillery, ten cavalrymen and one hundred and fifty infantrymen from the 24th Baluchis. A body of more than a hundred riflemen, untrained former gendarmerie under the command of Fraser Hunter, joined Twigg on December 23, and the two forces - Hunter's gendarmerie and Twigg's Indian Army soldiers - under Twigg's command with Hunter as Chief as Staff, advanced on Dasht-i-Arjan, six thousand eight hundred feet high in the mountains. There was no sign of the Kazeruni fighters. Around the small plateau on which Dasht-i-Arjan lies are precipitous mountains that rise up a further two thousand feet. These mountains, heavily wooded almost to their summits, are strewn with enormous boulders, some almost the size of a house, making communications difficult and maintaining direction a major feat. Beyond Dasht-i-Arjan towards Kazerun, the ground falls away and then rises once more rapidly to the Piri Zan Range - known as the "Range of the Hag". Beyond these hills is Miyan Kotal, a small village about ten miles short of Kazerun.

On Christmas Day, 1916, the Kazerunis fired on the advancing SPR. For about an hour and a half a company of the Baluchis and an SPR infantry company had been moving to the high ground of the Piri Zan range in order to guard the right flank of the main column. At ten a.m. the Kazerunis began firing heavily on this body and they were forced to take cover. The main column under Twigg halted at the sound of firing but could see no sign of their flank guard. Hunter and some of his Persians manhandled two old seven pounder mountain guns to where they hoped to be able to fire on the Kazerunis, but not only was the range too great but they also discovered that many of the shells were defective. The flank guard had to return to the main column since their commander, Captain Weldon, was unable to get his troops to advance into the Kazeruni fire.

Half an hour later Weldon and another SPR Officer, newly commissioned Captain Wittkugel who had back in the early days of the SPR been with the Indo-European Telegraph Company and had been such a help to Hunter in getting the camel and mule transport assembled, volunteered to have another effort to secure the higher ground and defend the right flank of Colonel Twigg's main column. The Persians went forward again in two sections, one led by Hunter with Weldon at his side, the other led by Wittkugel. The mountainside was steep, there were precipitous drops, and where there was any soil at all, the ground was covered by dense growth. Hunter and Weldon's party became separated from Wittkugel's but got to within two hundred yards of the summit before being stopped by the Kazeruni fire.

The Persian infantry, who had only a couple of weeks training, had little stomach for facing the heavy fire that was poured down on them by the Kazerunis at the summit and very soon Hunter found that his force had in addition to Weldon, diminished to a mere twelve men and a machine gun crew. Despite this, Hunter and Weldon began to make another attempt to reach the summit - Hunter effectively handling the maxim gun - when news reached them that Captain Wittkugel had been wounded and several Persian infantrymen with him killed. At the same time the Kazerunis, now reinforced, began still heavier fire on Hunter and Weldon's party. Sunset was at about 5 p.m. and Hunter realized that it would be impossible to take the summit before dark. He told Weldon that he would take three Persians and try to rescue Wittkugel who had got to within a hundred yards of the enemy before being hit.

Guided by a medical orderly from Wittkugel's party Hunter got close to Wittkugel and a wounded SPR near him before he was pinned down by enemy fire. Hunter was not sure where precisely the enemy fire was coming from so told his machine gunner to fire back whenever the enemy fired. This he did and in a series of short rushes between boulders and trees Hunter and one Persian finally reached the spot just short of the enemy where Wittkugel and the SPR soldier lay wounded.

Wittkugel was just alive though clearly though he was dying. He told Hunter that his back was broken and there was no hope of his surviving. He asked Hunter to request Sykes to ensure that his wife was looked after. They were his last words. Hunter tried to move him but he was a heavy man and as Hunter's Persian companion moved up to assist, he too was shot. He struggled closer to try to assist. No sooner did he move than he was hit again. Hunter moved and as he did so a bullet fired at him hit a rock by Wittkugel's head. It splintered, wounding Wittkugel still further and tearing into Hunter's arm. At this point the SPR on the machine gun giving Hunter supporting fire ran out of ammunition and shouted the news to Hunter. Unfortunately, the Kazerunis heard the message as well.

Keeping up rifle fire to protect the dying Wittkugel and the Persian soldier, Hunter withdrew and got a message to both Weldon and Colonel Twigg. Within an hour relief had arrived - more ammunition for the machine gun from Weldon and a platoon of Baluchis from Twigg. It was now dark and Hunter, Major de Vere Condon of the Indian Medical Service, and a Persian, Mohammed Gul, crawled back to the dying Wittkugel. When they reached open ground the SPR poured heavy fire into the Kazeruni positions and Hunter, Condon and Gul rushed across the open ground to Wittkugel. They made it safely and supported by heavy fire managed to drag Wittkugel and the wounded Persian to cover. They dragged their way back to base camp over the next two hours. Wrote Hunter,

"None of us who did that long toilsome descent, burdened with a heavy wounded man on a stretcher, crashing into trees and rocks, will easily forget it. The maxims went first and held positions to cover the 124th (Baluchis) who protected our rear. The 124th, as the South Persia Rifles and bearers became exhausted, were more and more called in as bearers. On all sides the enemy fire came nearer and every few moments shots were heard nearby. The slow progress took two hours...[25]

Brigadier-General Moberley, in his official history of the war in Persia, makes special mention of Hunter. "All ranks of the Indian troops behaved splendidly and, although two thirds of the South Persia Rifles had shirked fighting, the remainder had shown considerable gallantry. Colonel Hunter was specially commended for his intrepid and gallant attempt to bring in Captain Wittkugel..."[26]

By this time Twigg realized that he would have to withdraw since he would have suffered heavy casualties had he tried to advance with his flank exposed to the fire of the Kazerunis. Furthermore he had received information that more tribesmen, jubilant at the success already achieved, were reinforcing the Kazerunis. Hunter warned him that he had been told by the Persian officers to be on the watch for treachery on the part of the SPR soldiers who they expected to desert or go over to the enemy - several had already done so. Twigg could also see from the fires of the enemy that they were gradually encircling him and the column would be soon cut off unless they quickly withdrew back towards Khan-i-Zinian. Unfortunately the Persian muleteers began to desert in considerable number and this withdrawal took all night. On Boxing Day the withdrawal continued and they were frequently fired on. They reached Shiraz on December 28.

The snows closed the mountain passes shortly after this and the South Persia Rifles never succeeded in forcing their way through to Bushire. The tribes and the town communities of southwestern Fars remained supporters of Wassmuss and it was not until the end of 1918 that British troops from Bushire advanced through Tangestan.

Until after March 1917 Sykes' inability to cover those last miles probably did not concern him too greatly. He was not isolated. He could probably reach the sea by way of Lar and Bandah Lengah if he had to, and in any case his allies, the Russians, were to the north, in Isfahan. It was not until after the Russian Revolution and the disintegration of the Russian Army in Persia, that his isolation was a concern. The defeat of the column marching on Kazerun was of course serious. It strengthened the influence of Wassmuss, it nudged the Solat towards opened hostility, it probably made the Qavam uncertain that he was backing a winner and would have inclined him to an even more versatile political stance.

But why did it fail?

Well-armed tribesmen who knew the countryside well and were on the higher ground outnumbered the SPR. It was not possible for the SPR to take Kazerun in face of the opposition of the inhabitants of the countryside and in fairness to Sykes, the operation was really only a probing forward until it was certain just what the attitude of the Kazerunis would be.

Nevertheless, one must wonder why Colonel Twigg held back all but half a company of his experienced Indian troops while he moved forward the untrained men of Hunter's Fars Brigade - previously gendarmerie - to take the ground critical to the continued forward movement of the column. It would seem more reasonable to have used the best troops available - the Indians - to overcome whatever opposition there was while saving the men of the Fars Brigade for use as follow up or to escort the supplies through the mountain pass.

The early months of 1917 were principally concerned with the organization and training of the SPR in Fars province. Sykes was being criticized by both India and London for his inability to supply a coherent budget. Even after only a couple of months into the campaign his preliminary budget estimate to India was termed "so inaccurate and unintelligible as to be useless"[27].

Despite their fundamental disagreements Sykes was gracious towards Hunter before their final split. His report of March 17, 1917 stated,

"In conclusion I am especially indebted to Lt. Col FF Hunter who has been Staff Officer and later Officer Commanding Fars Brigade. To his energy, devotion to duty and capacity, the preliminary organization of the force is chiefly due. He has been ably seconded by Captain Hay Thorburn who has done the entire work of the Headquarters Office for the last two months. I think that it is only fair to these officers to give as my deliberate opinion that they have each done the work of two men with efficiency. Needless to say, the strain on them has been very severe."

But the animosity was growing and the final sentence of the above report may have been inserted by Sykes as part of a mechanism for getting rid of these two officers.

Hunter, as both acting Chief of Staff of the South Persia Rifles and head of the Fars Brigade of former Persian gendarmerie, became heavily involved in this planning process at a time when faced with a plethora of other duties. He worked at a constant disadvantage. The goals of the SPR - hunting down German agents, restoring order in the countryside, restoring British prestige, counter-balancing Russian influence, supporting Persian authority - were not mutually exclusive, but the combination of aims gave the force an ambivalent character and contributed to the controversies which developed. And India, of course, was particularly angry with Sykes because even by the beginning of 1917 he had not, despite frequent requests, presented a scheme for the organization of the force – a feature of the budgeting process.

London also was angry with Sykes because he too frequently ignored Marling's directives from Teheran. Sykes was fortunate in that neither India nor London wanted to appear to bow to the views of the other. The testiness that arose is recorded in surviving memorandum and illustrates not only the irritation of both London and India towards Sykes but also the different goals of the two headquarters. The Viceroy's office in India wrote in March 1917 "Sykes should understand that his permanent appointment will depend upon the satisfaction which he now gives and, in particular, that expenditure on the present scale cannot be tolerated." The same month, the Foreign Office in London wrote to India "....the hopeless chaos which envelops the present organization of the SPR which is due to Sir Percy Sykes' inability or reluctance to frame a general scheme in spite of our repeated requests." Sykes shied away from detailed planning - and in view of the more pressing concerns it is understandable that he did so. Someone, presumably Hunter, cabled to Delhi, "Send equipment for school for Persian officers and NCO's for Shiraz and Kerman - diagrams, chalk, copy books, etc". Two weeks later another followed this, presumably in response to a message asking for more detail. "Impossible to send detailed indent. Would suggest that Stokes (Former military attaché in

Teheran) advise and we can supplement it as required." Responded the Government of India, "Impossible for General Staff or anyone here to formulate this or any similar scheme without any data. Your proposal merely emphasizes necessity for a general scheme for the SPR for which we have pressed you many times."

Someone, presumably Marling, scrawled across the message from India, "The Govt of India is delightful. It begins by admitting distribution of forces is my job and Sykes'. And then unfolds a program knowing that Sykes will not dare disregard it. They clearly intend to keep up dual direction, i.e. muddle."

Fraser Hunter sent a detailed submission on the organization of the SPR to Sykes on April 1 1917. Sykes agreed with its aims and methods and forwarded it to India and to Sir Charles Marling, representing London in Teheran on 3 May, though it was not received until 7 June.

By May 19 1917 the Army department in India sent the Foreign Office in London a cable expressing two views of the Commander in Chief in respect of the SPR. The first of the two points was. "1. We have lost confidence in Sykes." Sykes was saved by the inability of London and India to agree as to what should be done about him. It was, however, finally decided that he needed, as indeed he did because the work was overwhelming Hunter and his meager resources, a trained Chief of Staff, one who could confine himself to that responsibility, had been to Staff College, and who had the resources to translate general concepts into detailed plans.

Colonel Orton arrived as the much-awaited Chief of Staff soon afterwards and prepared another plan - though he naturally used much of Hunter's material. But it contained some fundamental differences with Hunter's scheme. Sykes agreed with that one as well and forwarded it on the 26 May.

Sykes' force, though generating anger in India and London, was doing good work in the countryside during this period. Much of the brigandage had been quelled and order was restored in Fars and Kerman something that, although unappreciated by the Kashgai or the turbulent elements of the Khamseh, was welcomed by the settled rural and urban population.

In May Sykes sent a preliminary outline of the re-organization of the SPR to Marling in Teheran. In it he wrote,

"Until quite recently my British staff consisted of only two officers viz Lt Colonel F Fraser Hunter and Captain H Hay Thorburn. IMS. Their duties were the heaviest. There was the work connected with the column, military operations, taking over of German prisoners, translating and sorting German documents, account work including the preparation of a ready reckoner in krans and the ciphering and deciphering of hundreds of telegrams. Lt Colonel Hunter has had to take over and reorganize body of three thousand gendarmes scattered over some three hundred miles of country, who were disorganized and without discipline, and whose officers were hostile and prone to dangerous intrigue. In this task he had two young bankers with little military experience to help him. Moreover famine conditions added seriously to his task. Wheat had to be purchased and transported from the Bakhtiari country and barley etc from the south. Finally, he had to help Captain Thorburn in his duties, which consisted in doing the entire work of the Headquarters which is now being done by seven officers appointed to my staff. I consider that for Lt Colonel Hunter to produce the scheme which I now forward under such circumstances, is a remarkable piece of work and trust that this highly efficient officer instead of sharing the blame which is my lot, may be suitably rewarded."

In June Hunter and Sykes headed for Teheran. There had been some assassinations in the city and Sykes was convinced that both he and Hunter were slated as the next victims. Marling was not convinced. According to Sykes the French Minister in Teheran had personally warned him that dismissed officers from the SPR were trying to assassinate him and Colonel Hunter.

The Minister, Monsieur Lecombe, later claimed that he had never heard of such a plot, but Sykes was convinced and thought that Major Lundberg, who commanded the Swedish Gendarmerie in the north and had earlier been implicated in the take-over of Shiraz, was behind it. He sent Marling a sworn affidavit from a young Persian SPR officer concerning another proposed murder that Lundberg was alleged to be involved with. Marling sent all the material on to London. The MI.5 comment on the report after it reached London reveals the extent of the continuing antipathy towards Sykes as Inspector General of the SPR. The signature on the MI.5 comment is illegible. The words are not. "That Sykes should have forwarded this rigmarole is sufficient commentary on his methods to make it more desirable than ever to find a good officer to command the SPR. I wonder at Marling sending it on."

Marling wrote to Foreign Secretary, Arthur Balfour on 20 June that "he (Sykes) should confine himself strictly to duties as head of a branch of the Persian Government. I have endeavored to make it clear that there should be frank and full consultation between himself and H M Consul" (Marling)

Later that day, to Sykes,

"I have the impression that you have on several occasions addressed telegraphs to me on purely political questions. That you have been led, not unnaturally considering the circumstances of the commencement of your mission, in considering yourself in some degree as a political officer as well as Inspector-General of SPR and GOC H.M. Forces in south Persia and this impression has been confirmed both by conversations with yourself...Interference in political affairs by the British Inspector-General of what is officially a Persian force is most undesirable."

Marling then went on to reiterate the reasons for the formation of the force and add, "Political activities by the Inspector-General SPR implies encroachment on the sphere of work of the Consul – the officially accredited agent of HMG for local political questions. Encroachment means confusion – just as it would if consuls involved themselves with the organization of the SPR."

Marling was not trying to exclude Sykes from expressing views on political matters to consuls but simply to make him understand just who would make political decisions. In order not to lead Persians into misunderstanding the role of the SPR he also reiterated that the title of Political Officer held by Hunter should be Intelligence Officer, "which more correctly describes the function to be discharged". Marling sent copies of this letter both to the Foreign Office and the Government of India.

Hunter's spell as Chief of Staff had ended with the arrival of Colonel Orton whose background better suited him to the work. Hunter and Sykes bitterly disagreed about the real function of the SPR and on this they were never reconciled. Added to this, it is probable that their personalities and styles of command were totally different from each other. Sykes was autocratic and inclined to bombast. Hunter was ambitious - too obviously so in the eyes of some Indian Army officers - was fond of the Persian and saw the agonizing dilemma in which the war had placed them. He firmly believed that given the right leadership they would make good soldiers.

Towards the end of July Sykes cabled the Indian government (not Marling in Teheran)

"Matters have now, however, reached a pass where the interests of the service demand Hunter's immediate recall to India. Hunter has caused me much anxiety I regret to report that since the arrival of Staff....Colonel Hunter has shown himself persistently hostile to it.....He has been insubordinate in his written communications to Orton and (Major)Grant...who are unable to put up with the situation any longer. Before journey to Teheran position was considered very difficult by staff and self, but I deferred action, hoping the change might improve matters and, in view of his good services, tried to induce Hunter to accept the new order loyally."

It seems odd that Sykes should accuse Hunter, a lieutenant colonel, of being insubordinate to Grant, a major, which clearly by definition he could not have been but nevertheless it illustrates the intemperate situation that had developed.

It should be noted that Marling, at the Consulate, almost certainly sided with Hunter and also Hunter's poor view of Farman Farma – Sykes' "old friend" who was enriching himself at the expense of the peasantry. For face saving reasons, Sykes suggested that Hunter's return to India be "ostensibly on grounds of ill health."

Hunter remained loyal to Sykes. They had gone to Teheran - some say that Sykes was looking for a medal from the Shah - to meet and explain their activities to Sir Charles Marling. Marling was irritated by Sykes' constant concern with political matters - which were the exclusive mandate of Marling and the various Consuls. He also had to convey to Sykes the fact that the Indian government could not continue to tolerate such high spending by the SPR, although India's parsimonious views may not have been realistic in light of the circumstances. At any event, they do not seem to have curbed him because a year later he was requesting aircraft units.

The government of India believed that a general of high rank should replace Sykes with full control over civil and military authorities in South Persia and that the SPR should in some way be an adjunct to the Imperial forces. This was opposite to the views held by both Hunter and Marling. London had no interest in extending the Indian Empire to include Persia - for such would have been the consequence of implementing this proposal.

After a meeting with Sykes in which Hunter's and Marling's views predominated, Sykes acceded the point. Said Marling of India's concept of a general commanding the South Persia Rifles, "if they did not actually turn against him as I believe they would, would not support him but would desert with their arms - surely too much to expect that semi-mutinous troops taken over by us a few months ago will have become so loyal as to obey foreign officers against their own government – and his authority would have to repose on some two thousand Indian troops who still have to earn respect in South. Idea is wholly fallacious. Persian feeling is not with us and even if it were, mere appointment of such an officer would arouse suspicion we design to take over administration of South Persia."

Hunter's view – that of London and the Consul General - appeared to have won the day. Sykes, even if only to keep his job, now concurred in the view that his role as Inspector General of the South Persia Rifles was as a servant of the Persian government. Continued Marling,

"Sir P Sykes thoroughly understands this and I hope there will be no question of replacing him on account of dissatisfaction of Government of India with his work.....Sir P Sykes was set a task utterly out of proportion to means supplied him."

Sykes may have convinced Marling, but it was only temporary. Sykes' view of the SPR would change again.

Marling had written to the Foreign Office that, particularly since the Russian Revolution and its influence on the Persians, the only possible way of making success of the SPR was to make it a truly Persian force to be used by the Persian government. "If we try and impose it by such means as Government of India suggest, we shall have to send twenty thousand men for the purpose." The Russian Revolution was making the British government highly sensitive to what would today be called "people power".

However, the events did not have the same influence on the Government of India. Superficially, Hunter was to take some leave as he needed a rest. In fact the separation was far more acrimonious.

The arrival of Colonel Orton and Major Grant from India to take over the staff work had created bitter animosity. Sykes fell in line with Orton's views probably because not to do so would shorten his career as an officer of the Indian Army. In fact, according to Hunter later, while Orton and Grant were driving up to Shiraz with him they told him they were there from Simla H.Q India to "make or break" Sykes. Sykes probably guessed this and realized that his career would be better served by allaying himself unequivocally with his new Chief of Staff and the views of the Government of India.

Hunter earlier wrote that Sykes had suggested that he, Hunter, should become Inspector General if he resigned. Hunter countered this by proposing to the Minister in Teheran that in keeping with the size of the SPR Sykes should be promoted to Major General and that consequently both he and Colonel Farran with the Kerman brigade should be appointed to the rank of Brigadier General.

Hunter denied that he was only seeking his own advancement. "Far from having desired the big posts in the SPR", he wrote, "I have frequently expressed to the Inspector General and once to HBM Minister a desire to be permitted to leave the SPR. At present I have but one ambition and that has been placed frequently on record in India - that is, to fight for my own country, Canada, in any capacity or anywhere."

Captain Thorburn, Hunter's assistant, was equally embroiled. Wrote Major Grant, "I warned Captain Thorburn that he was coming more and more under Colonel Hunter's influence; partisanship often blinded his better judgment. Captain Thorburn at once flared up and told me that any unfavourable references to Colonel Hunter would be resented.....It became evident to me that Captain Thorburn regarded Colonel Hunter as some kind of superman."

The differences were never reconciled. Quite apart from clashes of personality, the concept of the organization of the SPR by Hunter was quite different from that envisaged by Orton. Orton wanted the SPR organized along Indian Army lines. Hunter totally disagreed. Such detailed organization might well have been appropriate in a fully organized Brigade in India with a supporting staff and highly developed civil and military systems. In Hunter's own Brigade there were only six regimental officers for the four thousand men and the loyalty of those men, some of them mutinous and disaffected by both the political turmoil in Persia and by the Russian Revolution, was only retained by the personal example of those six officers.

Hunter told Sykes that there was no loyalty by Persians to Britishers as such but that loyalty to chiefs was part of the Persian character and it was personal relationships that produced loyalty in his force. This was not simply a philosophical dispute. Orton, for example, wanted the Secret Service branch with its agents working from the six communities between Shiraz and Bander Abbas to work under an Indian officer. Hunter thought that would be unproductive and wanted a civilian, Dr Woolatt, who had long Persian experience and many local contacts, to head his secret service, one that would only be staffed by Persians.

Grant summed it up. "...both Colonel Hunter and Captain Thorburn have constantly expressed the view that the SPR is an irregular, or police force.......That they took their orders from the British Minister in Teheran, and not from Army HQ, Simla,...and hence opposed the organization of the SPR according to instruction received from Army HQ, Simla."

From this distance in time we must conclude that the break between Sykes and Hunter was in large part a consequence of the too vague initial orders concerning the role of the South Persia Rifles. Hunter's views coincided with those of London and Marling, Sykes' with those of Indian Army headquarters.

Hunter left, ostensibly on leave, intending to return to India via Russia and the Trans Siberian Railway. The axe soon fell on Hunter's allies. Major Grant wrote a lengthy criticism of Captain Thorburn. Thorburn told Sykes that he no longer wished to serve under him since Hunter had gone. Thorburn was "returned to India" a term that would be a stain on an officer's service record. Captain O'Connor, who had worked on Hunter's staff, also "returned to India". A couple of months later Sykes accused Dr Woolatt of insubordination and he too was returned to India. Sykes now had complete control of the SPR but the tragic events that soon followed suggest that Hunter's approach to the organization had been the wisest.

It is not at all clear from the remaining records whether Hunter, when he reached Teheran, ostensibly on leave on his way back to India, was delegated an observer of events in Russia by the Foreign Office or whether, as was later reported, he was to help Russian General Brusilov on the southern front. Whatever the intentions that August, Hunter like so many millions more, was soon caught in the tide of history. He was given three months leave. Three years would pass before he saw Persia or India again.

After Hunter left Teheran and headed north into Russia, the South Persia Rifles were afflicted by a series of misadventures. Although to the north of them the Russian Army in Persia was collapsing as a consequence of the Revolution in Russia, the SPR remained in South Persia, policing the countryside and continuing to chase the German agents - principally Wassmuss - and their tribal allies. Further north the dangerous gap in front of the Turkish Army caused by the disintegration of the Russians, was closed by a series of measures which were remarkable in that they succeeded.

A small force of Ford vans left Mesopotamia early in 1918 under the command of General Dunsterville - he had been at school with Kipling at Westward Ho and was the character upon whom Kipling modeled his hero Stalky. Dunsterforce, as it was called, included in its numbers some forty Canadian officers and NCO's as well as Australians and South Africans. Allied to it were the Russian General Bicherakov's Cossacks, and opposed to it, at least for a short while, were Kuchik Khan's partisans. Dunsterforce tried desperately to alleviate some of the ghastly famine that was sweeping Persia while at the same time trying to train local levies of Armenians and mountain tribesmen to fight after a fashion and so create a modest bastion against a Turkish advance. A large element of the force moved into Enzeli and took boats to Baku in Russia where, allied to the Communists and Mensheviks, as well as to the Armenian Dashnaks, they tried to organize a force which would keep the Turks out of Baku and thus deny them and their German allies the considerable volume of oil stored there. Part of this body moved across the Caspian and garrisoned Krasnavodsk - in liaison with Indian Army troops in Turkestan - and was briefly commanded by a Canadian, Major Gilmour.

In southern Persia Sykes continued attempts at pacifying tribes antagonistic to the British. All had not gone well after Hunter left and the shaky relationship with the Kashgai tribesmen deteriorated rapidly. The headman of the town of Abedah, Mohammed Ali Khan Kashgai became quite anti-British after Hunter left and began to stop food supplies from reaching Shiraz. At the instigation of the British he was replaced.

By May 1918 relations with the Kashgai had deteriorated so badly that the tribe declared war on the British and the South Persia Rifles and were quickly joined by the smaller tribes of the area.

The relationship of the SPR with the Persian government in Teheran remained ambiguous. In early March a British note was presented to the Persian government demanding that the force be recognized. It was not and the Persian response, hostile in tone, referred to the force as a menace and a danger to the independence of Persia. This was at a time when events in Europe suggested that the Germans might soon achieve victory. The Persian government attitude placed strains on the loyalty of the Persians serving with the force. These were not nomad tribesmen, indifferent to the attitudes of the government in Teheran, but sophisticated urbanites. Several Persian officers handed in their resignations, giving no reasons for them. On 18 April 1918, an NCO and ten men deserted at Abadeh, taking their rifles with them. At the same time another Persian NCO and a party of a dozen men returning to Abadeh from Dehbid deserted. The deserters from Abadeh left a document behind stating their action was politically motivated

Six were captured near Isfahan and Sykes ordered that they all be executed. Early in the evening of the 24 April, and with the assistance of the Consul's escort at Isfahan, all six Persians were shot to death. Also, a few days earlier, a Persian had deserted at Saidabad. Sykes thought it would be good to set an example and have this man shot as well. He was. Early in May the NCO who had deserted with his men at Abadeh was captured, sent back to his unit and executed.

These ferocious measures by Sykes should not have caused the authorities, either Persian or British, great surprise. Late in the previous year, in December, a party of Arab brigands had attacked an SPR caravan near Bandar Abbas and stolen some camels. Sykes believed that the headman of the village of Fin, a Persian named Rassulla, was implicated. He instituted an inquiry that decided that the headman was indeed implicated. A military patrol was sent to Fin, destroyed the fort there, captured the headman, brought him back to Bandar Abbas where he was shot. Earlier in April a Persian deserter who had been captured escaped from jail assisted by an SPR private. Both were captured and both shot.

Sir Charles Marling in Teheran, was appalled at the severity of Sykes' actions, describing them as being excessive, and considered it most injudicious that executions were carried out in Isfahan, which was not even in the British sphere of influence. Sykes replied that to return the men from Isfahan to execute them in Abadeh would have put the officer in charge in considerable danger. Sykes cabled Marling in Teheran,

"Protests from the Persian government who plot against us come badly and they themselves are responsible for the need for executions caused by their propaganda... Out of the total number of mutineers who have surrendered or been captured, only one third have been executed and these men were the ringleaders. Had greater leniency been shown than this it would have been dangerous and the action taken was only just sufficient to prevent an outbreak in Fars on a scale that would endanger the safety of the force and possibly Minister's position in Teheran."

The executions did not have the salutary effect that Sykes had hoped. Throughout the countryside the Kashgai tribesmen were drifting steadily towards a state of war with the SPR. Solat-u-Dola, chief of the Kashgai, sent a letter to the men of the garrison at Kaneh Zinian to the effect that the South Persia Rifles were not recognized by the Persian government and that orders had been received from Teheran to expel the British. On May 25 the garrison mutinied, killing their two British officers.

On July 6, three Persian officers and eleven men of the SPR who were implicated in handing Kaneh Zinian over to the Kashgai were publicly executed. As a final humiliation for their crime these men were shot by a firing squad composed of their own comrades. Others were publicly flogged twice and the rest were dismissed the service.

Farman Farma, the Governor, and Qavam-u-Mulk, Chief of the Khamseh tribes, tried to intervene and prevent the executions and the families of the men sentenced pleaded for their lives. They were unsuccessful. Sykes was convinced that it was not a time for leniency and the fourteen men were duly shot.

Two days later a messenger brought in news from Abadeh. Many of the Persians in the SPR garrison there had mutinied and joined the Kashgai chief, Mohammed Ali Khan Kashgai - the former chief of the village who had been earlier replaced by the British - who had encircled the fort and besieged the Indian troops there.

On the 10 July a relief column under the command of Lt Colonel Williams, who had taken over the Fars Brigade from Hunter, marched one hundred and eighty miles through the midsummer heat to lift the siege at Abadeh.

Even the city of Shiraz, headquarters of the Fars Brigade, came under attack from the Kashgai tribesmen. Irrigation water was blocked, cholera took its customary toll, pro-German tribesmen from the vicinity of Kaserun occupied the edge of the town and took the walled gardens near the edge of the SPR cantonment. There was a considerable gunfight, Kashgai tribesmen charging on horseback against the SPR positions. They held and the enemy horsemen suffered as many as two hundred killed and three hundred wounded. Solat's Kashgai were losing their impetus and there was frequent bickering over the distribution of loot.

The Kashgai would normally have moved their herds to the higher grazing for the summer but the campaign against the SPR in Shiraz had resulted in the sheep exhausting the lowland pastures and being debilitated by lack of food. The sheep were dying. With the assistance of the Kasam and the Arab Khamseh tribes, the Kashgai were eventually driven off, but it was not until October 1918, that the Kashgai were finally defeated by Indian troops of the SPR using the fire power of the Lewis gun to maximum advantage.

It was a short-lived victory. The great influenza epidemic which was afflicting most of the world reached Shiraz. One fifth of the population of Fars Province died. Ten thousand died in Shiraz. In the South Persia Rifles six hundred British and Indians were victims. Shortly after the sick men had recovered, Orton led a column southwards to link with British troops driving north from Bushire. He occupied Mian Kotal on January 27 1919, thirteen months after Hunter had been driven back. The force required to break open the route between Shiraz and Bushire amounted to some twenty thousand men.

The SPR certainly prevented the German agents and their tribal supporters from destroying all British influence in the southern towns of Persia. It is quite possible that after the Russian Revolution their presence also prevented the tens of thousands of repatriated German and Austro-Hungarian prisoners of war, released in Russia and Turkestan, from either joining their allies in Persia or organizing to join those Afghans who were belligerent to the British. It is also possible that the Punjab would have risen against the Indian government had the British force in south Persia been defeated. Nonetheless, the SPR left a residue of antipathy and exacerbated the growing alienation of Persians for all foreigners. The Turks and Russians had every reason to be hated for the atrocities they committed against the Persians. Yet Sykes too earned a legacy of animosity. Russians and Turks might rape, loot and murder in the violence of attack or victory. Sykes' violence may have seemed to Persians still more appalling, more malevolent, because it was seemingly dispassionate and implacable.

It is arguable that desperate times require desperate measures; that the spectacle of public execution was necessary to stem the disintegration of his force. If that was the intent, then it failed; the violence within and outside of the SPR was greater rather than less after his measures.

An argument can be made that during the First World War there were many executions for deserting with weapons and for mutiny - though not for stealing camels. That is true. During this war British Army courts martial condemned 3,080 men to death for offenses ranging from desertion and murder to sleeping at their posts or throwing away their arms. The men so condemned had formal trials with appropriate defense. Of the 3,080 men condemned, about eleven per cent, 346 of them were actually executed.[28] Many of the records of Sykes' management of the SPR no longer exist. From those that do it appears that the chief of the village of Fin was executed following an inquiry rather than a trial and that his principal offense was in aiding in the theft of camels. All the other executions were carried out following trials after which the appeal process appears to have been simple pleading by relatives or friends to Sykes himself - the man who initiated the trials and determined the sentences. One hundred per cent of those sentenced to death were executed - publicly and with a formality that would have horrified the Persian onlookers. Decades after the executions in Isfahan, Persians could point to the spot where they had taken place.

Unlike Hunter, it seems that neither Sykes, nor Orton, Hunter's successor, had any affection for Persians, those men they commanded. More likely, they held them it considerable contempt. Certainly Sykes liked those of the aristocracy and his references to His Highness the Farman Farma are tinged with sycophancy. Sykes appears not to resist any opportunity to refer to this highborn Persian either as a staunch ally or personal friend. Yet Sykes knew perfectly well that Farman Farma was robbing his own people and the British - and aided in doing so by the other ally of the British, the Chief of the Khamseh tribes, Qavam-u-Mulk. Supplies for the SPR were obtained through contractors at Shiraz and Kerman. During the SPR's most difficult period, the summer of 1918, Farman Farma used his power as Governor of Fars Province to control the distribution and disposal of produce from the estates of Qavam-u-Mulk and a couple of prominent Persian merchants. This was no small amount - it was half the agricultural produce of the province. Farman Farma stockpiled the grain in Firuzabad until he had forced the price up - this was at the time when famine was raging throughout Persia.

In a report to Sykes in August and September 1918 which was then forwarded to Indian Army headquarters in Delhi, it was estimated that the cost of supplies purchased by the SPR - then about two hundred thousand tomans a month - was double what it would be if Farman Farma was not forcing up the price. Throughout the year of terrible Persian starvation, Farman Farma used his political power as governor to force estates to sell him the grain, deduct the customary ten per cent, which was his right as keeper of the treasury, on all incoming and outgoing payments, then stockpile the grain until the price had been driven higher still. Sykes must have known that this was occurring.

Although Sykes expressed high regard for certain aristocratic Persians, his view of the urban Persian sounds frequently disparaging or patronizing.

It is reasonable to conjecture that the departure of Hunter from the South Persia Rifles was a major mistake and much of the turmoil that followed would have been avoided had Hunter remained. He appears to have been well liked by the Persians and he in turn, liked them. He felt that a meaningful level of command should be in the hands of the Persian officers of the SPR. These officers, educated and cultured to a greater extent that their Indian Army counterparts, had acquired a political consciousness in the preceding years which could influence the rank and file. This view was not shared by Hunter's successor, Lt. Colonel Orton. Far from admiring the well-bred Persians, Orton thought they were "too full of vices, too lazy to learn, and inordinately conceited."[29] He believed that they were always quick to think they already knew everything there was to learn.

Had Hunter's views prevailed during the difficult summer of 1918 - when the loyalties of the Persian officers were strained by the attitude of the Persian government in Teheran - the mutinies and desertions might not have occurred - at least not to the same extent. Hunter might have exercised a restraining influence on Sykes, and the death penalties, if passed, might have been commuted. But that was not to be. By this time Hunter was in New York and trying to get to the Western Front. The SPR managed to survive its crisis but, in doing so, contributed to the legacy of antipathy in which so many Persians to this day hold to all foreigners.

The South Persia Rifles did not survive long. After Sykes left, shortly following the end of the war, Orton became Inspector-General. At about the same time, Sir Charles Marling was replaced as British Minister in Teheran by the old eastern hand, Sir Percy Cox. Despite his skill and experience, Cox was quite unable to persuade the Persians to ratify the Anglo-Persian Agreement, a failure that certainly deprived the Persians of a opportunity to accelerate the modernization of the administration of their country. But nationalism and suspicion of all foreigners was rampant and the British, preoccupied by events in Egypt and Mesopotamia, lost interest in Persia. The South Persia Rifles were disbanded.

THREE CONTINENTS

"He travels fastest who travels alone." R. Kipling.

Hunter, in Teheran, wrote an extensive and feisty reply to Sykes' accusations. His response underlined the different views of the responsibilities of the South Persia Rifles - whether they were an extension of the Indian Army or an independent force.

While in Teheran Hunter probably stayed with Marling's family although had he stayed elsewhere he would certainly have socialized with him. Interestingly, records show that at this very time Marling had another houseguest. It was Grand Duke Dmitri Pavlovich Romanov. He had been exiled to Persia by the Czar because of his involvement with Prince Felix Yusupov in the murder of the holy man Rasputin[30]. Initially he was stationed with General Baratov's troops at Kasvin but later, as the Russian Army disintegrated, moved in with the Marlings in Teheran. Grand Duke Dmitri may have been the initial link between Hunter and Lady Muriel Paget.

Lady Paget and Lady Sybil Grey – daughter of the former Governor-General of Canada, Earl Grey - were joint leaders of the Voluntary Aid Detachment (VAD) in Russia. Early in the war Grand Duke Dmitri had given the first floor of his palace in Petrograd to be used as the Anglo-Russian Hospital. When, shortly after Prince Youssoupoff and Grand Duke Dmitri killed Rasputin some of Rasputin's supporters came to the hospital on the pretext of visiting the wounded but in fact hoping to gain access to Dmitri's apartments intent on revenge. Lady Grey had the foresight to have placed a sentry in the connecting passage and blocked their entry thereby probably saving Dmitri's life.

Two weeks later Hunter headed north into Russia. Today it is impossible to know just where he was at any particular time except that he was certainly in Petrograd where he wrote in the office of Oswold Lindley, the British charge d'affairs, suggestions about Russia that were forwarded to London. The initial plan was that he write suggestions for the re-organization of the Russian Army and although that was changed he would have visited the various army fronts on his way north. He almost certainly followed the route favoured by Persians seeking a western education at the end of the nineteenth century and went north from Teheran across the Elburz Mountains to the Caspian port of Enzeli then by boat to Baku in Azerbaijan, then to Tiflis in Georgia. From there his journey took him to Rostov on Don then west to Odessa where he may have met Lady Muriel Paget. After that north to Kiev and Moscow before continuing to Petrograd. It is quite possible that at some stage he traveled with General Kornilov's Savage Division, heading to Petrograd and the failed September counter-revolution.

Hunter soon saw that the Russian army, infected by revolution and demoralized by defeat, was collapsing. Viewed from Persia the extent of the collapse was not apparent. Russian troops in that country - Cossacks under General Baratov - were still not as infiltrated by radicals as had those further north. One unit, Cossack cavalry led by Colonel Bicherakov, kept fighting for a long time, continuing against the Turks after the war was technically over, and then against the Bolsheviks, and each man had sworn an oath of loyalty to his leader.

The further north Hunter headed the clearer were the signs of military and social disintegration. Even in the Caucasus the collapse had begun, although the October Revolution, those "ten days that shook the world", was still a couple of months away and the humiliating treaty that Lenin signed to save his revolution from the Germans, was still further off.

At more and more fronts Russian soldiers were being replaced by Trans-Caucasian volunteer units - principally Armenians with Russian officers. Russian soldiers were increasingly "self-demobilized", that is, they simply deserted and began the long walk home. Socialists in Baku - principally Armenian - were understandably terrified of a Turkish victory in the Caucasus. Even after the October Revolution most of the officers in Caucasian Red Army were Armenian Dashnaks (Armenians seeking freedom from both Russians and Turks.) and their chief of staff was a former colonel in the Tsarist army.

The Caucasus was a conservative area compared with other parts of the Russian Empire. It was, for example, the home of the notorious Savage Division, a predatory military unit composed of Moslem tribesmen from the mountains - Daghestanis, Chechnians and the like - who opposed the new order which they feared would withdraw from them privileges conferred by the Czar. Despite this, as early as September 1917, General Kornilov's reliance on them when he attempted to overthrow the Kerensky government proved to be a mistake.

Oil rich Baku, a city of contrasts where local entrepreneurs lived in splendor and Tartar oilfield workers in squalor, did not hold Hunter long. Word would have reached him earlier of the collapse of the Russian army on the south-west front and he hurried there to see what assistance he could give, if any, to General Brusilov. Brusilov, the most energetic and successful - and incidentally, the most socialist-minded of the generals - had recently been appointed Commander-in-Chief.

Kerensky's government had tried to keep up the fight against the Central Powers despite the appalling casualties suffered by Russia. Of all nations which participated in the First World War, none suffered as much as Russia which had called more than twelve million men to the colours. Casualties were in the millions. Millions more hoped that the March Revolution, now led by Kerensky, would bring them peace. The vast Russian Army, the largest force ever put into the field by any nation, was by the time Hunter got into Russia, "transformed" in the words of one Russian general "into an enormous, exhausted, badly clothed, badly fed, embittered mob of people, united by thirst for peace and general disillusionment".[31]

Brusilov's troops on the southwest front were hardly better. Though the general had a few months earlier mounted a successful attack on the Austrians, later attempts to consolidate these gains failed. The rout of Russian forces continued and Hunter soon was moving north again, a journey, which, although no records remain of it, must have been traumatic for Russia had by this time become an erupting volcano.

Kerensky, both initially as War Minister and later as Premier, was as aware as his allies of the consequences of the collapse of Russian resistance and tried to keep his troops fighting. He had commissars assigned to every army to act as a buffer between the conservative generals and the elected soldier's organizations. He made a tour of the front and in a series of rousing speeches tried to prevent the flood of desertion turning into a deluge - Kerensky was disparagingly referred to by some of his generals as "the persuader-in-chief."

Authority in the Russian Army must have been incomprehensible to both officers and men. Social Revolutionaries and Mensheviks broke the discipline and effectiveness of the army with their so-called reforms - for example, the infamous Order Number One which resulted in the dismissal of many of the best officers and, with the abolition of capital punishment prompted desertion by the hundreds of thousands. Yet at the same time these Social Revolutionaries and Mensheviks wanted to continue the war until victory. The Bolshevik position was at least clear - peace, immediately and whatever the price.

There were exceptions, and any hope surely fragile even as early as August, that the Russian army could be reorganized into an effective fighting force would have been based on these exceptions.

These few exceptions included volunteers such as those who had undertaken to fight to the death and were formed into combat units known as Battalions of Death. Soldiers in these units wore two chevrons on their right arms; one red symbolizing revolution, the other black symbolizing their willingness to die. One such unit was composed entirely of women and was led by Colonel Mariya (Yashka) Bochkareva, known as Russia's Joan of Arc. But even though these units may have been effective, there were far too few of them to offset the deterioration of Russia's military position. Yashka Bochkareva's women soldiers were briefly successful and Colonel Yashka returned to Petrograd, her battalion headquarters.

It was the collapse of the Gallician campaign, General Brusilov's July offensive, that finally devastated what was left of army morale. Ironically it was the initial success of the attack, spearheaded by reliable units of Finns, Siberians and Poles achieving advances of thirty miles against the Austrians, which made the subsequent retreat, when the Germans came to the rescue of their allies, all the more demoralizing. The offensive was futile and Russia's last.

It was following this debacle that Hunter arrived at southwestern headquarters. He did not stay long.

By the time Hunter reached Petrograd General Kornilov had been appointed commander-in-chief of the Russian armies. Kornilov, son of a Siberian Cossack, of somewhat Mongolian appearance, had had an early military career in Russian Central Asia. He spoke a number of Asian languages, had a flamboyantly dressed bodyguard of Turkmen warriors and preferred the company of Central Asians than European Russians. He was tough and intrepid. He was more comfortable with the revolution than many of the generals; he had been moderate in his criticisms of the excesses of the Revolution at the time when General Deniken, later to be leader of the Whites in the Civil War, was vitriolic. But he had little room for the Bolsheviks and told his staff that one way to cure Russia's troubles was to hang Lenin - Lenin was then in hiding in Finland following the failure of a Bolshevik coup in July.

Kornilov had considerable support. General Kaledin, leader of the Don Cossacks thought highly of him as did many other Cossacks. The British military attaché in Petrograd praised him and there is little doubt that Hunter would have found him a sympathetic figure. Kornilov wanted the discipline of the army improved and he tried to persuade Kerensky to give him the authority to do it. At the same time he positioned the Third Cavalry Corps and the Savage Division from the Caucasus within striking distance of Petrograd. It is possible that Hunter traveled north with the Savage Division who had shortly before been on the southwest front, but there is no way of verifying this.

In late August Kornilov attended a State Conference in Moscow and told the two thousand five hundred assembled delegates - the Bolsheviks had boycotted the meeting - that with the Germans at the gates of Riga the road to Petrograd would soon be open to them. And the army, said Kornilov "is a crazy mob". Ataman Kaledin, who followed Kornilov to the rostrum, demanded the abolition of soldiers' committees; those right-of-centre at the meeting clearly sympathized with Kornilov and Kaledin. But the great majority of delegates, Cadets who favored an English style parliamentary system, Mensheviks and Social revolutionaries, did not. They were prepared to continue with Kerensky rather than have a military dictatorship.

Believing he had key army units supporting him, Kornilov prepared to do by force what he could not do through the delegates. He believed that a street demonstration could be provoked in Petrograd that would give him the excuse to march on the city to save the government. In the city itself, two thousand army officers would act as a fifth column - although the phrase was still twenty years from birth - and arrest the socialist leaders.

When Kornilov ordered General Krymov to lead the Savage Division and march on the capital it soon became clear that neither side, not his own nor Kerensky's, had real power. That lay with the ordinary soldiers and with the Petrograd Soviet. They opted for Kerensky. Arms were handed out to the workers so that they could defend the city. The Bolsheviks, who were not prepared to fight for Kerensky, were prepared to fight against Kornilov to defend Kerensky. They accepted weapons - and when the crisis was over declined to return them. Barricades were erected; rail lines on the approaches to the city torn up.

When the Savage Division got close to Petrograd delegates from the Petrograd Soviet mixed among them and persuaded them to defy their officers. The Third Cavalry Corps abandoned the whole enterprise and sent representatives to the Petrograd soviet to seek instructions. Within the city, the fifth column fired not a shot. Kornilov's coup was an abject failure. It was likely that at this point Hunter abandoned his mission to devise a scheme for the re-organization of the Russian Army and wrote political suggestions instead. Unlike many British policy makers at that time Hunter saw no hope that any moderate party in Russia could successfully oppose the Bolsheviks unless there was outside intervention.

From the moment of that failure it was quite obvious to Hunter that any suggestions he had to contribute to the reorganization of the Russian army - apparently his original intention - were completely redundant. In retrospect it seems that the slide to the October Revolution (November in the new calendar) was quite inevitable.

Only days after Kornilov's failure voting in the Moscow Soviet revealed a Bolshevik majority. Three weeks later Trotsky was elected President of the Petrograd Soviet. There was growing public anger at all army officers - the people seeing them as potential traitors. Excesses became still more commonplace and incidents of throwing grenades into army officers' quarters increased. Even in the Caucasus, far from the mutinous atmosphere of Petrograd and Moscow, men murdered their own officers. This disintegration of Russia's armed forces seems now to have been a spontaneous eruption, the consequence of two and a half years of unsuccessful fighting under the harshest of conditions followed by a sudden relaxation of the old discipline and a government which failed to find what people most wanted - peace and land. No reorganization could have halted the collapse and the persistence of the middle class and the officer class in the formula of "war until victory" assured them instead of defeat until revolution.

On the eve of the Bolshevik Revolution life in Petrograd had acquired a fevered pitch. John Reed, author of <u>Ten Days That Shook</u>

<u>the World</u> and central character in the movie "Reds", wrote of life in Petrograd.

"All night, hundreds of soldiers slept on the floor. Holdups increased to such an extent that it was dangerous to walk down side streets....the committee rooms buzzed and hummed all day and wherever they could find room. Upstairs in the great hall a thousand people crowded to the uproarious sessions of the Petrograd Soviet.... gambling clubs functioned hectically from dusk till dawn with champagne flowing and stakes of twenty thousand rubles. In the centre of the city at night prostitutes in jewels and expensive furs, walked up and down, crowded the cafes."

The events of the second revolution of 1917, the revolution that overthrew the Kerensky government, have been detailed so often as not to require repetition here. Hunter was in Petrograd, in those fateful days and what is not always realized is that so were a number of other foreigners. There were even armed British troops in Russia, although they did not participate in the civil strife.

The so-called Locker Lampson Armoured Car Company, which had been fighting for two years on the eastern front from trans-Caucasia to Rumania and the Austrian border, was on its way back to England. One returning detachment passed through Moscow when reaction to the attempted Kornilov coup was intense. The English sailors, Royal Navy Volunteer Reserves (RNVR) who manned the armoured cars, had to be confined to the railway station area for their own safety. Most of this unit got back to England by the end of October but there was a rear party at Kursk, about halfway between the Black Sea and Moscow. No British-officered armoured cars were anywhere near Petrograd at the time of the October Revolution.

In <u>The Ten Days That Shook the World</u> John Reed reports that his friend Louise Bryant saw half a dozen cars of the disbanded British Armoured Car Division on the streets of Petrograd and that one fired indiscriminately into the crowd. When Russian sailors overcame it they found a dead British officer inside. Ms Bryant was almost certainly mistaken although there were reports circulating frequently at the time of British and French officers directing military cadets in the attack on the telephone exchange. There is now no possible means of verifying if any of these stories are true.

There were British officers in Petrograd at this time and Hunter was just one of them. Another was obviously the British military attaché. There were also the customary intelligence units, headed by Rex Leeper and Professor J Young Simpson. One of these units, MI.7, - concerned with publications and propaganda - a unit with which Hunter would soon be more closely involved, had three key figures in the city - a Dr Williams, Major Thornhill and the writer Hugh Walpole. Their head office in London included such other well-known writers as Patrick McGill, Lord Dunsany and A.A. Milne. The writer, William Somerset Maughan, had earlier been sent to Petrograd - by way of Japan and Siberia - by William Wiseman, the British Secret Service head in New York. Maughan's job - one which was impossible from the start - was to prevent the Bolsheviks from seizing power and assure that the Mensheviks held onto power.

Maughan had contacts and Wiseman hoped that he could "guide the storm". Maughan had once had a brief affair with Sasha Kropotkin, daughter of anarchist Prince Kropotkin, and he met her again in Russia where she introduced him to Kerensky. He also met Thomas Masaryk who was trying to organize Czech resistance in Russia. But Maughan had a problem. He had been instructed to send encoded cables from the British Embassy to Wiseman in New York who would forward the to Sir Mansfield Cumming ("C") in London. The British ambassador, Sir George Buchanan, was furious that he would have to forward cables, the contents of which he had no knowledge.

Hunter's approach was less obtuse. This was a result of the changing structure of MI.1(c) or the Secret Intelligence Service. Military intelligence changed its reporting line in 1917 when the need for strategic and political intelligence, rather that tactical intelligence, became apparent with the growth of revolutionary movements and the disintegration of Russia. Consequently it was removed from the control of the War Office and reported instead to the Foreign Office, just as the Embassy did. (Note: at about this same time MI.5, which previously had reported to the War Office, began reporting to the Home Office, which it continues to do) So, possibly adding to the confusion of the times, Hunter sent his messages, not to Wiseman in New York but direct to the Foreign Office in London.

This period appears to have been one of some confusion in intelligence services. Not only was there a plethora of agents, apparently unconnected with each other in Russia, but they appear to have had different reporting lines, some to the Embassy, some only to the Military Attaché there, others bypassing it altogether and going through the consul-general in Moscow.

Another British enterprise in Petrograd was the previously mentioned British Hospital in Grand Duke Dmitri Pavlovich's magnificent baroque palace at 41 Nevski Prospect run by Lady Muriel Paget and Lady Sibil Grey and their network of VAD's. The Voluntary Aid Detachment was begun early in the war by a Mrs. (later Dame) Katherine Furse. The Detachment operated throughout the European war zones and Muriel Paget headed the organization in

Russia. It provided volunteer help, mainly women but some men as well, to the more highly trained nurses in battle zones on all fronts. Lady Paget had left to visit another of her hospitals in Odessa, on the Black Sea, and she later laconically remarked that the train there was so slow that she sympathized with the soldiers who popped the engine driver into his own boiler.

Later in the year the hospital in Petrograd was left in the hands of the British surgeon but he soon found it impossible to continue and handed it over, along with seventy patients, to the Russian Red Cross, an organization that was itself disintegrating.

Hunter was working in Petrograd with the Honourable Francis Oswold Lindley, Charge d'Affairs under the Ambassador, Sir George Buchanan. Lindley was a man whose early career resulted in shared interests with Hunter. Four years older than Hunter he had been educated at Winchester School and Magdalen College, Oxford, before entering the Foreign Service. One of his earliest postings had been to Teheran where he soon passed examinations in the Persian language and shortly after that in Arabic as well. He had been in Russia since the summer of 1915.

Hunter completed his report in Petrograd - not however on the reorganization of the Russian army - but on how to retrieve something from the Russian debacle. On November 11, the day of an unsuccessful rising of Junkers – the military cadets - in Petrograd, Hunter's report went to London. Almost immediately it was in the hands of key government personnel including Lord Curzon, then a member of Prime Minister Lloyd George's all-powerful War Council.

At this time most SIS agents in Russia were principally concerned with keeping the Czarist armies fighting and they were telling their Chief, Sir Mansfield Cumming, that the Bolsheviks should not be taken seriously.[32] Hunter took the opposite view. He argued that the allied policy of non-intervention in Russia would have to be abandoned as there was no longer any possibility left that any moderate party could oppose Lenin.

Hunter made eleven suggestions.

1. The allies refuse to recognize the present government.

2. Troops from Maude's forces in Iraq be dispatched via Persia to the Caucasus to form a nucleus around which pro-allied elements might rally. (Quite unknown to Hunter, of course, since the event was almost a month away, was the eventual rallying of pro-allied elements around General Alexeev.)

3. Dispatch of allied men-o-war to Vladivostock combined with landings of Japanese and American troops.

4. The immediate occupation of Manchuria by the Japanese.

5. Landing of a small body of troops at Alexandrovsk as a threat to the Petrograd "anarchists".

6. Public notification that the allied armies will receive and employ in their ranks Russian officers and men who chose to join them.

7. Allied subjects in Russia be advised to concentrate in Manchuria or the Caucasus.

8. Selection and support by the allies of a Russian leader, such as Kornilov, Gurko or Kaledin, around whom the Russians could gather.

9. Announcement that in the case of a separate peace, Russians will not be admitted into allied countries.

10. Dispatch of transport material, already ordered in America, to Vladivostock with allied personnel to organize it.

11. Dispatch to the Caucasus and Siberia of large consignments of clothing and boots that would serve as a means of exchange for the purchase of grain now rotting in the fields for the starving towns.

The comments attached in London to this communiqué are revealing. Some thought that the suggestions might all be redundant since Kornilov and Kaledin might soon gain power. They were soon proved wrong. Lancelot Oliphant, Middle Eastern expert to the Cabinet, and General MacDonough, Director of Military Operations were, if not supportive, at least not derogatory. Curzon thought only the last two points were practical. Robert Cecil, the Under Secretary of State for Foreign Affairs, was more forthright. "Everyone in contact with Russia" he wrote over Hunter's report, "appears to be insane."

Yet within a short time most of Hunter's proposals were followed and only six weeks later British General Dunsterville was being briefed in India to lead a small force from Maude's positions in Iraq, through Persia and into the Caucasus.

Hunter now had the problem of getting out of Russia and avoiding the turmoil all around, particularly since Riga had fallen and, as Kornilov had predicted, the Germans were on the road to Petrograd.

Just how Hunter got out of Russia is not clear nor is it clear why he chose to head out eastward instead of going through Finland, as some of the Embassy staff did later. But there are reports that just before he left he acquired the Russian military ciphers and handed them over to the allies when he got to New York. What is known is that, until the Russians changed their codes in 1920, the misleadingly named Government Code and Cipher School (GCCS) which was, in 1923 absorbed by the SIS, was able to intercept and decrypt wireless messages from the Soviets to their representatives in London. Someone had secured the ciphers and passed them to British Intelligence.

Hunter left Petrograd and traveled by train to Moscow where he may have met Lady Muriel Paget again. She was still recovering from the effects of typhoid fever caught earlier in Kiev, but after inspecting her VAD Field Hospital in Odessa had traveled north again and reached Moscow where she awaited the hospital staff following her up from the south. While there she made all the arrangements necessary to take the train across Siberia to the Pacific Ocean and the final party which she gathered around her - some forty British in all - may have included Hunter, who certainly traveled that route either at about that time or, more likely, some weeks earlier.

The Paget party certainly included the future President of Czechoslovakia, Thomas Masaryk, who had been in Petrograd when Hunter was there, along with five Red Guards who were persuaded to travel with the party as far as Irkutsk in Western Siberia. Hunter's later friendship with Lady Paget and his association with Thomas Masaryk reinforce the probability that he met them at this time or in Odessa or Moscow before their departure. The party left with two coaches at their disposal, a second and third class, for the long journey across Russia. While this also is uncertain, the passengers may have also included Colonel "Yashka" Botchkareva, of the all-women "Battalion of Death".

Lady Paget and her party traveled in the third class coach since, being wooden, it could more easily be washed down. She looked after the food for the whole group and managed to obtain just before departure a supply of black bread and eight sucking pigs. As darkness came to Moscow on the evening of March 7 1918, their train began its long journey across Russia.

After a few days they reached Zlatousk, a small town in a valley of the Ural Mountains, the range that separates European Russia from Asia; then through the mountains to Chelyabinsk, a rail junction with the line from the mining centres in the northern Urals and the main line to Vladivostock. At this time Russia had been the source of some 95 percent of the world's supply of platinum, most of which was mined in the Urals. To the north of Chelyabinsk, on the railway line, is the town of Nizhne-Tagilsk, a major mining centre for platinum - the largest specimen of platinum ever found, 310 ounces, had come from the vicinity. Later stories say that Hunter, in his flight from Russia somehow acquired, in addition to the military ciphers, 20,000 pounds (presumably in sterling) of platinum. If this is so then Hunter, when the other passengers were restocking with provisions and filling themselves with cabbage soup and goose, was loading the platinum from Nizhne-Tagilsk onto the train at Chelyabinsk.

Then began the long haul to the Pacific and it took Lady Paget's party more than a month to complete the journey - in the intense Siberian cold - to the sea by way of Lake Baikal, Harbin in Manchuria and through to Vladivostock. However, it is likely that both Hunter and Muriel Paget left their trains at Harbin and connected with the Chinese Eastern Railway Company traveling south to Port Arthur, then the territory of the Japanese, at that time allies. From Port Arthur they crossed the Yellow Sea to Japan where they promptly caught a steamer to Vancouver, carrying on as quickly as they could to Toronto. Lady Paget and Hunter left Toronto for Montreal and then went on by train down to New York with Lady Paget continuing onto Washington, D.C. While the route was identical Hunter was likely a few weeks ahead of Lady Paget and her party.

On May 14 Lady Paget was taken to meet President Wilson by Mrs. J Borden Harriman, widow of the Manhattan banker who was active in support efforts for the allies. Lady Paget spent fifteen minutes with the President telling him of the need for intervention against the Bolsheviks. Mrs. Harriman had dinner with the Pagets (Lady Paget's husband had now joined her in America) on 21 June and two days later took Colonel "Yashka" Botchkareva to meet President Wilson.[33]

Hunter had immediately reported to the British authorities in New York City and, partly because he was ill and the Medical Board ruled against him getting into action, was appointed the British Assistant Provost Marshall to the United States. This function was not what its title suggested. He was principally concerned with propaganda work in the United States which was being conducted by MI.7(b) and which reported to the head of the Intelligence Bureau in London. This was Captain Mansfield Cumming, R.N. - the original "C" of spy story fame. His principal people in the States were Sir William Wiseman[34], head of the British Purchasing Commission and Major Norman Thwaites, who a year earlier had recruited the now famous agent, Sidney Reilly and had sent him up to Toronto and then onto London to join the Secret Service and become Britain's best ever known spy.

Wiseman (Willie to his friends) was an ebullient character. Thirty-two years old at this time, he looked younger. He held an ancient baronetcy and was a Cambridge boxing blue. He had sought his fortune in enterprises ranging from Mexican meat packing to Canadian property development. When war began he volunteered and was soon gassed on the Western Front. Cumming (who had known Wiseman's father) thought him just the sort of man for intelligence operations and sent him to the United States as his station chief there to keep an eye on German and other enemy activity. Thwaites ran the New York office.

However, after America joined the war the needs of a military intelligence activity in the States was much reduced with the Americans taking over most of the work. Thwaites was then required to reorganize the Military Mission office in New York reducing the number of employees drastically; the problem with this was that such a reduction would mean abandoning the work done combating activities of Indian "seditionists". It is possible that Hunter joined the Mission as Assistant Provost Marshall - the first to be appointed - as a means of circumventing the direct order of Military Intelligence. Technically Hunter had a Provost function - arranging for the Americans to pick up deserters or people masquerading as senior officers - but most of his activities appear to have been in propaganda work as part of MI.7.

Clarifying which department was responsible for what in Military Intelligence is made more difficult by the frequency with which numbers were changed - sometimes it must seem that the changes were made simply to confuse future researchers. "C", that is, Captain Mansfield Cumming, sent Wiseman to the United States in November 1915, while the States was still neutral, to organize a branch of MI.1c. Its duties in the United States were to investigate the activities of those who were suspect by London. It was also responsible for a general watch over the Irish movement in the United States and the investigation of Indian sedition. This later work resulted in a major court case in San Francisco that did much to discredit the Indian movement in the United States.

Gradually Wiseman's work in the United States transformed into his becoming liaison between President Wilson's aide, Colonel House, and the Foreign Office and so he handed over the control of the New York office of MI.1c (frequently known as Section 5) to Norman Thwaites. When America entered the war it was decided in London that the organization of MI.1c (espionage) should be taken over by MI.5. - the counter-espionage agency headed in the United States by Colonel Packenham. Espionage could not be carried out in an allied country.[35] The Provost work, an entirely new position that required, in addition to the approval of London the concurrence of Ottawa, appears to have been principally concerned with propaganda - although there were certain provost functions. Policy was decided by the Department of Information in London at that time headed by the writer John Buchan - later to be, as Lord Tweedsmuir, Governor-General of Canada. The Department would soon become a Ministry headed by Canadian Lord Beaverbrook.

British propaganda efforts in the United States, though highly successful, had not always been aware of American sensitivities. Wrote John Buchan, "It annoys Americans that England should sometimes fail to understand that American ideals are not necessarily English ideals, and that America is the best, and in fact the only judge of what her action ought to be in the present crisis." That crisis was profound. Buchan's memorandum was written towards the end of February 1917. In January the British government had given to the Americans a copy of an intercepted telegram from the German Foreign Minister Zimmerman. This telegram had been sent to the German Embassy in Mexico. It proposed a German-Mexican-Japanese alliance against the United States with the Mexicans being rewarded on the successful completion of hostilities with the re-conquest of "the lost territory in Texas, New Mexico and Arizona". It was, of course, in code. The code, a complex one, had been broken by cryptographers working for Admiral "Blinker" Hall in Room 40 at British Naval Intelligence. They had been able to break this code as a result of two outside events. A young man named Alexander Szek - of British birth but Austro-Hungarian parentage - was working at a radio transmitting station in Brussels when the Germans occupied the city. Allied Intelligence was able to persuade - with difficulty - this young clerk to copy the German diplomatic code piece by piece. The copies were forwarded to Room 40. Subsequently Szek disappeared. What happened to him is no longer known. Some believe that the Germans caught and shot him. His father, after the war, claimed that the British had him murdered in order to prevent the Germans from discovering that their code had been broken.

At much the same time, Wilhelm Wassmuss had entered Persia on his way to Bushire. The British at Bushire had failed to catch him but they had seized most of his baggage and this was sent back to India and, from there, to the India Office in London. Later in the year a British naval officer, invalided home from the Gulf, was telling Admiral Hall of the events there and the increasingly infamous Wassmuss. Hall had a hunch and sent searchers to locate Wassmuss' baggage. They found among the papers the German diplomatic code book Number 13040. With the aid of Szek's information and Wassmuss' codebook, British cryptographers were able to decode the "Zimmerman Telegram".

When the British leaked the contents of the telegram to the American administration it had a profound effect on Washington's attitude towards intervention and the American people's view of where their interests lay. (Note: the acting British Consul at Bushire, C.J. Edmonds, in a paper to the Journal of the Royal Central Asian Society in January, 1960, relates that because of Wassmuss' escape, the British decided to arrest – illegally, since Persia was neutral - the German consul in Bushire and that the code was found wrapped in several pairs of long woolen underpants.)

Early in February, following a German decision that their submarines would attack any vessels in the so-called war zone, the United States severed diplomatic relations. On February 25 a German submarine torpedoed and sank the British liner "Laconia" which had several Americans on board and also sank a number of American vessels. President Wilson went to Congress on April 2 saying that "the world must be made safe for democracy" and on April 6, the United States was formally at war. From that point on British propaganda and intelligence efforts clearly changed from countering German propaganda in the United States to reinforcing the success of earlier efforts.

An indication of the enthusiasm with which many Americans supported the Allied cause appears in a report written by John Buchan to Sir Edward Carson.

"Our war films have been shown throughout the length and breadth of the USA and it is calculated that over the past three months (prior to September, 1917) over ten million people have seen them. At the first exhibition of the battle of Arras in New York last week 6,000 people had to be turned away. In the Middle West the success was even more striking. In Omaha the opening of the pictures was made an occasion for a public holiday and it is estimated that 75,000 people tried to gain admission to the different shows. In St Louis a service was held beforehand by the clergy of all creeds.

Long lists of articles so placed are filed in the Department and so great a propaganda medium as the Saturday Evening Post is full of our material. Mr.Butler arranges lecture tours by British visitors such as Captain Beith (Ian Hay), Dr Parkin of the Rhodes Trust, M Delaval, (who defended Nurse Cavell who was executed by the

Germans) all of which have been highly successful. I think that there can be no question but that the British propaganda organization in the United States is being managed with very exceptional ability and energy."

Hunter was lassoed into the propaganda team and required to make fundraising and stirring speeches. This was shortly after the German Spring offensive when the situation looked dire for the allies on the western front. The New York Times reported at least three speech-making occasions of his towards hundreds of contributors in the city. At about the same time he reportedly traveled with Jan Paderewski, the Polish pianist and patriot who raised millions of dollars and immense support for the allied cause among Polish-Americans. Then came for Hunter one of those remarkable coincidences that occur in wartime.

When Hunter's former unit, the South Persia Rifles, was formed, one of its initial instructions was to go to Persia and rescue William Frederick Travers O'Connor, consul at Shiraz who, along with the other British residents, had been imprisoned by pro-German tribesmen. He and the others had been released in an exchange before Sykes and Hunter got to Shiraz, and he went back to India. But his health had been severely affected and it was not until the Fall of 1917, by then in a sanatorium in Scotland, that he was again pronounced fit for duty. O'Connor knew John Buchan and Leo Amery, Assistant Secretary to the War Cabinet, and through them got an appointment with the new Minister of Information, Lord Beaverbrook. Beaverbrook gave him a job. It was to go to Siberia and take over propaganda work there on behalf of the allies.

O'Connor crossed the Atlantic and arrived in New York, overwhelmed by the vibrancy of the city. He wrote,

"New York was amazing. The States had been our allies for a year but hitherto no troops had been sent over. But the great German breakthrough of March 1918 had thoroughly aroused the country. I have never seen such martial enthusiasm as then prevailed. Great crowds thronged the streets and all down 5th Avenue and elsewhere orators on stages bellowed through megaphones exhorting everyone to support the current "Liberty Loan". A British officer in uniform was almost mobbed when he showed himself. All down 5th Avenue allied flags were flying. The terrible crisis in France (Germany's March offensive.) had sent its reverberations all through America - one was embarrassed by the avalanche of friendly greetings and offers of hospitality from perfect strangers....I was much struck by the deep seated feeling evoked in shops, offices, etc. I have known the most prosaic-looking shopman dart into his back premises to rout out some poem or heart stirring speech he had cut from an English newspaper and an assistant in a bookshop said to me, 'Well at any rate we shall never have this old anti-English stuff about George III taught in our schools again. We're friends now at last, in spite of all the mischief makers.'"

O'Connor goes on to describe early incidents there, "One of my first visits was to the British consulate. The Consul-General (Bayley) was out but I was shown into the Vice-Consul's office where I was delighted to recognize Mr WA Smart, from whom I had taken over the Shiraz Consulate and whom I had last met halfway between Shiraz and Isfahan."

They compared notes and congratulated each other on the enjoyable coincidence. Then Smart decided O'Connor should make yet another call, to the man who had just been appointed Assistant Provost Marshall. "It was Colonel Frazer(sic) Hunter who had accompanied General Sykes' column for the relief of Shiraz as its Chief of Staff. It was extraordinary."[36]

There were many advantages living in New York rather than being on active service. There were many pleasures to be had from the quasi-diplomatic duties. Hunter was in contact with numerous influential American businessmen anxious to set up shop in Persia after the war and even had discussions with Morgan Shuster, the man who had proposed a Persian Treasury Gendarmerie and had wanted Claude Stokes to lead it. Nonetheless, the job was not to Hunter's liking. He wanted to be on his way again, back in the war, not involved in some part diplomatic, part secret role in sophisticated New York.

After talking to O'Connor he saw an opportunity. Lord Beaverbrook's Ministry of Information in London was unaware, when they appointed O'Connor to the Vladivostock office, that he was already committed by the Indian government to be the British Resident in Nepal later that year. He was an experienced Political Service officer and before being captured at Shiraz had, in addition military service on the Northwest Frontier, diplomatic experience as secretary and interpreter to the Commissioner, Francis Younghusband, in Curzon's Tibetan adventure. He spoke Chinese, Parvatiya, Persian, Pushtu, Russian and Tibetan and the Indian government did not want him, after his health had returned, at some job for Beaverbrook in Siberia.

As O'Connor saw it, Hunter would make an ideal replacement for him. He wrote John Buchan enthusiastically on July 3 "In the event of intervention taking place I would strongly recommend that Colonel Frazer Hunter, whom I met in New York and about whom

I wrote you, should be sent here. He could work with me while I am here and replace me when I leave. He is a most useful type of man and could take on my job. Consul (in New York, Bayley) knows him and entirely agrees. Will you discuss matter with Lord Beaverbrook."

At the end of July, in a telegram to the Director of Military Intelligence in London, O'Connor who had now arrived in Russia said, "I do not at present require any other British subject for military staff work which is much better conducted by Russians. But I shall require a larger staff and experts in various lines if my proposals are approved (they weren't). I urgently require meantime one suitable assistant. Some weeks ago I telegraphed John Buchan asking whether Colonel Frazer Hunter could be spared from New York. He would, I think, like to come and is just the type of man we want here. Will you try and arrange this please?"

On August 1st Sir Henry Mill Pellett, senior partner at Pellett and Pellett, stockbrokers at the Bank of Hamilton Building in Toronto, builder of Toronto's Casa Loma, and, like Hunter, a graduate of Upper Canada College, wrote a lengthy letter to Lord Beaverbrook warmly endorsing Hunter's efforts to serve in Russia[37]. Wrote Pellett, "....I thought you might be glad to have your own opinion regarding Colonel Hunter's merits confirmed by one who has had a lifelong opportunity of observing them, as I have."

At this point the British Medical Board in New York looked as if it might succeed in upsetting all of Hunter's and O'Connor's plans when they said that Hunter simply was not fit enough to strenuous duty and extended his sick leave, which was due to expire on August 16 to November 16. Hunter was appalled and made a special appeal to them. As a result they modified their recommendations to permit him to travel and serve in Russia. They were particularly anxious that he not serve in the tropics.

Hunter was getting impatient. A telegram to Lord Beaverbrook from Geoffrey Butler in New York - he would soon be succeeded by Sir John Hay Beith, who wrote novels under the name 'Ian Hay' - contained the terse sentence, "Unless you obtain immediate modification of his present orders he intends to act for release from his present duties and proceed to England forthwith."

Beaverbrook replied that they had asked for Hunter's services from the Indian government but had not received a reply. "I think it advisable that he should stay in New York until reply received since if he is going to Russia it is undesirable that he should cross the Atlantic twice. For a week longer Hunter, irritated and anxious, waited in New York. On July 31 the death knell sounded for his application. Said Beaverbrook, "....owing to the changed situation in Eastern Siberia we shall have to forego our requests for Colonel Hunter's services."

The British, in conjunction with their allies, had decided on military intervention in Siberia, as had the Americans and the Japanese - Canadians would join later. British troops of the Middlesex Regiment arrived in Vladivostock from Hong Kong on August 3 closely followed by the Japanese, then the French from Indo-China and the Americans from the Philippines. The Ministry of Information job became a civilian concern with O'Connor being replaced at the end of September by a John F Blair. One British army officer took over propaganda work in Western Siberia, but he was a subaltern.

Hunter, angry and disappointed, left for England on the liner "Empress of France". The voyage brought an unexpected bonus. There were many Americans on the voyage, one of them being a Red Cross nurse with the American Expeditionary Force, Katherine McFarland. She was from Illinois - born in Marseille, Illinois and educated in Ottawa, Illinois. Most important, she was passionately interested in horses, in riding and in racing. She and Fraser Hunter found they had a lot in common and the friendship flourished.

In London Hunter still hoped that he might be able to continue onto Russia, albeit at a later time. The only record that remains is from Hugh Walpole who had been one of the last British out of Petrograd. Walpole wrote, "Lord Beaverbrook would be glad if Mr Crookson would see Colonel Hunter who is at present at the Cavalry Cub to soothe his feelings."

What Crookson said to Hunter is not recorded yet a couple of days later, on October 2, Hunter went again to the Ministry of Information with a request to take a party of Americans to the Western Front. On his admission pass to the Ministry building he noted that he would probably required later for Russia, Persia or the USA.[38]

The American party which Hunter saw as an opportunity to get into a more active area included William Edgar, editor of the Minneapolis Bellman and Northwestern Miller and an expert on raw materials for warfare, Herbert Hoover, the American Food Comptroller and future President, Dwight Morrow, lawyer and future ambassador whose daughter would marry the aviator, Charles Lindbergh, and the lawyer, Clarence Darrow, all of them regarded by the British as "ardent patriots".

Hunter did not get to take the Americans to the Western Front. One of the irons he had warming in the fire glowed hot for him. Quite out of the blue - metaphorically and almost literally - he was on October 14 appointed Assistant Chief of Staff (G2) to the First American Army Air Service - the same day that his new commander, "Billy" Mitchell, was promoted from Colonel to Brigadier General reporting to General Hunter Liggett who had just stepped into the shoes of General John Pershing - now Army Group Commander - as commander of the First American Army. Pershing was named Army Group Commander.

Back in Siberia O'Connor ran afoul of authority. He had to go to Nepal on behalf of the Indian government - something the Ministry of Information had not been aware of when they appointed him. Instead of traveling by sea to India and then overland to his new post, O'Connor had the grand idea of traveling overland all the way - Vladivostock to Samara, then on to Orenburg and through Turkestan to India distributing propaganda material all the way. Beaverbrook's office was not amused. "Seeing that you have already drawn in full salary and expenses up to 3 October, all we can agree to is the actual cost of your journey by shortest route from Vladivostock to nearest Indian port. We disclaim all responsibility in the event of your pension from Indian government being in any way prejudiced by your late return."

O'Connor gave up. He decided upon reflection that his journey was impractical and that he would return by sea. Not all considered it impractical or impossible. On 30 September 1918, General Knox, head of the British Military Mission in Russia, sent a message to the War Office which showed that among generals "dreams may exceed their grasp" and that the "Great Game" still loomed large. "I suggest", he wrote, "you consider feasibility of employing our Brigade or part of it immediately on arrival (Bn from India will reach Vladivostock Nov 15 and Canadians at end of December.) to clean up Turkestan in combination with Dutov's Cossacks. Our troops would rail through via Samara and Tashkent. In the meantime we could gain control of the Kaspian; Turkestan and northern Afghanistan would be permanently protected from German influence. Canadians would be railed back to Rov Vollga in time for spring operations."

One must wonder if O'Connor seeded this idea. The DMO had noted, "Unfortunately there appears to be no prospect of getting this excellent project accepted." Various staff notes were attached. One of them may have been enough to ensure that the Canadians did not take this train ride through Asia. It gave the distance for the journey via Vladivostock, Cheliabinsk, Samara, Orenburg, Tashkent, Samarkand, Bokhara and Merv to Krasnavodsk as 7,089 miles.

In New York, meantime, Colonel Norman Thwaites, senior Secret Intelligence Service operative in the USA had, as part of the whole reorganization of the Intelligence function, been appointed Assistant Provost Marshal to the United States, the second one, taking over where Hunter left off.

While O'Connor was heading direct for Katmandu, Fraser Hunter was heading by rail across France to the headquarters of the First American Army Air Service at Verdun. The Argonne-Meuse offensive was underway and he wanted to be there.

Western Front

Even today flying has a glamour not shared by other branches of the service and during the First World War it attracted young men over all other forms of military service. Aviation was the elite branch; fliers moved in a mysterious technical world of their own and the heroes were romantic aces who, flying ten thousand feet high at a hundred and fifty miles an hour, engaged their enemy in a combat to the death somewhat after the style of medieval knights.

Nowhere was the appeal of combat aviation more keenly felt than among the young Americans. Late into the war the American zest and enthusiasm were a tonic for the exhausted allies, numbed by three years of fruitless slaughter. Americans who had joined the war earlier by becoming soldiers in the French Foreign Legion were formed into the famous Escadrille Lafayette Squadron. Just about every young American volunteer, hard drilled in the boot camps prior to embarkation, looked skyward and was convinced that his future was in flying and not the infantry. There were quite literally thousands of volunteers for the Air Service.

When Hunter arrived in France it was to join this glamorous elite. He had been appointed Assistant Chief of Staff (G2) to the United States Air Service commanded by Brigadier General William Mitchell, and his particular duty was to assemble military information about the enemy, prepare and issue maps and have done the survey work necessary for the accurate pinpointing of targets. Staff officers in the American Air Service at that time had the additional responsibility of commanding the troops in their branch. Unlike many other staff officers, and this was probably influential in obtaining the appointment, Hunter may have been able to fly, and possibly had learned to do so with his friend Shakespear back in India. This put him in a particularly advantageous position with the young flyers who milled around headquarters; although an old man - after all, he was by then forty two - he would have learned to fly in the earliest days of aviation, when his young Americans were scarcely out of their prams.

Hunter immediately reported to the American headquarters that had recently moved to the shattered city of Verdun. Verdun was the location of one of the longest and bloodiest battles of the War. During 1916 it had absorbed most of the energy of both France and Germany and more than seven hundred thousand were killed or wounded there. In the Meuse Valley, between the forests of the Argonne and Woevre, it commanded the route to Paris and had been a fortress since the days of the Romans. The French fortifications there included artillery turrets set in concrete forts lying almost at ground level and were the linchpin of the entire allied trench system, extending from the English Channel to Switzerland. The German General, Von Falkenhayn had attempted to smash the French army at Verdun, to turn the city into a vast slaughterhouse and break the will of the French army to resist further. The French, under General Petain, held despite appalling casualties. An Anglo-French offensive on the Somme in July had compelled Falkenhayn to divert forces northwards and the German offensive had failed - yet it was the immense casualties suffered by the French in holding Verdun and blocking the road to Paris that triggered a series of military mutinies in the French army a year later.

The French had held at Verdun because of the calm and methodical leadership of General Petain and because the narrow road from Bar-le-Duc, forty miles to the south and the main artery for supplies, held. Because the road was held, Verdun held, and the road that saved it acquired the name of la Voie Sacree - the Sacred Road.

Two years later, in the summer of 1918, the French were still in Verdun, the Americans were holding the front further south, and the land between, the Germans held the St-Mihael salient. In September the Americans attacked northwards into this salient. General Pershing's troops performed excellently and by the end of the first day had captured most of their second day objectives. There is little doubt that the Americans could have kept on advancing but they had to be halted - Pershing was committed to the Argonne offensive and his men had to be quickly moved to a new location. Before the Argonne offensive could be launched nearly a quarter of a million men of the French Second Army in the vicinity of Verdun had to be moved out of the sector to allow six hundred thousand Americans to move in. Brilliant staff work accomplished this prodigious move smoothly and nine American divisions prepared to attack.

In the early hours of September 26 Pershing's First Army moved forward. By evening the Germans had been driven back five miles along the Meuse and two miles into the Argonne Forest but after that the Americans, and the French further along the front and the British at Cambrai, were reduced to a grueling series of frontal attacks.

It was during this period of incessant frontal hammering that Hunter arrived at Pershing's headquarters. General Pershing occupied the same room in the town hall where Petain had directed the defense of Verdun. The road that passed in front of the town hall was "the sacred road". The American divisions, all of them, within a few weeks, were victims of a condition familiar to all allied infantry - the autumn rains turned the roads into a quagmire of mud.

Once the planes were in the air mud was not a hazard for the Air Service - but the weather conditions that caused it - the rain, fog and low cloud - were. They made Hunter's responsibilities for mapping and survey reconnaissance particularly difficult. The Americans depended on allied planes - piloted by Americans - for combat and pursuit work and the Americans supplied the allies with Liberties for observation and bombing. While the infantry struggled in the mud, steadily pounding the southern flank of a German pocket extending into France, the Air Service was active day and night in the final offensive of the war. Two squadrons were assigned to day work and one to night reconnaissance. Airplanes penetrated deep behind enemy lines. The Germans were kept under constant surveillance. Hunter's work was invaluable. Four command teams were kept constantly on duty at the Air Service headquarters and were called upon to perform almost every class of mission.

During this period Hunter, although a staff officer, was in one of the planes either as gunner or pilot. He took off, apparently attacked the enemy and shot down three enemy Fokkers. He received from the French the Croix de Guerre.[39]

It was the meticulous reconnaissance work that was great valuable.

To cite the history of the American Air Service, American Expeditionary Force,

"Of particular value were photographs taken before and after fire on these points by army artillery at Montmedy, Longway, Spincourt, Dommary-Baroncourt and Conflams. Though these important stations were protected by concentrations of anti-aircraft artillery and pursuit planes, they were successfully photographed, allowing (our) artillery to fire effectively during the attack.....Air photographic units made an average of from 2,500 to 3,500 prints day for each army corps. Photography was found to be of great advantage not only in keeping track of the enemy, his operations, concentrations and movements, but also the greatest advantage in advising our staff of the location of our own units."

"With relatively green troops, unaccustomed to keeping in touch with one another in such a large operation as at the Argonne and working in heavily wooded, rough country, and in which there were few roads or channels of communication, it was of great advantage to have pictures from the air.....In one of our Air Service operations during the Argonne it was learned that a large German force was massing for a counter attack at a time which was critical to our forces which had advanced materially but had not yet consolidated. The Air Service stepped into the breach and by the use of 170 planes conducted a major offensive from the air against the ground troops who were massing for the counter-attack. During that operation 39 tons of bombs were dropped. We suffered no loss of our planes and in addition to tremendous destruction on the ground of the enemy troops, twelve enemy airships were destroyed and a large number of others driven out of control. The counter-attack was prevented."

With the German surrender on November 11 the long process of repatriation of enlisted soldiers and their return to their homes began. For far too many, in particular Canadians, it took far too long. The year immediately following the war was often one of disappointment and anguish. Once the initial jubilation was over disappointment became widespread; disappointment that military affairs took too long to wind down, disappointment that the brave new world was eluding the victors, was added to anguish caused by a worldwide and massive influenza epidemic that took thirty million lives.

"HE IS CERTAINLY A CANADIAN..."

While most army officers were considering their options for civilian life, Hunter's view of the future was less uncertain. He had a regular commission in the Indian Army and was also a member of the prestigious Survey of India, a membership that had been interrupted but not ended by the war. Before he returned to India to rejoin the Survey he wanted to examine some of the alternatives. His first military duty after war's end was in Paris for a couple of months as the American Air Service, headquartered on the Rue de Constantine, had more than eleven thousand men to demobilize. After that, England.

For the first week in England he stayed at his club, the United Services Club on Pall Mall in London and for a while after that with Admiral Sir David Beatty, the First Sea Lord, at his home in Brooksby Hall in Leicestershire.⁴⁰ It is probable that Admiral Beatty knew of Hunter because of his views on both Russia and India and may well have been aware of Hunter's report from Russia on actions that could be taken, actions that included intervention.

The principal international issue that Beatty was involved in at this time was the War of Intervention in Russia since it involved keeping a large number of warships in the Baltic, at Archangel, in the Black Sea and the Caspian as well as in the Far East. There was also a strong possibility that King George would offer the Vice-Royalty of India to Beatty in succession to Lord Chelmsford. However, according to Beatty's mistress, Eugenie, the King knew that Beatty's wife's health was poor and a stay in India would make it worse.

While in London Hunter was invited to dinner at Lady Paget's new home. Muriel Paget, before her marriage to Sir Richard Paget Bt, had been Lady Muriel Evelyn Vernon Finch-Hatton. She was the only daughter of the 12th Earl of Winchelsea and a bundle of dynamic energy. Since returning from Russia this formidable lady had been living at the former home of an old friend, Sir Starr Jamesson - of the "Jamesson Raid" fame or notoriety - who had died while Lady Paget was in Russia.

Lady Paget had finally got back to England from the United States in May of 1918. Her work with the Voluntary Aid Detachment in Russia was ended by the Revolution and her hospitals closed down. She now concentrated her energies on relief work in Slovakia and with the Rumanian Red Cross. Harold Nicolson, who was one of the British delegates to Paris for the Peace Conference, remembers meeting her there in February while she was heading by train to Slovakia. He recalled, "Her energy is terrifying. She sends Prime Ministers scuttling at her behest."

Two weeks after this she back in London again and arranging a small dinner party. Among the guests were Lady Curzon, wife of the former Viceroy of India who was at that time Lord President of the Council and in the War Cabinet and was soon to be Foreign Secretary, and Fraser Hunter.

The conversation at the dinner party would have been wide ranging. Certainly included would have been the lively and popular topic that had been raging since war's end and had been first raised in the Cabinet by Lord Curzon - the topic of "Hang the Kaiser". The popular demand to punish Kaiser Wilhelm was both spontaneous and vigorous; throughout the war the Kaiser had been vilified as the man most responsible for all the misery and all the suffering of the world's worst war. Why, the public demanded to know, should an ordinary soldier who, because of exhaustion or falling asleep on duty, have been executed - and many were - while the man who was responsible for it all be allowed to live in luxurious exile? Another topic would have been reparations - the extent to which the Germans should be made to pay. Another was the slow pace of demobilization and the fear - terribly real at the time - of "red revolution". It is easy now to disparage a fear that never materialized. Yet the war had wrecked the western world's social system; there was brooding and growing anger in the air and the possibility of revolution may not have been quite as remote as some now believe. Wrote Kipling – "All the world over, nursing their scars/ Sit the old fighting men, broke in the wars;/ All the world over, surly and grim/ Mocking the lilt of the conqueror's hymn."

There were mutinies in the army at the slow pace of demobilization and some units had formed Soldiers' Councils. In Luton in northern England there were riots and the Town Hall was burned down by a mob. A full-scale mutiny had broken out in Calais at the end of January, there were riots in Glasgow and Belfast, while in London, three thousand soldiers returning to France, had marched on Whitehall to express their grievances.

One topic, which may not have received attention at Lady Paget's, was India. Lord Curzon was not at the occasion and Lady Curzon had not been to India. She had married Curzon a couple of years earlier. His first wife, the former Mary Leiter of Washington, who had been Vicereine of India, died shortly after their return to England. It was not until 1916 that Curzon remarried, again to an American. Hunter did not have too much in common with her

- except that he knew the United States quite well, had traveled it from coast to coast, and his fiancé - by this time the shipboard romance had blossomed into a formal engagement with Katherine McFarland - was also an American. But the subject of Persia did crop up and Lady Curzon remarked to Hunter that her husband, although he had not been there for several years, was still deeply interested in the country.

A few days later Hunter wrote to Lady Curzon saying that he would like the opportunity of meeting her husband to discuss some ideas he had on the subject of Persia and that Lord Curzon might remember him as having worked with the late J.G. Lorimer on maps of the Persian Gulf for the Foreign Office in India. Hunter would be staying until the end of the following week with Sir David Beatty at Brooksby Hall but would then be back in London and at the United Services Club in Pall Mall.

Curzon and Hunter did not meet on that occasion, but did so socially about a week later, although Hunter did not have the opportunity to discuss Persia with Curzon since Hunter was called away from the party early in the evening. (What called Hunter away is unknown but it must surely be unusual that in those more formal days a "half colonel" would leave a function before a man second only to the Prime Minister)

On March 28 Hunter met with the Cabinet's specialist in Middle Eastern affairs, Lancelot Oliphant, who took Hunter's nine-page memorandum back to Curzon and also had a lengthy conversation with him. Oliphant knew quite a lot about Hunter and made a significant comment - for one so guarded in his words. "I have never met anyone" he wrote "who did not say that he (Hunter) did not have amazing influence over the Persians." Oliphant, who probably knew more about Persia than anyone in the British Civil

Service at that time added "From such reports as I have received Colonel Hunter has a very great influence over all Persians with whom he comes in contact and although somewhat impetuous himself has I think a very good working knowledge of the Persian. He is exceedingly keen and energetic."

Oliphant did not tell Hunter but did remark to Curzon that Hunter's views on the best course of action in Persia coincided in great measure with Curzon's own. Oliphant also remarked to Curzon that when Hunter had been in the United States the heads of about a dozen of the biggest commercial undertakings in the States had approached him regarding trade prospects in Persia after the war. All the Americans expressed the view that for successful commercial enterprises there need be a stable government and secure communications in the country. One of Hunter's fears, said Oliphant, was that once the Americans were in the country - and that might be inevitable - should there be any disorder then there would be political pressure upon Washington to intervene - it seemed that Morgan Shuster had touched upon this when he had met Hunter in New York. Oliphant agreed strongly with Hunter that there would be trouble if Persia were exploited by various independent commercial enterprises that were not necessarily in touch with the government.

Hunter told Oliphant that the two posts that must be held by Englishmen in the country were Financial Adviser and Commander in Chief of the Persian forces - a position he would be glad to hold himself - one of his assets was that he personally knew virtually all the prominent Persians. He added that he felt that Colonel Stokes might be better known in the north of the country. Hunter also drew Oliphant's attention to the presence in London of others who knew Persia well, and named particularly Major Thorburn - who had been his assistant when Chief of Staff with the South Persia Rifles - and Colonel Kennion.

Hunter impressed Oliphant. He saw in him the commander of some unified force in the country. Said Oliphant, "I do not disguise from myself the fact that he is so enthusiastic...that he is apt to be carried away.....He had differences of opinion with Sir P Sykes from whom he subsequently parted (but) his general views on Persia and the line which it would be desirable to take coincide in a very great measure with the line you are adopting." Lord Robert Cecil, brother of the young Lord Salisbury and at that time Under Secretary at the Foreign Office (Prime Minister Lloyd George was also Foreign Secretary and Lord Cecil reported to him), commented "He seemed to me, when I met him, to be an enthusiast but to have much sound sense."

The memorandum that went to Curzon covered nine pages and was entitled, "Suggestions for Action in Persia." The emphasis was to help Persia help herself. Hunter saw Persia as an advanced civilization compared with her neighbours, but the political weakness of the country made her vulnerable to Mesopotamia (now Iraq) and to turbulent Afghanistan, and also, and this was not without significance at the time, "to the ambitions of unseen movements in Central Asia." - Hunter was referring to the Pan-Turanian movement.

"Persia," he said, "cannot remain an unguarded route for freebooters on their way to the Mesopotanean plains, or a field of adventure for other raiders...." Hunter pointed out that Britain before the war had considered Persia left as a desert as the best safeguard against Russian and German intentions towards India. "This", said Hunter, "was unpardonably selfish. The policy of sacrificing weaker neighbours or of getting them to pull the chestnuts out, in order to avoid facing the costs of our own insurance stood us in little stead in 1914-15. No nation, either from her own point of view or from that of humanity, has any right to stifle and strangle the progress of another." These were strong words for an Indian Army half colonel to be writing to the most senior member of the Cabinet, next to the Prime Minister. Hunter was not prepared to leave it there. "Had Persia possessed sufficient railways and had Britain and Russia, instead of dismembering and bullying her, given her a helping hand in 1906, what a different story might have been written of the Russian front in 1917." Hunter continued, giving a lucid description of the potentials of Persia - oil was not excluded - and the ability of the country to raise much of the necessary capital itself, providing dishonest officials could be prevented from stealing so much of it - was Hunter thinking of Sir Percy Sykes' good friend Prince Farman Farma?

Hunter made cogent arguments for the regeneration of Persia and the need for British influence to predominate there and made suggestions that - either because he was listened to or because such ideas had already been formulated in London - were to materialize. Yet Hunter displayed directness of the type that had and would earn him enemies. "In the light of past events," blandly stated this Indian Army officer, "it is strongly urged that the control of the British mission in Persia should, under no circumstances, be placed in the hands of the Government of India but should be vested in that proper department of the Home (British) Foreign Office...... the actions of Indian officials in Persia will always be subservient to the aims of India."

Far from being shocked by these outspoken views, Curzon thought it encouraging that the minds of those who knew Persia - Major Hay Thorburn had been in touch as well - should be exercised over the future of the country. Wrote Curzon, "One point of Col

Hunter's is of importance. We hope to have a financial and military policy for Persia. We ought also to have a commercial. I do not mean that we should bag every concession for ourselves, but we should know in advance what industries we intend to push, and should organize the forces to do it. I trust that when the time comes we will find some employment for all these enthusiasts."

Hunter's memorandum achieved results.

Little more than a week later a confidential memorandum was sent from the Foreign Office to the Department of Overseas Trade stressing the need for a commercial policy towards Persia and raising the matter of railway construction in that country - something which would improve the general conditions of the countryside and facilitate commercial relations.

By this time Hunter's interest in Persia was temporarily distracted by forthcoming domestic events and on Saturday, May 17, he and Katherine McFarland were married at St George's Anglican Church in Hanover Square - the fashionable Mayfair church where Bernard Shaw's Eliza Doolittle would see her father married, if he could get to the church on time. Earlier weddings at St George's had included those of Percy Shelly, Benjamin Disraeli and Theodore Roosevelt.

A few months later Hunter, although slated to return to India, was expressing considerable interest in being appointed to the Anglo-Persian Military Commission being organized by the Foreign Office. Hunter was being advocated by no less an authority on the Middle East than Sir Percy Cox - by that time High Commissioner in Mesopotamia who had recently earned favour at the Foreign Office by preventing the Persians from formally attending the Versailles Peace Conference. Sir Percy, who would soon be appointed to Teheran himself, recommended as Chief Military Adviser to the Mission either General Dunsterville or General Dickson and Fraser Hunter as either Chief of Staff or Political Officer. Cox promoted Hunter's appointment forcefully. "Colonel Hunter" telegrammed Cox "has a strong personality, popular and sympathetic with Persians. Reason for trouble with General Sykes was latter's attitude in regarding SPR a British force. This should not militate against Hunter." But it did, although Oliphant wrote, "I venture to think that some of these characteristics would be of great utility to the Military Mission and Col Hunter's use to us in Persia should not be rendered impossible merely on the grounds that he did not hit it off with General Sykes, even though his CO there."

Lord Curzon said "a man of (Hunter's) nature would materially strengthen the body and in these circumstances cannot agree to his name being withdrawn." But there was strong objection to the appointment of Hunter, particularly from General Thwaites who had taken over as Director of Military Intelligence and Operations from General MacDonough.

Why Thwaites was so opposed to Hunter is not recorded but his opposition was determined and ultimately successful.[41] Nor did Thwaites want Dunsterville in command and proposed instead General Thomson. The Government of India had its views on the subject as well. They wanted Dickson to head the Mission rather than Dunsterville and felt that Hunter had displayed a lack of tack when with Sykes in Persia and would therefore not recommend him.[42]

Both Oliphant and Curzon strongly supported the nomination of Hunter. Said Oliphant, "I have seen a good deal of him and have formed a high opinion of his knowledge and experience of Persia and the Persians, with whom he gets on remarkable well. His position as Chief of Staff to General P Sykes was a difficult one and certainly they did not hit it off. I think, however, it would be most unfortunate if Col Hunter's experience etc were not used and with great respect I would urge that we support Sir Percy Cox's candidature of this valuable officer."

Lord Robert Cecil concurred and remarked that he had a rather favorable impression of Hunter. Curzon was supportive. "I always knew," he said "that the War Office would object to General Dunsterville... I think we should find out rather more about him (Hunter) before consenting to (Thwaites') abrupt extinguisher." Yet Thwaites continued in his opposition - although not in writing. There remains only a scribbled note after a meeting between the Foreign Office and War Office on the subject of the appointments. Said the Foreign Office notation – "They (Thwaites and the War Office staff) adhere to their view about Colonel Hunter. I understand they doubt he could work with other officers. He is certainly a Canadian and they seem bent on resisting his inclusion as likely to upset the Com (illegible but presumable Commission). They regard him as very much out for his own advancement. I have recorded before my views of this officer but do not wish to cause further delay in the dispatch of the Mission."

Hunter's difficulties with General Sykes was the obvious reason for the impediments to promotion. Yet perhaps not all. Hunter's earlier determination to leave the Indian Army and join the Survey of India gives some additional clues. He felt that he had "pressing reasons" which could have been financial for although Indian Army officers were paid at a higher rate than those in the British Army the cavalry of both armies expected their officers to have private (that is, unearned) income. This may seem odd today when being an army officer is to civilians much like being a member of any other profession. But in late-Victorian and early-Edwardian military society the officer class was about fifty percent composed of the aristocracy and the "landed gentry", generally people with private incomes derived from rural land, and by about fifty percent by sons of the professional middle class. Elite regiments generally had higher percentages of aristocrats and landed gentry. Hunter may well have had a Canadian or non-professional middle class aversion to those who received income they did not earn. Just as likely, perhaps even more likely, was that his friction with other officers was a consequence of "style".

In both the British and Indian army of that time there was an affectation, peculiar to the English, of seeking to achieve excellence without appearing to try very hard, to do well without being a specialist. Understatement was understood and appreciated. Self-deprecation and the laconic manner rather admired. Appearing to be too keen would have been disparaged as poor taste. Many army officers sought to appear as gentlemanly amateurs. This would have been quite alien to Hunter who saw himself as a professional. Hunter's professionalism could have been interpreted as self-advancement and instead of being understood for what it was become instead a major obstacle on the road to high rank.

The assignment left for Teheran with Major-General Dickson as "President", and Colonel Stokes as Chief of Staff - he would come down from Baku. Hunter would not have been aware of all the controversy surrounding his appointment but he would have known that his candidacy was being pressed. He and his wife were to have sailed from England to India on September 27th but Curzon and Oliphant only abandoned their efforts on his behalf on October 10th and Hunter's departure had been postponed until it was clear where his destination would be. The Royal Geographical Society had asked Hunter to give a paper on his making of the map of Arabia. He agreed and delivered his lecture in October, shortly before leaving for India.

It is only possible today to conjecture at Thwaites adamant rejection of Hunter as a member of the Mission. He hardly knew him personally. Possibly, but not likely, the objections emanated from Norman Thwaites, the man who had been running the Secret Service in New York and who followed Hunter as Provost Marshall in the USA after Hunter left New York for England. Despite their name, there was only a distant relationship between Colonel Thwaites and the DMI, General Thwaites. Yet they did know each other and in his autobiography, Colonel Norman Thwaites comments on meeting with General Sir William Thwaites before leaving for New York to take up the post as Assistant Provost Marshal. Superficially at least, Hunter and Colonel Thwaites had areas of strong common interest. Both were cavalry officers - Thwaites had been a cavalryman in the South Africa War - both were keen polo players - Thwaites mentions Hunter in his book, Velvet and Vinegar, as playing polo with him in some prestigious game in the States. Both would ultimately try for political office – though unlike Hunter Thwaites was not elected. Both were keenly interested in flying and coincidentally, Thwaites as well as later becoming editor of "Air" magazine, also became Secretary of the Air League in England while Hunter became President of the Air League in Canada[43].

It is more likely that the objections to Hunter by General Thwaites were rooted in the stylistic differences noted earlier as well as the controversy between Hunter and Sir Percy Sykes and the fact that Hunter, not one to call a spade by any other name, would have antagonized many by the forcefulness and possibly even the abrasiveness of his opinions.

There is some mystery concerning Hunter's activities at this time. In replying to the Royal Geographical Society accepting their invitation to present a paper, Hunter asked for Colonel Lawrence's address (Lawrence of Arabia) as "Colonel Hogarth is anxious that I meet him". Why Hogarth - head of the Arab Bureau in Cairo during the war - and as such the chief of allied intelligence in that area - and now involved with Middle Eastern events at the Peace Conference in Paris - should have wanted Hunter and Lawrence of Arabia to meet is not clear. Nor is it known whether or not they did. Hunter was a longstanding and active member of the RGS by this time and would certainly have known another active Fellow at this period. This was Coote-Hedley, formerly of Map Publications in the Survey of India and subsequently head of MI4 in London.

Despite the ambiguities in this period of Hunter's life, what is known is that he and his wife Katherine left for India in the late Fall of 1919 and that both of them turned up in Teheran in the following Spring having reached there via India and Baghdad - Hunter was be the liaison between Norperforce and the Persian Cossacks led by the flamboyant Russian, Colonel Starosselski, a move probably engineered by Sir Percy Cox.

WITH THE COSSACKS

The war had resulted in horrifying consequences for Persia. Although Persia was ostensibly neutral, Russian troops had rampaged their way through the northwest into Turkey and to the Mesopotamian borders. Turkish troops had invaded the west, Russian had occupied the northeast and the British the borders of Afghanistan - and after the Russian Revolution had taken over the area that had been controlled by the Russians. The British had occupied parts of southwest Persia and the British officered South Persia Rifles had patrolled and enormous area of southern Persia. In the Gilan forests of the northwest an Iranian nationalist leader, Mirza Kuchik Khan, controlled the countryside with a body of partisans called Jangalis dedicated to ejecting foreign forces from their country. Predatory tribesmen throughout the country harassed townsmen and villagers, and German agents - in particular Wassmuss - led tribal levies trying to dominate the countryside. After March 1917, the disintegrating Russian army brought still more havoc to the countryside as deserting soldiers, and often whole units, killed their officers, struggled northwards, an undisciplined and murderous mob, back towards Russia, on their way robbing the already famished villagers of food and other supplies.

As a direct consequence of war two million of Persia's twelve million population died. Many succumbed to the great influenza outbreak and others starved to death when ruined farms and looted warehouses failed to feed them. Unlike Russians, Turks or Germans, the British in Persia made efforts to alleviate the starvation – Dunsterville's force on its way north from Baghdad to Baku made enormous efforts to stave off starvation in the towns and villages through which it passed. But the scale of the problem was simply too great for their efforts to make much of an impact.

The Revolution in Russia had inevitable consequences upon Russians in Persia. The principal one was the gradual but total disintegration of the Russian army – the army that had fought its way into Turkey and, further south, to the borders of Mesopotamia. Only one body of Russians remained intact – these were Cossacks under the command of Colonel Bickerakhov who had all taken a personal oath of allegiance to their commander and who would follow him when he allied himself with British General Dunsterville who briefly occupied Baku and later, when he tried to join his brother who was fighting with the White Army against the Bolsheviks. But Bickerakhov's men, though allied to the British, were really a band of independent marauders, representing no one save themselves.

In northern Persia there remained one force which, though inefficient and riddled with intrigue, was a legal body with a legitimate association with Russia – whatever its government – the Persian Cossacks, a force of about five thousand Persian cavalry and infantry at that time, with both Persian and Russian officers and under the command of a Russian.

Fraser Hunter may well have known its commander from his days in Russia and the collapse of the Kornilov coup outside Petrograd. The notorious "Wild Division", which Kornilov had relied upon to seize Petrograd, was composed entirely of Moslems from the Caucasus and officered by Caucasians and Russians. Being exempt from military service, the Moslems were volunteers and the Division was organized into six cavalry regiments – according to the tribes they contained. Thus there were Tatar, Daghestan, Chechnyn, Ingush, Osset and Kabarda regiments. The commander of the Tatar regiment was Colonel Starosselski. Kerensky fired Colonel Starosselski - along with many other officers of that Division - when Kornilov's coup collapsed, and he was sent home. In another, quite unconnected event, Kerensky ordered the replacement of the commander of the Persian Cossacks, a right-wing member of the old guard and no longer representative of the new Russian government. Kerensky put in his place a liberal officer named Colonel Clerge.

Heading south to take up his new appointment Clerge passed through Tiflis where he met an old friend - none other than Starosselski, who was kicking his heels in forced retirement and looking hard for a new appointment. Starosselski persuaded Clerge to arrange for his appointment as second-in-command of the Persian Cossacks.

Clergue was something of a liberal. Furthermore, his views about the Persian Cossacks were similar to Hunter's views of the South Persian Rifles. Clerge believed - and did not hesitate to expound his views to the Persians - that Persia was a sovereign nation, not an extension of Russia, that the Persian Cossacks were a Persian force formed to serve Persian interests, and that the Russian officers training them were serving Persia and would ultimately return to Russia. Starosselski kept silent at first, but to him this smacked of treason against Russia and he was able to persuade some of the Persian officers that Clerge was not a liberal but a communist preaching ideas that would result in their own eventual downfall as well as that of their division and their country.

Starosselski confided his fears in one particular Persian officer - a forty-one year old Iranian whose twenty-year old wife had just given him twins, one a boy named Mohammed. This officer, a forceful and impressive personality, was Colonel Reza Khan - later he would adopt the name Pahlevi. Reza Khan, with Starosselki's encouragement, decided that Clerge must go. Early one evening, while Clerge was having tea, Cossacks surrounded his quarters and arrested him. Reza Khan had a carriage take Clerge to the port of Enzeli (later named Pahlevi) and put on a boat to Russia. Starosselski placed himself in command of the Cossacks and Reza Khan was promoted to the rank of Brigadier commanding the Teheran Brigade.

The military and financial missions from Britain arrived in Teheran in the spring of 1920 and, although he was not a member of them, so did Fraser Hunter and his wife, Katherine. Hunter's position was somewhat ambiguous. He had been appointed by the British to the Imperial Persian Army; a liaison officer between British troops in the country (Norperforce) and the Persian forces - essentially the Cossacks - and the likelihood is that this position had been engineered by Cox, supported by Curzon, and was designed to keep an eye on Russian activities in the north. Curzon feared - and with good reason - that although the Cossacks were Persian and their officers not well disposed to the Bolsheviks at home, their loyalty was nonetheless still to Russia, whatever its government. The end of the war and the collapse of Russia presented Britain with an admirable opportunity to extend its influence, and thereby offset the advance towards India made by the Russians through the 1907 Convention. Hunter was the man to do the job and to report on Starosselski's activities.

Britain had signed a very favorable treaty, the Anglo-Iranian Treaty, but it had not been ratified by the Persian Parliament - the Majles - nor would it be. British troops were still in Mesopotamia where many of the tribes were in revolt against them, but the military position in Persia was patchy. In the northeast corner of the country, a British force - Indian Army - known sometimes as "Malmis", after the mission commander, General Malleson, was stationed at Meshed. Further north the Bolshevik Revolution had spread throughout Central Asia, and there was a Bolshevik government firmly in control at Tashkent enthusiastically supported by the Russian settlers. Nevertheless, in the deserts surrounding the towns the Turkomen tribes had totally rejected communism. In the spring and summer of 1918 - when, on the Western Front final victory was nowhere in sight - the British had sent a small force under General Dunsterville north from Mesopotamia into Persia where it was to rally the tribes as a force to prevent the Turks from moving eastward into the vacuum created by the Russian collapse. Dunsterville went onto Baku - with a number of Canadians in his force - and briefly held it. As an extension of this block against the movement of the Turks eastward - and ultimately into Afghanistan and India - Malleson's force was in Meshed.

To Malleson's south, patrolling the Persian-Afghan border as far south as Baluchistan was the so-called East Persian Cordon, a small military force to prevent gun-running to the tribes of Afghanistan and to prevent German agents, such as Niedermayer, from reaching Afghanistan where they sought to bring the Afghans to war. This body was for some time commanded by General Dyer - soon after the war ended to win notoriety by firing on and killing many Indians in the city of Amritsar. Before the war ended General Dickson had taken over and thus, when he went to Teheran in 1920 leading the Military Mission, he knew a great many Persians well.

On the western side of Persia the military problem was compounded by events in Mesopotamia. At the end of the war Mesopotamia, along with other segments of the Ottoman Empire, was to be a Mandate administered by the British. The area of

Mesopotamia had for years been of critical importance to the British. Before the war the Persian Gulf had almost been an English pond and British commercial interests predominated in the Mesopotamian area of the Ottoman Empire. When Turkey was friendly with the British there was sufficient security for the route to India. However, when Turkey joined Germany in the war it was essential to British interests - oil in particular - and the security of India that the lower Tigris and Euphrates Valley be secured.

During and following the war the growth of Arab nationalism, and Bolshevik-promoted resistance to imperialism, was felt throughout the Arab lands. This complex situation was made still more difficult by the rivalry between London - and the Cairo "Arabists" such as Hogarth, Lawrence and other officers of the Arab Bureau - and the Indian government officials who were openly critical of them. In July 1920 an Iraqi rebellion broke out. The Iraqi nationalists murdered many British political officers who were manning lonely posts and quite unprotected, and scores of soldiers, most of them under-trained recruits were killed.

While the Iraqi revolt was raging - Cox who engineered the throne for the Hashemite emir, Faisal, eventually ended it - Hunter was in Persia. Part of the British Mesopotamian force was a substantial body under General Champain, known as Norperforce and stationed in North-West Persia. The Iraqi revolt isolated it from its base in Baghdad and it was uncertain of any support it might receive from the Cossacks should it ever need any. This uncertainty can be seen in a note which survives from those days and was written by a junior company officer of the Gurkha Rifles about six weeks after Hunter had joined the Cossacks. "18th May. 1700 hrs. Armed and mounted Persians Cossacks, about 25 commanded by one Russian officer, arrive verst 12 from Resht. I train Lewis gun on them and go out and ask them what they want. They go back to Hasanrud Bridge and stay there until dark."⁴⁴ Not the words of trusting allies.

The Russians with the Cossacks had reason to be distrustful of the British. One of the first actions by General Dickson, after the Military Mission reached Persia, was to ask the Russian officers to hand over their force to the British. They naturally refused - though of course they knew that their wages were being paid, via the Persian treasury, by British subsides.

Events in north Persia were complicated by two disturbances - one world shattering the other local. Russia had been embroiled in civil war since shortly after the Bolsheviks had seized power and White Russian resistance to the Bolshevik seizure of power had centred, in the south, on General Deniken. Some of Deniken's ships on the Caspian Sea had escaped, as the White forces were being driven back, to the Persian port of Enzeli, occupied at that time by British troops of General Champain.

Starosselski saw an opportunity to redeem himself in the eyes of the new government of Russia and the Bolsheviks informed him that, if he would help their forces in the invasion of Persia, then he would be allowed to pass through Russia with all his considerable wealth on his way to anywhere in the world he wanted to settle. Russian troops, a small body of them, landed in Mazanderan province and Starosselki and his Cossacks went ostensibly to drive them out. Starosselski told the Russians that they had landed in an unsuitable place if they wanted to be able to march on Teheran; they would do better to land at Enzeli from where they could not only recover their ships but also, if they chose, march on Teheran. The Russians agreed and withdrew. Starosselski was hailed as a hero in Persia for defeating the invading force and promoted to command all Persian forces. Then the Russians landed at Enzeli.

The Bolsheviks told Champain that they wanted the ships back and were prepared to invade to get them. Champain decided that he did not have sufficient strength to resist and withdrew inland placing his troops at Kasvin and at Zanjan on the Kazvin to Tabriz road.

On May 18 the Bolsheviks landed at Enzeli, took the town and the ships. The Cossacks attacked - this time seriously - and captured several prisoners while others of the invading force continued to hold the town or fled into the forests and joined the partisans.

It was in the forests that a local enterprise complicating affairs in Persia was active. This was the nationalist uprising of Kuchik Khan that had begun in 1915 and had received German and Turkish support. Kuchik Khan and his partisans were called the Jangalis. Kuchik Khan's closest advisor was the German agent, von Paschen,

The Jangalis dominated Gilan province, robbed banks and landowners to finance their operations and captured the British intelligence agent, Captain Noel - the same Noel who had almost captured Wassmuss and who had attempted the rescue of the prisoners of Shiraz. When General Dunsterville went through the area in 1918 on his way to Baku, Kuckik Khan was compelled to allow them passage and to release Noel - and to expel his German and Turkish advisors. With the war ended, Kuchik Khan needed new allies. He found them in the Bolsheviks across the border. Yet he distrusted these revolutionaries. A Moslem and an Iranian nationalist, alliance with the Bolsheviks was not to his taste at all but after the Russian invasion and against his personal inclinations, he declared the Soviet Republic of Gilan and telegrammed Lenin his support.

Kuchik Khan's fears were soon realized. Bolshevik agents dominated the Iranian nationalist Jangalis. There were numerous and perfunctory trials, many hundreds of property owners, army officers, intellectuals, merchants and schoolteachers were executed. Kuchik Khan was horrified by the excesses of his Bolshevik allies and determined to break with them. On August 12 he did so and while the Iranian nationalist element of the Jangalis reasserted control the Bolshevik supporters fled to Resht, looting and burning as they went, then to the port of Enzeli, to wait a better opportunity.

Starosselski, with Hunter alongside, now struck hard. First the Bolsheviks in Resht had to be driven out. They not only dominated the town but were holding the Italian consul prisoner. On August 24 the Cossacks, with Hunter at their head, stormed into Resht. Within a few hours the town was recaptured, Starosselski had gathered up a considerable quantity of loot, including a large number of rifles, ammunition, bombs and gasoline. The Italian consul was freed, and five hundred Bolshevik troops of the 11th Russian Army that had been organized in Azerbijan, were taken prisoner; thirty had been killed in the attack. The Cossacks lost only one man.

The details of Hunter's actions in that attack are not recorded in detail.

Starosselski recommended to the Persian government that he be awarded the Persian Military Medal for gallantry while part of the advanced guard of Cossacks attacking the town. Hunter was modest when describing events to a reporter in Toronto many years later (to Frederick Griffin, Feb 23, 1935) It was, he said, for capturing four guns with cavalry at Resht. "I was commanding the Persian Cossacks. Instead of sticking to the road we went around through the swamp and bush. There was nothing much to it. Just horse sense, but the Persians thought it was good."

The Persian government approved the award of the Nishan-I-Shujahi-I-Tala'a (the sign of bravery in gold) and a year later, long after Starosselski had fallen from favor and left Persia, this award was confirmed by a warrant from the government." It was said to have been the only time this medal was awarded to a British officer. (A year later the question of Hunter receiving this award was raised with Curzon. Regulations had been enacted stating that "fighting services subsequent to the signature of the German Peace Treaty cannot be considered grounds for acceptance of foreign decorations" Hunter was told to return the medal." He did not do so and today, his award called "the Gold Medal of Persia" is on display, along with his many other awards, at the Canadian Legion building in Durham, Ontario.)

Starosselski's good fortune did not continue. Kuchik Khan had not moved to support his erstwhile allies in Resht and seemed set on maintaining a neutral attitude for a while so the following day Starosselski moved on towards the port of Enzeli not realizing that the Bolsheviks had been reinforced by substantial supplies, in particular heavy trench mortars and four inch howitzers from Baku.

When the Cossacks advanced from Resht about eight miles along the road to Enzeli they came under heavy fire. At this point the road reaches the sea, curves left and runs parallel with the coast until it reaches the port. The Bolsheviks on the land bombarded the Cossacks with mortars and howitzers while from the Caspian, Russian ships hammered their rear and a flotilla of armed small craft manned by Reds fired on their flanks from the lagoon of Enzeli harbour.

Later, reminiscing in Toronto, Hunter claimed that the fighting had won them the fishery station of Sufid Rud and "the finest caviar in the world. "We fought," he said, "seven battles to get that caviar."

Reza Khan, standing on an exposed hill with the bugler, tried to rally the Cossacks whose morale had remained quite good despite the setback. Yet once the order to withdraw was given the retreat became a rout. The Cossacks streamed back into Resht, through the town and out onto the road to Kasvin - where a British force was stationed. Technically the British were neutral in what was seen as an exclusive concern of the Persians. In reality they were not. British aircraft, which had not been able to help the Cossacks in their attack on Resht because of low cloud, were now able to take off and made a bombing raid on the Russian ships in Enzeli Harbour, and made two direct hits on oil boats there.

Hunter, Reza Khan and the other Persian Cossacks who had initially captured Resht, reorganized south of the town on the Kasvin road just north of the Manjil Bridge, which was held by a small body of British troops as an advanced guard from Kasvin. Hunter may never have become aware of a strange coincidence that now occurred. While he and the Cossacks were on their bleak hill between the Menjil Bridge and the Bolsheviks were in Resht they were cautiously observed by the British detachment holding the bridge. These were men of the Chestnut Troop of the Royal Horse Artillery. Major van Straubenzee commanded them. A Canadian, Arthur Bowen van Straubenzee had graduated from the Royal Military College of Canada in Kingston in 1911 and was commissioned into the Royal Artillery. His father had also been at Kingston and had joined the Royal Engineers - he was later acting governor of Bermuda - and his uncle, Casimir Cartwright van Straubenzee was also a cadet at Kingston and was an instructor in artillery there at the time when Hunter was a cadet.

Major van Straubenzee would later report that he had made no contact with the Cossacks forward of his position and it is unlikely that he knew that one of the Kingston alumnae was part of what probably appeared by that time to be a disorganized rabble.

Starosselski called his officers together and made a passionate speech on the need for self-sacrifice and struggle against the Bolsheviks. There was a surprising objection from the assembled officers. Reza Khan was not prepared to be so easily coerced. He demanded to know what Starosselski's long term plans were before he was prepared to sacrifice anything more of himself. The meeting broke up. It has been suggested that the junior officers, who knew nothing of Starosselski's earlier dealings with Bolsheviks, supported him, while Reza Khan had been tipped off by the British that Starosselski was still dealing with the Bolsheviks in order to keep his options open. Dickson, the head of the British Military Mission, had met Reza Khan and was impressed by him. It certainly suited British interests to have the Russian officers discredited. Hunter was a Persian nationalist and if Starosselski was double dealing it is likely that Hunter told Reza Khan of it and gave some impetus to Starosselski's decline and Reza Khan's rise in power.

The Cossacks continued desultory skirmishing around Resht but they were demoralized. Not only had they been driven back after the elation of their victory at Resht but they were being badly affected by malaria. Only a few months earlier they had been held in considerable esteem by the Persians, government and people - largely because an earlier success had followed upon the dismal showing of Norperforce. It had certainly not gone unnoticed by the Persians that the British had withdrawn from Enzeli and Resht in the face of Bolshevik threats despite considerable strength. Brigadier General Champain's North Persian Force, the 36th Indian Brigade consisted of the Chestnut Troop of the Royal Horse Artillery, the Guides Cavalry, two batteries of Indian mounted artillery, a company of sixteen armoured cars, the 2nd Battalion the York and Lancashire Regiment, the 1st Battalion the Royal Berkshire Regiment, the

2nd Gurkha Rifles, the 122nd Rajput Regiment, the 42nd Deoli Regiment and a flight of RAF. Where this force had failed - in the eyes of the Persians - their Cossacks had succeeded. Now they too had failed. Morale was declining fast.

A neat opportunity had presented itself for the British to finally get rid of the Russian officers of the Persian Cossack Brigade. The recent failures were a consequence of the incompetence of the Russian officers, said the British. More than that, they were also corrupt, robbing the Persians to supplement their pay. The British held the trump card; they were paying the Cossacks through subsidies to the Persian government. Britain did not want to be involved in any fighting in Persia so that while the Reds still threatened Teheran or while Kuchik Khan's partisans in Gilan appeared able to topple the government it was essential that the Cossack force be maintained.

The War Office had also decided to replace General Champain and by the end of September his replacement, General Edmund Ironside, had arrived in Teheran. Ironside had had an incredibly romantic career. He was probably the man upon whom John Buchan's principal hero of "The 39 Steps" - Richard Hannay - was modeled. Ironside was a determined young general on the rise - by the beginning of the Second World War he would be Chief of the Imperial General Staff - and he was not going to have British activities in Persia complicated by Russians in the north. Events had presented him with the perfect opportunity to rid northern Persia of Russian influence. He was determined that Starosselski must go. Like Dickson, he too was impressed by Reza Khan. Events were working in his favor; some four hundred of Kuchik Khan's men were openly assisting the Cossacks and the inhabitants of the countryside were clearly anti-Bolshevik. At the end of September a General Tolstov, Ataman of the Ural Cossacks, and some two hundred officers, remnants of the Ural Cossacks fighting for the Whites in Russia, escaped into Persia after great difficulties and privations getting through the Caucasus. They had seen the Bolshevik suppression of a Tartar rising in Azerbijan where estimates were that the Bolsheviks had, while suppressing it, massacred some fifteen thousand Tartar men, women and children. The Ural Cossacks were very pro-British and offered their services to Norperforce. Furthermore, on September 22 the Persian Cossacks again captured Resht with a force of three hundred cavalry and eight hundred infantrymen. But they soon they lost the town again. Starosselski claimed to have fought long and hard to hold on to the town. Hunter contradicted this. He reported that in fact there was very little resistance at all to the advancing Bolsheviks, that the Cossacks suffered no casualties at all and simply pulled out because, for whatever reason, morale was bad.

The campaign of the British to end Russian control of the Persian Cossacks was nearing an end. To add to the mystery of that time, Wolseley Haig, a British official in Teheran, reported that "a British officer who had been in Riza Khan's confidence" may have been passing information between the British and Riza Khan. Who that officer was is not now known. It was likely Hunter but could also have been some unidentified figure.

The Shah wanted the Cossacks to stay but since British subsidies were paying them his wishes were not paramount. He agreed to fire the Russians but suggested that Persia should grant small pensions to them in recognition of past services. As the Shah saw it not all the Russians had the opportunity of enriching themselves at the expense of Persia as had their commander. The British did not agree. Norman, now the British Minister in Teheran, contended that rather than give the Russians pensions they should instead be compelled to return the money they had already stolen. The Shah disagreed;

to force them to return their loot - and Starosselski had amassed a considerable quantity - would be an act of ingratitude for past services. Norman was cynical. "The truth is", he said "that the Shah has...ed(indecipherable but should probably read "participated") in Colonel Starosselski's depredations and has lately received from him a pearl necklace worth 35,000 tomans." The Russians did not get any pensions but were able to retain whatever wealth they had acquired in the service of Persia.

Hunter's services were no longer needed in Persia. Ironside, who was determined that British officers would not replace the Russians, met him in Teheran on October 25, told him that Starosselski was going and that the time had arrived for Hunter and his wife to return to India. Starosselski was on his way out and the Shah appointed a political supporter, Sardar Homayun to command the Cossack Division - with operational control by Reza Khan. Some of Dickson's staff were loaned to the force for the purposes of reorganization.

The new Prime Minister gave Starosselski and the other Russian officers two hours to quit Teheran. They could not return to Russia, they had double-crossed the Bolsheviks and the Whites were collapsing, and France initially appeared the most appealing destination. Norman in Teheran gave Starosselski a letter assuring him and his family free passage and non-molestation by the British as they traveled to Paris. In Baghdad, a few days after they had left Persia, Madame Starosselski told the British commander in Mesopotamia that they had decided to settle in America rather than France and gave him a formal letter from her husband seeking assurance that the promise of "non-molestation" would be extended to their new route - to the States via India and Japan. The assurance was given and while most of the Russian officers headed for Paris, the Starosselki family - possibly accompanied still by Fraser and

Katherine Hunter – traveled to Baghdad then down to the Gulf and the mail steamer to Bombay. The Hunters headed to Calcutta and the offices of the Survey of India, the Starosselskis to the United States where they disappeared from the pages of history.

Shortly after Hunter returned with his wife to India, Reza Khan, the new effective commander of the Cossack Division, moved his troops closer to Teheran. On the night of 20 February there was some sporadic shooting in the streets of the city. Reza Khan used this as a pretext to intervene and Teheranis woke the following morning to read posters on the walls of the city announcing that order must be maintained and signed by Reza Khan. As a precaution he arrested a considerable number of Persian nobles and politicians who were kept at the Cossack headquarters.

Only about a week earlier Ironside had met Reza Khan. Ironside knew that with the withdrawal of British forces Teheran was vulnerable to attack by Kuchik Khan's partisans. Internal turmoil was imminent. He told Rheza Khan that Norperforce would not oppose any effort by him to seize power provided that the Shah was not deposed. Reza Khan gave him this assurance. A day or so later Ironside was instructed to leave for a conference on the Middle East in Cairo called by the new Minister at the Colonial Office, Winston Churchill.

Reza Khan entered Teheran at the head of a force of three thousand Cossacks and was shortly afterwards, on the orders of the new Prime Minister, appointed head of the army. By the end of the year virtually all the recently appointed British civil and military officers were dismissed from the Persian service.

The India to which Hunter and his wife returned had profoundly changed in the few years he had been away. Relations between Indian and British had soured. Indians made immense efforts on behalf of the allied war effort. Hundreds of thousands had volunteered. Tens of thousands had died. The Indian Army that had been designed by Kitchener to defend India had learned to fight across the world. Its soldiers had battled in Europe, in Mesopotamia, in East Africa, in the Sinae and Palestine, in Trans-Caspia, the Persian Gulf, Kurdistan, Somaliland, the Cameroons, Salonika and Gallipoli. One regiment even went to north China and participated in the capture of a German colony there. By November 1918, India had sent more than a million three hundred thousand men, soldiers and civilians to serve the allied cause. Politically conscious Indians expected that they would be well rewarded for the country's sacrifice. They were not. Indians who had been taught that the control of the sub-continent by morally advanced Europeans would prevent the Indian races from resorting to old barbarities and fighting among themselves had discovered during the war that Europeans could be just as savage as Pushtuns or Pindaris. Civilization, it would seem, even in Europe was only skin deep.

Two great allies of the British, Russians and Americans, had given Indians another perspective. Russians had rebelled against the old autocracy and the new government there was calling for an end to colonialism and the freedom of all subject peoples. President Wilson enunciated his Fourteen Points and called for both national freedom and self-determination. In 1917 Edwin Montague at the Indian Office made a declaration in Parliament - it was partially drafted by Lord Curzon – "The policy of HM government, with which the government of India are in complete accord, is that of increasing association of Indians in every branch of the administration and the gradual development of self-governing institutions, with a view to the progressive realization of responsible government in India as an integral part of the Empire." This declaration was cautious. It would take years to implement.

Before the war ended a committee presided over by Judge Rowlett made recommendations to combat subversive activity in the country. Judges would be empowered to try political cases without juries; provincial governments could intern suspects without trial. There was no caution about passing these recommendations into law - even though every Indian non-official member of the Imperial Legislative Council voted against them.

In fact, the powers they allowed were never used. Nonetheless, their passage had inflamed public opinion and seemed a paltry reward for the efforts made throughout India to assist the allied cause. Then there was a new man on the scene, one very concerned with what he perceived as moral issues - and this was one of them. He was a forty-nine year old lawyer just back from South Africa and he launched a series of public meetings to protest the Rowlett Acts. His name was MK Gandhi.

Among Moslems in India there was considerable anxiety at the breakup of the Ottoman Empire and the future of the Caliphate, traditionally vested in the Sultan of Turkey. Many Moslems asked themselves, "Would they be denied access to the Holy Places of Islam?" In the Punjab there were numerous disturbances and there were plans for insurrection - the Afghan postmaster in Peshawar, for example, was preparing a local rising. In Amritsar there had been riots and number of assaults against Europeans. During April of 1919 the main railway line from Bombay to Peshawar was frequently attacked. Buildings were burned down, tracks torn up. There were disturbances in a number of cities, including Delhi. Martial Law was proclaimed, assemblies prohibited.

The new Amir of Afghanistan, Amanullah - he had recently replaced the assassinated Habibullah, the man who had been able to prevent a German-sponsored invasion of India - saw in the troubles in India a chance to unite his disunited country. He declared that in order to ensure that the troubles in India did not spread across the border he would move his own army up to the Durand Line. British intelligence got wind of the Amir's plans - and also those of the postmaster of Peshawar - and knew that an uprising in conjunction with an Afghan invasion was likely during the first week of May. Tension was rising and the disorders in the Punjab were spreading. On April 11 troops under the command of Brigadier General Dyer opened fire on a large crowd assembled in an enclosed area in Amritsar. 379 Indians were killed and many more injured. Believing that his drastic action had had a salutary effect - which it had - Dyer went off to participate in what came to be known as the Third Afghan War. Amanullah had attacked, some of the border Pathans rose in his support, units of the South Waziristan Militia mutinied in the Kurrum Valley - although the British major commanding them managed to fight his way out with the support of loyal militiamen. Indian opinion was divided - as was British - as to where Indian loyalties should be directed, but on no subjected was it more fiercely debated than that of Dyer's severe methods.

Dyer performed admirably against Afghans and Pathans and his determined actions may have saved the frontier region for India. But none of this saved him from losing his command, enforced retirement and an early death from multiple sclerosis. His action at Amritsar had polarized opinions - too often along racial lines - and the killing at Amritsar was a watershed. From then on a considerable body of Indian opinion was irrevocably committed to freeing India from British rule and the charismatic holy man, Gandhi became a beacon which appealed to Indian emotions and which the British could not extinguish save by resorting to methods which would have been anathema to them.

The Russians had not been simply watching events. Thousands of Moslems from across the Middle East and Central Asia gathered at the Caspian port of Baku for a weeklong harangue by Bolshevik revolutionaries determined to inspire colonized Moslems –particularly those from India - to revolt. The Comintern – whose leadership included Lenin and Trotsky - was committed to the international spread of communism, initially thought Lenin, starting in Europe as a result of war weariness. Later, after the Red Army was repulsed in Poland, Asia and particularly India, was perceived as a more promising plum. Agitators attempted to cross the borders into India while further north, with Malleson's Mission withdrawn, Soviet troops advanced further into Central Asia. In February 1920, even the semi-independent Khanate of Khiva fell to the Red Army. Official India was deeply alarmed.

This was the India that Fraser and Katherine Hunter returned to. They went immediately to Dehra Dun in the Punjab where he was appointed Deputy Superintendent of the Trigonometrical Survey Office. This was a paper appointment and two weeks later they both moved to Calcutta where Hunter was made Deputy Superintendent of the Number One Drawing Office. A year later he was placed in charge of the Map Record and Issue Office and two years after that became Superintendent of Map Publications, and later Director. He simultaneously held the post of Deputy Director of Surveys for Mesopotamia.

The Number One Drawing Office had been the department originally designated responsible for topographical intelligence gathering but the entire Map Publications Office - of which the

Drawing Office was a department - was soon involved. Coote-Hedley, for example, was with Map Publications before returning to London to head MI.4. Despite its intelligence function the department also assiduously concerned itself with those overt functions for which it was responsible. For example, in 1927 it printed more than a million sheets of maps, which included sheets of 327 newly mapped areas.

Hunter was also involved in the American flight around the world. In April 1924, four Douglas World Cruisers left the United States returning there on September 28. American Army Air Service officers had piloted them the 27,553 miles in 175 days. Starting from Santa Monica, California, their journey took them to Alaska, then onto Asia and across India where Hunter was responsible for the logistical arrangements necessary to speed the record-breaking flight along. For his assistance he later received a special citation from the United States government recognizing him "As a principal contributor to the success of 'the First Around the World Flight of the American Air Service'"

Horse racing continued the principal off-duty interest for himself and Katherine. On New Year's Day, 1925, in Calcutta, Katherine's horse "The Gift" won the Indian Grand National, second greatest steeplechase in the world. Katherine, ill with typhoid, had to be carried to the grandstand to watch the race. As her horse flashed over the final jump and on to victory, the excitement was too much. She collapsed.

Hunter's experience flying and mapping, allied to his experience as G2 with General Mitchell may have resulted in the emphasis given by the Survey of India to the Canadian method of using aircraft for mapping purposes. The first time that aircraft were used on a large scale for mapping was during the War, not only on the Western Front but also in Egypt and Mesopotamia. The maps were made from strips of photographs and there was distortion whenever there was any relief on the ground or if the camera was tilted. In Mesopotamia, in areas where the ground was flat, the maps proved to be quite accurate and its success contributed to the enthusiasm in the Survey of India to use air surveys in India after the war.

The Survey of India decided on the Canadian "oblique method". The Canadians had developed a system of air survey tailored to their own needs and topography. Canada, with large areas of forest and nearly level country intersected with lakes and waterways, needed detailed maps so that the best way of opening up the country to development could be determined. Canada had soon discovered that ground surveys were far too expensive and slow.

The Canadian method, which was adopted in India, was to use oblique photos. Knowing a position of two points in a photo on which a horizon appears it was possible to rule a grid on the photos corresponding to a grid on the map. The detail was then transferred square by square to the map. Using an airplane and a camera, obliques were taken every five miles from a height of five thousand feet, one looking straight ahead and two from either side covering an arc of ninety degrees on either side of the line of flight. The width of the strip that could be mapped from one flight was about ten to twenty miles. A grid was drawn on the first photograph from two fixed points established by ground surveyors; the position of two or more points in the middle distance of this photo could be used to rule a grid on the second photo and a series could be joined together quickly and cheaply. The constraining factor was that this method only worked successfully in flat country with bold features and a clear atmosphere - Baluchistan and Mesopotamia, for example.

Hunter was active on the technical side of his work. In addition to his leadership role in introducing air surveying, he also brought in new methods in engraving and in photo-lithography in map making. Records of his principal work during this period, topographical intelligence in India and adjoining countries, no longer survive.

It is unlikely Hunter played any role in Persia, something for which his background made him suitable, after his return to India. It would certainly not have been an official one. Reza Khan was concentrating on building up an army free of foreign influence; even foreigners from long standing neutral countries were removed and military matters were surrounded by considerable secrecy. However, it is known that at this time German, French, and Russian pilots were involved in building up the air-force and that negotiations were conducted with various countries, including Britain, regarding the provision of weapons and military training.

It was a period during which Reza Khan became Minister of War and the army moved into a dominant position in Persian life - a position that it would retain until the fall of the Shah and the take-over of Iran by Ayatolla Khomeini. It was also the period when Reza Khan moved vigorously against Kuchik Khan and the so-called Soviet Republic of Gilan (Kuchik Khan had once again moved into an uneasy alliance with the Bolsheviks). Kuchik Khan's forces were routed and he fled into hiding in the forests where he froze to death. Later his head was carried in triumph to Teheran. Reza Khan's ambition at this stage was to rid Persia of foreign dominance - particularly that of the British and Russians. He succeeded for a while in eliminating the dominance. His greatest success, however, was the pacification of the countryside.

All around Persia the control of the central government had vanished or diminished. Kuchik Khan was not the only rebel against central authority. The Azerbaijani tribes were in open revolt. The Kurds had proclaimed an independent Kurdish state. The tribal leaders across the country refused to pay taxes. In the southwest the Sheik of Mohammarah, who had become sheik by murdering his brother, had made as far back as 1910, an arrangement with Sir Percy Cox whereby the Anglo-Persian Oil Company would be able to build and operate a pipeline from the oil fields to Abadan Island on the Shatt-el-Arab where they could build a refinery. In return the British government guaranteed his autonomy.

The Bakhtiari tribes west and southwest of Isfahan, traditionally pro-British and subsidized by the Anglo-Persian Oil Company, were not actively hostile towards Teheran, but were determined to maintain their independent and nomadic status. Some years later a daughter of the Bakhtiari, Soraya Esfandiari, would marry the son of Reza Khan and become world famous as the beautiful Queen Soroya. Ironically, two of her uncles were so independent and rebellious that Reza Khan had them executed. There was also major unrest in Fars Province and it was here that Hunter, because of his deep experience, could have exercised influence.

The principal troublemakers were still the Kashgai, but they were not the only ones. The entire province had become a haunt of highwaymen, outcasts from their tribes or former road guards and dismissed gendarmerie. They assisted in a flourishing trade running guns from the Arabs of the Oman Sheikdoms to the interior tribes of Persia. Farman Farma, who had tried to control the Province while he was governor during Sykes period as Inspector-General of the South Persia Rifles, was replaced by the Shah. Apparently Farman Farma's greed was too great for even Teheran to ignore. Replacing him was Dr Mussadiq who thirty years later would become Prime Minister and cause the British considerable difficulty with his attempts to nationalize the Anglo-Iranian Oil Company - as it had become. Like Soraya, Mussadiq also became world famous.

The editors of "Time" magazine chose Mussadiq over John Foster Dulles and Dwight Eisenhower as "Man of the Year" for 1951. His weeping, fainting and theatrical tantrums had turned the spotlight of the world on Teheran.

The Farman Farma family remained powerful in Iran until the fall of the Pahlevi Shah and accession of Khomeini and the ayatollahs. It was reported in the <u>Fall of the Peacock Throne</u> that the Farman Farma family influence had become widespread; seventeen of them have earned PhD's, and they are in engineering, law, architecture, banking and government. One was a professor at the University of Texas.

The tribes were subdued. The old enemy of Hunter and the South Persia Rifles was Solat-u-Dolah, Chief of the Kashgai. Mussadiq allied himself with Kazam-u-Mulk, head of the Khamseh tribes, who had also been a lukewarm ally of the SPR, and attempted to reduce Solat's raiding and robbery. Solat was finally captured and, on orders of Reza Khan, imprisoned. He died in jail.

Years later, when Reza Khan lost power himself, the tribal chiefs were released from imprisonment or house arrest. They returned to their old nomadic ways. Solat would have been proud of his heirs. His four sons succeeded him as Khans of the Kashgai. During the Second World War they were openly pro-German and, like their father before them, defied the Central government and the allies and gave shelter to numerous German agents.

In his final years with the Survey of India much, most of Hunter's work was concealed from public vision and so remains.[47] From his offices in Calcutta and Simla he and his surveyors played some of the closing rounds of "the Great Game", as well as the routines of conventional surveying. Information was gathered and assessed. The routes by which the Russians, this time Soviets, might move through

Afghanistan and Persia and reach India were carefully documented and relevant information about these routes - and the people who lived along them - was assembled. There were many who scoffed. The Russians, so they said, would never advance on India, would never invade Afghanistan or Persia. But Hunter and his co-workers could not agree and Hunter remained suspicious - some might say realistic - of Russian intentions for years. They would argue that Russian policy towards adjoining countries had not changed. Under Czar or Bolsheviks, the goal was still the warm water ports of the Indian Ocean; led by flamboyant General Skobolov or a taciturn commissar, Russian imperial policy remained basically unaltered.

On 16 January 1925, two weeks after his wife Katherine had her horse racing success at Calcutta in the Indian Grand National, Hunter went "on leave" for two years, three months and twenty seven days. It appears that this was the time for his retirement from the Indian Army, but not necessarily from the Civil Department and the Survey of India. During this leave period he was listed, in addition to his other duties with the Survey, as "Assistant Director of Surveys in Mesopotamia". What happened during his long leave is today largely unknown except that at some point he was involved in real estate speculation and development in Florida. However, three days after returning to Calcutta he was appointed Director of Map Publications.

Going Home

"God gives all men all earth to love
But since man's heart is small
Ordains for each one spot shall prove
Beloved over all."
                                        Rudyard Kipling

When Hunter finally retired from the Survey of India he was only fifty-three years old. He had reached the senior ranks of the Survey of India - only one man, the Director General, was senior to him and Hunter frequently acted as Director General in his absence. Certainly he had no intention of retiring to a life of reminiscing. But first he and Katherine would have a holiday, see the world, decide just where they would finally settle.

They thought Mexico would be a fine place to live. After some months there they changed their minds and moved north into the United States. The United States seemed to be the most promising. Katherine was an American and her family lived in Illinois, while Fraser had traveled extensively in the country and had some business interests there - the Missouri Slope Land and Investment Company of North Dakota and Hunter's Chlorine Hot Springs in Lakeview, Oregon, that had been founded by H A Hunter in 1925, as well perhaps continuing other real estate interests in Florida. But genial travel without some purpose at hand was not to their liking and in 1932 they returned to Canada and set up house at "The Hedges", the home in Durham, Ontario where Hunter had been born. Life was soon active.

He briefly held the position of Substitute Director of Military Studies" at Toronto University - the Director, Brigadier General Cartwright, had been ill and took a year's leave of absence - and he lectured extensively on eastern affairs. He was made an honorary member of the 111th Battalion, the Toronto Regiment, he was a founding member of the Imperial Officers' Association of Canada, a Vice President of the Royal Military College Club of Canada, an honorary member of the Governor General's Horse Guards, was active in the Eglington Hunt, and was on the executive committee of the Toronto Horse Show.

In 1934 he ran for political office from his other home in Poplar Plains Road and was elected the Liberal member for the St Patrick's riding in Toronto. It was not the first time his thoughts had turned to politics for it was reported that when in London immediately after the end of the war he was offered a Labour Party nomination but was unable to accept because he was still in the army. He may have retained a childhood interest in politics since his father was in the Ontario legislature for many years as a supporter of the Mowat government. More than that the impression is given that Hunter was not cast in the mold of the typical army officer of that time, generally of a conservative inclination. His early determination to leave the Indian Army, his sympathy for the much-derided Persians and his reiterated wishes to join the Canadian forces may give authenticity to his wish to compete for a Labour Party seat in the British elections

The Toronto result was surprising. The Tories had been confident of victory and had assiduously courted the constituents; they had, for example, contributed generously to the construction of a Talmud Torah for the large number of Jewish residents of the riding, and they had comfortably won the previous election. Hunter entered into the fray only a couple of months before Election Day and his chances were held to be poor. Yet after a flamboyant campaign he squeaked in after a recount and a final majority of just fourteen votes. At the next election his majority was substantially increased. His political career would last for a decade and prove to be as turbulent as some of his Persian years.[49]

Many thought Hunter would receive from Premier "Mitch" Hepburn one of the cabinet posts generally given to Toronto. He was not. "Saturday Night" commented that "...his claims to that honor on the grounds of character and intellectual ability are beyond dispute. Some may doubt that he has the necessary pliability for cabinet timber(sic)" Instead he sat on committees concerned with the well-being of veterans.

A Liberal in Ontario, when Mitch Hepburn was premier, Hunter could not restrain his criticism of Mackenzie King's federal Liberal government. Though Hunter was a Liberal he openly advocated the wartime policies of Arthur Meighen's Opposition Conservatives, though his criticism of the provincial Liberals began well before that. He was convinced that in 1934 Harry Nixon, then Minister of Game and Fisheries, had "used his power to turn disabled men and soldiers who had served their country and province well, out of jobs they had been assured of by legislative enactment. He had no hesitation in destroying the livelihood of soldiers... leaving them and their families penniless."

In 1936 Hunter was in Europe again. On 26 July, along with many other former Canadian soldiers, he attended the opening of the Vimy Ridge Memorial on land given to Canada by France. In 1917 Canadian forces recaptured the high ridge from German control, following the failure of British and French troops to gain the ridge. Some 3,598 Canadian soldiers were killed and 7,004 injured. Inscribed on a series of long walls are the names of more than seven thousand Canadians who were killed in France but whose resting place is unknown. Brigadier General Alexander Ross, who commanded the 28th Battalion at Vimy Ridge said it "was Canada from Atlantic to Pacific on parade. I thought then that in those few minutes I witnessed the birth of a nation." Hunter, along with other assembled dignitaries, heard King Edward speak of Canada's great loss and tremendous contribution to victory in the war.

Back in Canada the feud about jobs for discharged soldiers continued throughout his political career. In 1937 however events of a more lively nature occurred. Although General Motors had earned its largest profit in history, in 1936 it decided to cut the wages of its workers in Oshawa, Ontario. The body-shop workers at the General Motors plant in Oshawa went on strike in February, halting production throughout the plant and by mid-April more than four thousand workers struck. "Mitch" Hepburn, the premier feared that the strike might spread to mining companies and was determined to stamp it out. He ordered the creation of a special police force – the federal government would not increase the number of RCMP stationed in Oshawa – and appointed Hunter to raise the force, soon to be called Hepburn's Hussars[50] or "sons of Mitches". Why Hunter cooperated in this venture is uncertain at this late date, for two cabinet ministers resigned rather than go along with the scheme. The new police were paid $25 a week and Hunter recruited a substantial number of war veterans and it may well have been his opportunity to find employment for the veterans that overrode other concerns. However, shortly after the recruiting office opened in Toronto "standing room only" signs were erected and Hunter was able to report that Hepburn's quota had been reached. The strikers in

Oshawa were not rioting, no emergency existed and after two weeks General Motors, fearing the loss of markets to competitors, accepted the union's demands.

His concerns for war veterans and the soldiers of the new war, declared in 1939, remained paramount. In 1943 he battled again over proxy voting for soldiers that, he said had been so grossly mishandled that thousands were disenfranchised. He criticized the moving out of the province troops in training, depriving them of their vote there and said that many who did receive the return proxies would be deprived of their vote through relatives changing their addresses. Said Hunter, "Thousands upon thousands of our Ontario citizens in the armed forces have been robbed of their votes in this election." He found it hard not to believe that this "gross incompetence was not deliberate." He continued, "Call it an accident, the result still condemns the government responsible more strongly than any words I can think of."

Hunter's political career came to an end in 1943 after years of bitter disputes with Nixon, who had become party leader. There were rumours that Hunter would run again in the St. Patrick's riding as an "independent Liberal" but he put those rumours to rest in a radio broadcast, "paid for by myself" and which he described as his political swansong. He attacked Nixon for "the betrayal of our armed forces by the Liberal Party machine"

He said Harry Nixon had made a promise in July 1943. He had said, "I give my solemn promise on behalf of the Province of Ontario that we will stand by our men of the Navy, Army and Air Force to the utmost of our responsibility now, in time of war, and in the after period when peace is restored. To the faithful discharge of this high duty I pledge my health, my strength and my sacred honour." Responded Hunter, "I'm afraid I can't take Mr. Nixon very seriously…I'm still waiting to be shown where his sacred honour was in 1934 or, for that matter, where it is in 1943." He said that Nixon was one of the worst offenders in the matter of firing ex-service men. He quoted several examples of hardship "to give you some idea of how much Mr. Nixon's sacred honour is worth".

In his radio broadcast castigating the Liberal Party he read a newspaper report of the St Patrick nomination for the forthcoming election. "It seems he (Hunter) has not met with the wishes of some of the party heelers in Toronto. The claim is that he has not done them enough favours, has not got more in the way of patronage for the little bosses. So the machine went to work to get rid of Colonel Hunter by packing the convention meeting and ousting Hunter in favour of Controller Hamilton. The machine thinks Hamilton will better serve its purpose."

Hunter concluded his radio address saying that he had never understood that, as a candidate, "I must do things I would be ashamed to do" and that he regretted that he would now be unable to serve soldiers returning when war ended but that "there were things a man could not do for political office when young Canadians are offering their lives in hope that a cleaner, better world may come into being". Hunter predicted calamity for Ontario if Nixon won the election.

Nixon did win the election but the St Patrick's riding reverted once again to the Conservatives.

In the last years of his life, in the late nineteen fifties, his thoughts undoubtedly drifted back over the event-filled years. Sometimes he must have wondered that he survived so long. So many died young serving in the east, yet Hunter, an old man now, had seen action in India and China, on the Western Front, and in Persia. He had been a close onlooker of the Russian Revolution and had ridden into action alongside Englishmen and Indians, Americans, Russians and Persians. He had earned the Distinguished Service Order, the Persian Medal of Valour, the Americans had given him the Order of the Dragon and the French the Croix de Guerre. He had been mentioned in dispatches fourteen times. And he had survived it all, being wounded, and only slightly, just once.

Fraser Hunter was deeply disappointed and angry at not being able to return to service life when war resumed in 1939. Although he was in his sixties he believed that his knowledge of Iran and many of the people there, as well as his ability to speak several languages, were attributes that could be useful. But it was not to be.

On November 30 1939, the Russian Red Army, at that time allied to Hitler's Germany, invaded Finland. The Finns put up a surprisingly successful resistance and many in the West wondered what could be done to help them. Bizarre though it must now seem there were even those in the War Cabinet who contemplated going to war with Russia to help Finland. Beaverbrook, recovering from an asthma attack in his home in the south of France, proposed that the British government should attempt to stir up public opinion in the USA in support of the Finns, then others would join in ultimately nudging public opinion to favour help for Britain. He wrote to the secretary for war "If the United States decides to help Finland, help to Great Britain may not be far off."[52] Seen in the light of those days Hunter's actions in Durham are understandable. He armed and trained a contingent of volunteers to go to Finland and fight with the Finns in the defense of their country against the Russians.[53] An anxious letter from a Major Collins, who was in charge of the local Legion of Frontiersmen to RCMP Superintendent Kemp in Toronto wondered if their drilling with arms (loaned to them by the Provincial government) would be regarded as an offense against the

Criminal Code. Major Collins was eventually assured that there was no necessity for any action to be taken.[54] The volunteers drilled and trained in the Frontiersmen's Hall in Durham and although today it may seem extraordinary that Canadians should even think about fighting for the Finns against the Russians, it was in the earliest days of the war an idea which was widely supported. But events overtook the idea and the volunteers did not get to Finland.

Hunter was also involved in a scheme to train pilots for France.[55] He was desperately anxious to be of use in a time of world crisis. A Liberal in Ontario when the ebullient "Mitch" Hepburn was Premier, he would not restrain his criticism of Mackenzie King's federal government and he consistently and openly advocated the wartime policies of Conservative Arthur Meighen. Partly because of this his party had declined to re-nominate him. His political career had ended.

WHERE DID ALL THE SOLDIERS GO?

William Shakespear. His friend of his early days in India, William Shakespear, had been less fortunate than Hunter. His life was short and yet during his few years he made an indelible impression upon the nomadic tribesmen of Arabia. It is said that when in later years Ibn Saud was firmly established on the throne of Saudi Arabia he was asked by a distinguished English visitor which European he most admired. The King replied without hesitation, "William Shakespear". The Englishman was amazed that this desert nomad should be so well versed in literature until it was explained that King Saud was referring to Captain William Shakespear of the Indian Political Service.

Captain Shakespear did not live long enough to see Arabia shake off Ottoman domination. He was killed, fighting alongside Ibn Saud's men in a desert battle against the forces of their pro-Turkish enemy, Ibn Rashid. His last sight was of the enemy cavalry, camel and horse, charging over the sands towards him, exposed on a slight hill. He stood alone in the end until overwhelmed by Ibn Rashid's bedouin followers. First he was struck by a bullet in the leg; then another in the arm. Finally, as he emptied his revolver into the charging swarm, a bullet struck him in the head. He was thirty-six years old. An English newspaper, "The World", wrote of him, "He was one of those Englishmen Kipling delighted to picture.

Nothing daunted him; he lived for enterprise and rejoiced in the handling of men; the more difficult and dangerous the job, the better it pleased him. He bore an English name not easy to add glory to, yet he succeeded."

Colonel J C Lorimer. Soon after Shakespear's death Colonel J.G. Lorimer, Hunter's partner is the making of the map of Arabia, died somewhat mysteriously. He had been British Resident in Baghdad but had been transferred to Bushire on the Gulf. He was killed in his office by a self-inflicted shot through the head. Apparently this occurred while he was cleaning his own gun, something that must be considered remarkable for so experienced a soldier.

Lord Curzon. Lord Curzon died soon after the war, a disappointed man. Beaverbrook said of him that he had entered heaven too soon and that everything afterwards was a letdown. Beaverbrook was referring to all the pomp and glory that went with being Viceroy of India, when Curzon was only forty years old. After the war he was appointed Secretary of State for Foreign Affairs, but Lloyd George, the Prime Minister, kept a firm grip on all foreign policy decisions. When Bonar Law became Prime Minister in 1922, Curzon had a freer hand. Yet he never achieved his greatest ambition, which was to become Prime Minister, and he died, after many years of poor health, only in his middle sixties, in 1925.

Oskar von Niedermayer. After six months in Kabul von Niedermayer realized that his efforts to have the Emir support Germany were fruitless and he began his long journey home. He went north initially into hostile Russia then west to Turkey. After three months he was back with the German military mission to the Ottoman Empire, but finally, in March 1918 got back to Germany. Here he saw in action on the western front. After study and posting to the German embassy in Moscow after the war he became something of an expert in Russian affairs. During the Second World War he commanded Caucasian, Georgian and Tartar troops in the OstLegion fighting partisans in the Balkans. It was reported that he made disparaging remarks about Hitler's eastern policy and was arrested and court marshaled. After Germany's surrender he was arrested, this time by Soviet troops and sentenced to twenty-five years imprisonment. He died in jail 1948.

Wilhelm Wassmuss. Perhaps the saddest end was that of the indomitable Wassmuss, Hunter's quarry in south Persia. He had succeeded in keeping his Tangestani and Kashgai allies until the war ended and was a constant thorn in the side of the British forces. His fame became almost legendary. The British newspaper, the Daily Mail, said of him in 1919,

"The name of Wassmuss is a symbol of all the bold, skilful and daring methods adopted by Germany for the purpose of influencing the East. In November, 1914, we tried in vain to capture this young man, but he escaped us like the 'Goeben' and, like a human 'Goeben', he remained throughout the war a constant menace, a political force which we were obliged to take into account....His success in grappling with the difficulties he encountered is marvellous as the work of one man. We were attacked by tribe after tribe."

Wassmuss was repatriated in 1919 and went home by way of Baku and Batuum to Saxony. There he married and moved to Berlin where he had been promised a prominent position in the German Foreign Service. He was appointed head of the eastern section and discovered that the old way of life, the purposeless feuding and poverty, had returned to the Bushire hinterland.

Wassmuss became obsessed with the idea that he personally was responsible for what was happening between Shiraz and Bushire. For four years the tribesmen had followed him; he made them promises and had so far been unable to keep them. He began to receive letters from the tribal chiefs demanding compensation for their efforts on Germany's behalf during the war - claims for money far in excess of that which Wassmuss had ever promised. Wassmuss decided that they must be paid - not the exaggerated claims but the original commitments. There was little sympathy in the foreign service for his pleading on behalf of former allies. Germany had lost the war and claims against her were coming in from all over the world.

He took some leave in 1923 and he and his wife traveled back to the Persian Gulf. The tribesmen flocked to welcome him and although he told them that Germany had no money to pay them now, he assured them that the day would come when they would be. In fact, he devised a scheme to help his former comrades. He applied for the post of German consul at Bushire and planned to buy a farm near there and use the profits and half his own pay to pay off the tribesmen in installments. But the German government refused. The British were at the time having problems in the east and Germany had no wish to antagonize them by appointing Wassmuss to Bushire. Any other post he could have; but not Bushire. Wassmuss told his government he would resign if the tribesmen did not get compensation. The German government gave him about twenty thousand dollars (five thousand pounds sterling in 1923) to pay off his former allies. To the surprise of the German government he resigned anyway and bought a farm that he could work to pay off the tribes gradually.

His honorable efforts failed. He and his wife had arrived back in Bushire in December 1924. By 1928 he was ruined. Even worse, he was convinced that the tribesmen he was trying to help were deliberately damaging his crops for no other reason than ignorant maliciousness. The Governor of Isfahan offered him the post of manager of a large prosperous farm near that city - but on the condition that any receipts from the sale of his old farm not go to the southern sheiks. But Wassmuss was adamant. The sheiks must have the money. It was a German war debt that he had incurred and if the German government would not pay it then he must himself. Wassmuss' honest intentions did not deflect the inevitable. He was declared bankrupt and in April, broken hearted, he left Persia finally. In November 1931, he became seriously ill but just before he died heard from Persia that there had been a final judgment in his favor and some money from the sale of his property would come to him - or as it happened, to his wife for he died shortly afterwards.

Major General Sir Percy Sykes. Sykes' career after leaving the South Persia Rifles at the end of the war officially ended in 1920. He continued active. In 1923 he delivered the Lowell Lectures in Boston and ten years later came to Canada, lecturing under the auspices of the National Council of Education, coincidentally during the same period that Hunter too was lecturing under their auspices.

In November 1934, Sykes delivered a lecture on Persia and the Great War to the Canadian Military Institute. He made a passing reference to Hunter. From the wording it appears that Hunter, hardly surprisingly, was not present.

All had not been tranquil for Sykes. "The Times" of London had published a lengthy article by a staff reporter on the South Persia Rifles and, in particular, the defense of Shiraz during the rising of the tribes against the Rifles in 1918. The article was warm in its praise of the force but contained information that could only have been obtained by talking to Sykes or indeed have been written by him. Curzon, by then Foreign Secretary, was furious with Sykes for not only abetting in the production of a newspaper article which contained confidential material but also for doing so in such a way as to give Sykes more credit than was his due. Curzon wrote to Edwin Montague, Secretary of State for India, of his growing irritation of "a glowing account of the performance of Sir Percy Sykes at Shiraz which gave in many respects a quite one-sided view of the operation... As these communications could only have emanated from or been inspired by Sir P Sykes himself, and as the latter had already been warned at Foreign Office against any publication, I instructed Oliphant to write and ask for an explanation"

A formal letter to Sykes stated, "Lord Curzon directs me to state that your action in supplying the information in question to the Public Press without permission from this office, and indeed after categorical warning against it which Mr. Oliphant communicated to you seems to him to have been of a very reprehensible character and he viewed it with the utmost surprise."[56]

Curzon later modified his language but remained convinced that Sykes had distorted the facts in comments to the press for his own benefit.

Sykes was a tireless writer and his <u>History of Persia</u> remains something of a classic. In 1932 he was appointed Honourary Secretary of the Royal Central Asian Society. In 1940 he wrote a history of Afghanistan. Although heartily disliked by many who had contact with him - Hunter's distaste was shared by Gough, the British Consul in Shiraz and others - he did contribute to western understanding of the immense and wonderful span of Persian history. Sykes was certainly a bombastic bully in his earlier years and in his retirement was regarded by his family and those who were not his contemporaries as a crashing bore. On a hot day in 1945 he collapsed while walking to his club. He died a few hours later.

Captain Hay Thorburn. Captain Thorburn returned to India then to his regiment, The Cameronians(Scottish Rifles)and later to North Africa. He had long been interested in that continent and had attended meetings of the Africa Society in London in his youth. Shortly after the end of the war he was placed in command of the Tenth Sudanese Rifles, part of the Egyptian Army, and in 1922 gave a detailed paper to the Royal Geographical Society on some of the tribes in the Sudan.

Lancelot Oliphant. Lancelot Oliphant continued in the Foreign Office and was eventually appointed Deputy Under Secretary of State for the Foreign Office. In 1939 he was made Ambassador to Belgium and, during the retreat of the allied forces was captured by German troops. Despite pleading diplomatic immunity he was imprisoned by the Germans until September 1941. After his release he continued his duties towards the Belgium and Luxembourg governments in exile until retiring in 1944. He died in 1965.

Lady Muriel Paget. Lady Paget continued the work she had begun with the Voluntary Aid Detachment. After the Russian Revolution she returned and traveled widely in that country. She set up a house in Leningrad where impoverished former servants of aristocrats were supplied with food and clothing. She also helped many destitute in the Slav and Baltic states with free meals, medical aid and clothing.

More than a decade later her name became prominent again. At the most notorious of Stalin's Great Purge Trials in Russia, Genrikh Yagoda, former head of the NKVD (Russian Secret Service, later to become the KGB), was charged along with several co-conspirators with murder, treason and espionage by Prosecutor Vyshinsky. One of these co-conspirators - the last survivors of the old Bolshevik guard - was Christian Rakovsky, who in 1924 had been Soviet Charge d'Affairs in London. During this time, he said, "Two Englishmen named Armstrong and Leckhart came to me in London with a letter which, though a forgery, seemed to say that I had served the German secret police during the war." Rakovsky said that he was given the option of serving the British Secret Service or shown up to his Soviet masters as a traitor and he chose the former course. Later, he said, Trotsky (who had been banished to Central Asia) told him "the British Secret Service are going to help me escape from Alma Ata across the desert and mountains. When I asked Trotsky "How?" he said that since 1926 he had been in communication with the intelligence service through a representative of the Lena Goldfields.

Rakovsky said that he had delivered a considerable amount of information to the British up until 1936. In this, he said, he was helped by Lady Muriel Paget serving as a link between him and the British Secret Service. British Prime Minister Neville Chamberlain dismissed these allegations in the House of Commons. "Lady Muriel Paget" he said "has no experience with the British intelligence service and anybody who knows anything about her knows that her work is purely unselfish and humanitarian."

Unlike most of the others at Stalin's show trial Rakovsky, though found guilty, was not executed. He was sentenced to twenty years. Later though, in 1941, he was shot. Who now knows if any of the allegations were true? However, it is true that about the only way of surviving a purge trial was to plead guilty on all counts and give whatever "evidence" the prosecution wanted. A few months after the trial Lady Paget died in her sleep. She was 61.

Colonel "Yashka" Botchkareva. "Yashka" Botchkareva left Washington and wrote her memoirs in New York – Mrs. Harriman had promised to have them published. After the war she returned to Russia and eventually her home village. The Cheka, Bolshevik security police, found and her and she was executed.

Brigadier William Mitchell. Brigadier Mitchell returned home from France a hero. His promotion to brigadier general was soon made substantive and before long he was the major exponent in the United States of the future of air power. But the government was budget conscious. On three occasions Billy Mitchell demonstrated the potential effectiveness of aircraft in war - sinking the former German battleship "Ostfreisland", the obsolete American warship "Alabama" and the obsolete "New Jersey" and "Virginia" with aircraft - and arguing that the age of the battleship was passed. He also warned that one day the Japanese would attack - and do so without warning. In 1925, tired of his constant harping on this theme, the war department had him transferred to a minor post in Texas with the rank of colonel. From there, after the destruction of the navy dirigible "Shenandoah", Mitchell charged the war and navy departments with "incompetence, criminal negligence and almost treasonable administration of the national defense." For this he was court marshaled. He was able to use the trial as a sounding board for his opinions but was nonetheless, found guilty of making statements to the prejudice of good order and military discipline. Wide circulation was given to the rumour that one member of the court's panel of judging officers voted not guilty. This member was General Douglas MacArthur. Billy Mitchell resigned from the army in 1926 and became a farmer in Virginia. From his home he continued to write of the need for air power and the danger of Japan attacking without warning. On December 7, 1941, almost six years after Mitchell's death, his prophesy came true.

Major Claude Stokes. Hunter's acquaintance, Claude Stokes, after considerable controversy in his early career, not something to set one on the path to promotion, fared well. After serving with Dickson on the short-lived military mission to Persia he was appointed Chief British Commissioner in Trans-Caucasia. He retired in 1922 and married Olga, the daughter of a White Russian General. From 1931 to 1940 he held what must surely have been a plum in consular appointments. He was the British Vice Consul in Nice, on the French Riviera. He died in 1948.

Field Marshal William Edmund Ironside. General Ironside took over command of the British troops in Persia from Brigadier-General Champain and assisted in the career of Reza Khan in the Persian Cossacks. He became commandant of the Staff College at Camberley in 1922. Thereafter he received a series of commands and promotions that culminated in his appointment as Chief of the Imperial General Staff in 1939 and later his promotion to the rank of Field Marshal. In 1941 he was created the first Baron of Archangel and Ironside. He died in 1959.

Reza Khan Pahlevi. After the march of the Cossacks on Teheran, Reza Khan was appointed Minister of War and Commander in Chief of all Persian forces. He made himself Prime Minister in 1923 and at the end of 1925 the Persian Parliament acknowledged him the new Shah of Persia. One of his decrees introduced to speed the westernization of Persia - now to be called Iran - was that Iranians, who formally went only by their given names, should take a family name. He chose the name Pahlevi. He soon broke with the orthodox mullahs by a series of measures which included the banning of the old style of dress - Reza Shah was a great admirer of Kemal

Ataturk - raising the age of marriage for a girl from nine to fifteen and compelling men to tell prospective wives how many wives they already had.

He transformed Iran, but he alienated tens of thousands in doing so and was also accused of following the Persian leadership tradition of looting the public purse. Whatever his faults, and they were many, he made considerable progress in freeing Iran from foreign domination. But he failed to free it entirely, as he discovered in 1941. Germans were active in the country again. In the First World War they had claimed that the Kaiser had become a Moslem and was now Haji Wilhelm. In the Second World War the German propaganda machine made much of their common "Aryanism" - from the name "Iran". There were more Germans in Teheran than any other foreign group, Iranian students poured into German universities, and Iran's principal trading partner was Germany. But the Allies needed a route through Iran to re-supply the Russian Army struggling to slow the German drive on Moscow and they wanted the Germans out of Iran. Reza Shah refused. On August 25 1941 British, from the west and south, and Russians from the north simultaneously attacked. On August 27 Iranian troops were ordered to cease resistance and to return to their barracks. Less than three weeks later the Shah abdicated in favor of his son.

Reza Shah and his family traveled by British boat towards Bombay[57] but the Indian government, realizing that there could well be riots if the ruler of so ancient a Moslem state, who had been deposed by force, were to appear in any Indian city, managed to have his destination changed. He was transferred to another British ship a few miles out from Bombay and taken instead to Port Louis in Mauritius. The climate did not suit him. He had first thought that he would be sent to Canada but now was moved to South Africa and took up residence in Johannesburg. He died in July 1944 at the age of sixty-six. In 1950 his remains were returned to Teheran for a state funeral. His son, Mohammed, who became shah at the age of twenty-one, also died in exile, deposed by the forces of Ayatollah Kohmeini.

Lieutenant Colonel Frederick Fraser Hunter. The nineteen fifties saw Fraser Hunter pass into amiable old age. Katherine had died in 1939 after a long struggle with cancer and they had had no children. The Hunters had taken to wintering in Florida and when Katherine Hunter became ill Fraser found a nurse for her, Mary Walsh, who lived with the family. After Katherine's death Mary stayed on. In his will Hunter left everything to Mary Walsh but there was little left save memories and Mary Walsh herself died a few months after Hunter.

Fraser Hunter, "the Colonel" is still remembered for displays of his collections in the downstairs of the public library - a library which his father had helped organize - and explaining to the school children who visited it with their teachers what all the artifacts meant and where they had come from. Most of the military memorabilia was stored in a garage behind the Hedges and a fire destroyed virtually everything in it.

Hunter died after a lengthy illness on December 14, 1959, aged 84. His sword rested on the flag draped coffin, carried by eight officers and NCO's of the Grey and Simcoe Foresters Regiment. The casket was placed on a gun carriage and escorted to Durham cemetery. The Last Post was sounded, and Frederick Fraser Hunter was laid to rest alongside his wife Katherine.

Nearby lay other Hunters, including his father, James Hill Hunter, his mother, Kate MacDonald Hunter, his grandmother,

Elizabeth, and grandfather, Archibald Hunter who, one hundred and seventeen years earlier, had struggled through the Queen's Bush, found a deserted wigwam and spent his first night at what would become Durham.

> I'd not give room for an Emperor-
> I'd hold my road for a King.
> To the Triple Crown I'd not bow down-
> But this is a different thing!
> I'll not fight with the Powers of Air-
> Sentry, pass him through!
> Drawbridge let fall - He's the Lord of us all-
> The Dreamer whose dream came true!
> (Rudyard Kipling)

BIBLIOGRAPHY

PRIMARY SOURCES.

Arfa, General Hassan. <u>Under Five Shahs</u>. New York, 1975.

Dunsterville, Maj-Gen LC. <u>Stalky's Reminiscences</u>. J Cape, 1928.

Foreign Office Records FO 371/2981 – 99734. FO 248/1186.
 Public Records Office London.

Haig, Wolseley. <u>Making a Shah in Persia</u>. The Living Age. January –
 March 1926. Boston.

Harriman, Mrs. J Borden. <u>Pinafores to Politics</u>. Henry Holt and Co
 New York 1923.

Hunter, Lieut- Colonel FF. <u>Reminiscences of the Map of Arabia
 and the Persian Gulf</u>. Royal Geographical Society, 1919.
 <u>India in Transition</u>. Empire Club of Canada. Oct 1931.
 India Office, London. Political and Secret Records
 L/P&S/10/690, and L/P&S/10/580 and L/MIL/17/15/23

Ironside, Sir Edmund. <u>High Road to Command</u>. Leo Cooper,
 London.1972.

Lorimer, J C. The Gazetteer of the Persian Gulf, Oman and Central Arabia. 2 vols.India Office Library and Records, London.1915.

Newby, Eric. A Short Walk in the Hindu Kush. Pan MacMillan Ltd. 1958.

Niedermayer, Oskar von. Under the Burning Sun of Iran. Unicom Office, Dachau, Near Munich. 1925.

Shuster, W Morgan. The Strangling of Persia. Greenwood Press, New York.1968.Skrine, Sir Clarmont, World War in Iran. Constable, 1962.

Survey of India Reports. Series V19/71 through 88 and V19/227 and V19/231.

Survey of India Records, Vol XX: The War Record, 1914-1920. Dehra Dun; Survey of India 1925

Sykes, Sir Percy. History of Persia. (2nd vol). Routledge and Kegan Paul. 1969.
South Persia and the Great War. Royal Geographical Society, Vol 58.Aug 1921

War Office Diaries. WO 106/928,931, 935, 939, WO 371/2736, WO 371/2981 Public Records Office, London.

SECONDARY SOURCES.

Abella, Irving. (ed) <u>On Strike</u> Six Key Labour Struggles in Canada 1919-1949. 1974.

Andrew, Christopher. <u>Secret Service</u>. Sceptre (Hodder and Houghton Paperbacks. 1987.

Blunt, Wilfred. <u>Lady Muriel</u>. Methuen and Co, London. 1962.

Branch 308 Royal Canadian Legion. <u>Lest We Forget</u>. Royal Canadian Legion, Durham Ontario. 1990

Bridger, Professor. The Second Decade. and <u>The Third Decade</u>. RMC Canada.

Brinkley, George A. <u>The Volunteer Army and Allied Intervention in South Russia, 1917-1921</u>. University of Notre Dame Press. 1966.

Burrell, R M. <u>Arms and Afghans; An Episode in Anglo-Persian Relations 1905-1912</u>. Bulletin of the School of Oriental and African Studies, University of London. Vol 49. (1986)

Buxhoeveden, Baroness Sophie. <u>Alexandra Feodorovna</u>. C Trade Paper, 1996.

Canadian Who's Who. 1937.

Caroe, Olaf. <u>The Pathans</u>. Oxford University Press, 1984.

Chamberlin, William Henry. The Russian Revolution. (2 vols) Grosset and Dunlap. New York.1965.

Collier, Peter. The Impact on Topographic Mapping of Developments in Land and Air Survey: 1900-1939. Cartography and Geographic Information Service. Vol 29. 2002.

Dilks, David. Curzon in India. (2 vols) Taplinger Publishing Co. New York.1969.

Dodds, Ronald. The Brave Young Wings. Canada's Wings Inc. Stittsville Ontario. 1980.

Durham Historical Committee. History of the Town of Durham, 1842-1994. Durham Historical Committee, 1994.

Edmonds, CJ. "The Persian Gulf Prelude to the Zimmerman Telegram" *Royal Central Asian Society Journal*, January 1960.

Edwardes, Michael. Playing the Great Game. Hamish Hamilton, London.1975.

Encyclopedia Britannica. 11th Edition. Cambridge University Press.1910.

Forbes, Wm H. Fall of the Peacock Throne. Harper and Row. 1980.

Fowler, W B. British-American Relations 1917-18. The Role of Sir William Wiseman. Princeton University Press, 1969.

Garrod, Oliver. <u>The Qashgui Tribe of Fars.</u> Royal Central Asian Society Journal, Vol 33. July-Oct 1946.

Gudgin, Peter. <u>Military Intelligence, The British Story.</u> Arms and Armour. 1989.

Heffernan, Michael. <u>Geography cartography and military intelligence: The Royal Geographical Society and the First World War.</u> Institute of British Geographers, Vol 21. 1996.

Hills E H. <u>Report on the Survey of Canada.</u> The Geographical Journal. Vol 24, No 2 (Aug., 1904)

Hopkirk, Peter. <u>Setting The East Ablaze.</u> John Murray, 1984.
<u>The Great Game.</u> Oxford University Press. 1990.
<u>Quest for Kim.</u> John Murray, 1996.
<u>On Secret Service East of Constantinople.</u> Oxford University Press 1995.

Kazemzadeh, Firuz. <u>Russia and Britain in Persia, 1864-1914.</u> Yale University Press.

Keown-Boyd, Henry. <u>Boxer Rebellion.</u> Dorset Press, New York. 1991.

Masaryk , Thomas G. <u>The Making of a State.</u> Howard Fertig. 1970.

Mackey, Sandra. <u>The Iranians.</u> A Dutton Book (Penguin Group) New York. 1996.

Mason, Philip. A Matter of Honour. Jonathan Cape Ltd. 1974.

Meyer, Karl E and Brysac, Shareen Blair. Tournament of Shadows. Counterpoint, Washington. D.C. 1999.

Moberley, Brigadier-General F J. Official History of the War. Operations in Persia 1914-1919. HM Stationary Office, London. 1987.

Moorehead, Caroline. Durant's Dream. Harper Collins.1998.

Morgan, Gerald. Myth and Reality in the Great Game. Asian Affairs, Journal of the Royal Central Asian Society. Vol 60. February, 1973.

Neilson. Keith. "Joy Rides" British Intelligence and Propganda in Russia, 1914-1917. The Historical Journal. 1981

Niedermayer, Oskar von. Under the Scorching Sun. Dauchau 1923.

Olson, William J. Anglo-Iranian RelationsDuring World War 1. Frank Cass and Co, London. 1984.

O'Connor, Sir Frederick. On the Frontier and Beyond. J Murray, 1931.

Perrett, Bryan and Lord, Anthony. The Czar's British Squadron, William Kimber, London. 1981.

Pethybridge, Roger (ed) <u>Witnesses to the Russian Revolution</u>. George Allen and Unwin.1964.

Preston, Richard Arthur. <u>Canada's RMC</u>. University of Toronto Press. 1969.

Read, Anthony. <u>Colonel Z</u>. Viking Penguin, Inc. New York. 1985.

Roskill, Stephen. <u>Admiral of the Fleet Earl Beatty</u>. Atheneum London 1981

Safiri, Floreeda. Unpublished doctoral these. <u>South Persia Rifles</u>. Edinburgh University.

Siegel, Jennifer. <u>Endgame</u>. I.B. Tauris and Co, Ltd. London and New York. 2002.

Skrine, Sir Claremont. <u>World War in Iran</u>. Constable and Co Ltd. London. 1962.

Stockdale, Melissa K. <u>"My Death for the Motherland is Happiness" Women, Patriotism and Soldiering in Russia's Great War, 1914-1917.</u> American Historical Review, Vol 109 2004.

Sykes, Christopher. <u>Wassmuss, The German Lawrence</u>. Longmans Green and Co London .1936

Taylor, AJP. Beaverbrook. Simon and Schuster, 1972.

Thwaites, Norman. <u>Velvet and Vinegar</u>. Grayson, London. 1932.

Tuchman, Barbara. <u>The Zimmermann Telegram</u>. Balantine Books, 1966.

Ullman, Richard H. <u>Anglo-Soviet Relations, 1917-1921</u>. Princeton University Press 1961.

Viereck, George Sylvester. <u>Spreading Germs of Hate</u>. Duckworth, 1931.

Wilber, Donald Newton. <u>Iran, Past and Present</u>. Princeton University Press. 1976. <u>Riza Shah</u>. New York, 1975.
Winter, Denis. <u>Death's Men</u>. Penguin Books. 1979.

Winstone, H.V.F. <u>The Illicit Adventure</u>. Jonathan Cape. London. 1982. <u>Captain Shakespear</u>. Jonathan Cape. London. 1976.

Wright, Sir Denis. <u>The English Among the Persians</u>. Heinemann. London.1977.

Wynn, Antony. <u>Persia in the Great Game</u>. John Murray. 2003.

Yapp, M E. <u>The Near East Since the First World War</u>. Longman. London .1991.

Youssoupoff, Prince Felix. <u>Lost Splendor.</u> G P Putman's Sons. 1954.

ENDNOTES.

1   Dodds, Ronald. The Brave Young Wings. P.233.

2   The general description of the tribes used at that time rather than the current and more correct term "Pushtun".

3   The Third Decade. P 33.

4   Christmas Review Royal Military College of Canada, December 1934.p.67.

5   Public Archives of Canada M6Z6.G.Vol 84.

6   Letter from Curzon to Hamilton quoted by Dilkes p.58

7   Encyclopedia Britannica. 11th Edition. Vol 6. P.172.

8   By the end of his career he could speak French, Russian, German and Japanese and had passed official tests in Hindustani, Chinese and Pushtu.

9   Canadian Who's Who. 1937.

10   Now Thailand

11   Simla Memorandum # 142-2-CCS (MO3)

12   A further intelligence agency, Indian Political Intelligence, (IPI) was added in 1921 because of the growth of Indian anarchist activity in England. It employed both Indian police and army officers and maintained close contact with Scotland Yard and MI 5.

13   Royal Geographical Society, 1919. Reminiscenses of the Map of Arabia and Persian Gulf by Lt Colonel FFHunter. IA

14 Apparently, more than 22 million tons of coal were discovered near the port of Sur in Oman

15 By 1912 British blockade efforts were so successful for local manufacture to flourish again in Afghanistan. Fifty years later this author saw industrious Afghans manufacturing bullets with simple equipment and primitive molds.

16 Letter from Hunter to Dr Scott Keltie, the Royal Geographical Society, March 17 1910.

17 Named after the Empress of Austria, Hungary and Bohemia it is said to be still used in parts of the Middle East and Africa.

18 Letters to Hunter dated Jan 28 and Feb 22nd. Royal Geographical Society archives.

19 Viceroy to Indiia Office 15 March, 1910.

20 Hunter to Sir Richmond Ritchie 6 April, 1910 received Political Department, India Office 20 April, 1910.

21 Letter Lord Morley to Viceroy, India 22 March 1910.

22 Zair Khidhar Khan to O.C. Bushire. 23 February, 1916.

23 Wynn, Antony. Persia in the Great Game. p 266-267. Skrine's letters to his mother found in the Oriental and India Office Collection at the British Library.

24 Ibid. P 268-269.

25 Memo from Lt Col Hunter to OC Kazerum Column Dated Shiraz 1st Jan 1917 in WO 106/928

26 Moberley, Brigadier-General. The War in Persia. P.221.

27 Safiri. Chelmsford to Chamberlin (Austin Chamberlin private papers University of Birmingham) AC/20/4/46.

28 Winter, Dennis. Death's Men. P.43.

29 Wynn, Antony. P 276.

30   The Marling's became fond of Dmitri and, contrary to regulations, managed to have the Grand Duke return to England with them.

31   Chamberlin

32   Knightly, Phillip. <u>The Second Oldest Profession</u>. P.56

33   Reportedly an emotional meeting with "Yashka" on her knees weeping with pleas for "intervention" causing the President to break into tears as well.

34   Wiseman was also in Washington ding with Mrs. Harriman who said, "He is a sort of super-head of the British secret service here". Pinafores and Politics. Page 282.

35   A view less energetically observed in Russia.

36   O'Connor. <u>On the Frontier and Beyond</u>.

37   Sir Henry Mill Pellatt. C.V.O. of Pellatt and Pellatt Share brokers and Financial Agents Bank of Hamilton Building, Toronto. To Lord Beaverbrook, London. August 1st, 1918.

38   Ibid

39   Royal Military College of Canada Review. Deember, 1934.

40   Letter from Hunter to Lady Curzon from United Services Club March 13, 1919.

41   General Thwaites had some connection with Major Thwaites at the time Major Thwaites became the second, Provost Marshal in the US. following Hunter. Major Thwaites had been previously with MI5 in New York. In London he had lunch with General Thwaites and attended a conference at the War Office. It is possible that in their discussions about the New York posting Major Thwaites may have displayed a negative attitude about Hunter to General Thwaites. But this is conjecture. See, Supplementary Memp on Relations of New York Office (Section V) and MI.5. October 3, 1918.

42   Telegram from Viceroy of India 26 August 1919

43   <u>Who's Who</u>. P. 516.

44   War Diary Norperforce, 18/19 May

45   Letter (No 223) from British Legation Tehran to Lord Curzon dated Dec 28, 1921.

46   Reply to above from War Office Decorations file 297. Dec 28 1921.

47   In an address to the Empire Club of Canada in 1931 Hunter was introduced as "Late of the Indian Secret Service."

48   University of Toronto Archives A73-0026/163(10)

49   Hunter's slim majority increased in 1937 to 762.

50   The Eglington Hunt offered to lend the force sixty horses.

51   Toronto Star, July 28, 1943.

52   Taylor, AJP. <u>Beaverbrook</u>. P. 400. Public Archives of Canada. File 8054-86-N/2262.

53

54   Public Archives of Canada 8054-86-N/2262.

55   The Department ofNational Defence was apparently ready to lend two aeroplanes to the Toronto Flying Club for training pilots. Public Archives of Canada 8054-86-N/2262

56   Lord Curzon to Montague March 4 1919.

57   Escorted by Hunter's early admirer, (Sir) Clairmont Skrine.